How to Spot a Dangerous Man
<u>Before</u> You Get Involved

ABOUT THE AUTHOR

Sandra L. Brown holds a master's degree in counseling. She is the founder and former executive director of Bridgework, Inc., a multifaceted nonprofit center for victims of violent crime. There, she provided both administrative leadership and clinical service through individual and group counseling.

She has worked as a therapist at hospital inpatient programs, residential treatment facilities, intensive outpatient programs, and other nonprofit treatment programs. She has been a keynote speaker, conference teacher, and workshop and retreat leader. She has taught counseling courses at the college level.

Sandra has provided consulting for human-service agencies in the area of program development for trauma-related disorders. She has assisted in international program development for the abandoned street children in Rio De Janeiro, Brazil. She is a frequent guest of radio call-in shows and has hosted and produced her own TV show, *A Voice for Victims.*

She is the author of the books *Counseling Victims of Violence* and *The Moody Pews,* as well as numerous articles on clinical counseling and personal-growth issues.

DEDICATION

To my husband, Ken, whose insights into men have fueled the concept for this book; to my precious and priceless daughters, Lindsay and Lauren, because I still dream of a day when your dating and marriage choices can all be danger-free; to my mother, Joyce, and sister, Linda, who understand all too well the face of danger; and to all the women I have met over the past fifteen years who shared their stories of dangerous men with me—may their honesty reward all of our lives with more insight, knowledge, choices, and, most of all, safety.

Ordering

Trade bookstores in the U.S. and Canada please contact:

Publishers Group West
1700 Fourth Street, Berkeley CA 94710
Phone: (800) 788-3123   Fax: (510) 528-3444

Hunter House books are available at bulk discounts for textbook course adoptions; to qualifying community, health-care, and government organizations; and for special promotions and fund-raising. For details please contact:

Special Sales Department
Hunter House Inc., PO Box 2914, Alameda CA 94501-0914
Phone: (510) 865-5282   Fax: (510) 865-4295
E-mail: sales@hunterhouse.com

Individuals can order our books from most bookstores, by calling **(800) 266-5592**, or from our website at **www.hunterhouse.com**

How to spot a dangerous man

a dangerous man before you get involved

Sandra L. Brown, M.A.

Hunter House PUBLISHERS

Hunter House Inc., Publishers
PO Box 2914
Alameda CA 94501-0914

Library of Congress Cataloging-in-Publication Data

Brown, Sandra L., 1957-
How to spot a dangerous man before you get involved / Sandra L. Brown.—
1st ed.   p. cm.
Includes bibliographical references and index.
ISBN 0-89793-447-4 (pbk.)
1. Man-woman relationships. 2. Dating (Social customs) 3. Abused women—Psychology. 4. Abusive men—Psychology. 5. Violence in men. 6. Self-esteem in women. I. Title.
HQ801.83.B76 2005
646.7'7—dc22   2004023841

Project Credits

Cover Design: Brian Dittmar Graphic Design
Book Production: Hunter House
Developmental and Copy Editor: Kelley Blewster
Proofreader: John David Marion
Indexer: Nancy D. Peterson
Acquisitions Editor: Jeanne Brondino
Editor: Alexandra Mummery
Publishing Assistant: Antonia T. Lee
Publicist: Jillian Steinberger
Foreign Rights Coordinator: Elisabeth Wohofsky
Customer Service Manager: Christina Sverdrup
Order Fulfillment: Washul Lakdhon
Administrator: Theresa Nelson
Computer Support: Peter Eichelberger
Publisher: Kiran S. Rana

Printed and Bound by Bang Printing, Brainerd, Minnesota
Manufactured in the United States of America

9 8 7 6 5 4 3 2   First Edition   05 06 07 08 09

Contents

Important Note

The material in this book is intended to help women identify dangerous and potentially dangerous relationships. Every effort has been made to provide accurate and dependable information. The contents of the book have been compiled through professional research and in consultation with other professionals. However, the reader should be aware that professionals in the field have differing opinions.

Therefore, the publisher, author, and editors, as well as the professionals quoted in the book, cannot be held responsible for any error, omission, professional disagreement, or dated material. The author and publisher assume no responsibility for any outcome of applying the information in this book in a program of self-care or under the care of a licensed practitioner. If you have questions about the application of the information described in this book, consult a licensed therapist. If you are in a violent or potentially violent relationship, please call a domestic-abuse hotline.

Foreword

Diana Ross, the Supremes, and my mother were right: Trying to "hurry love" causes women to find out the hard way that love doesn't come easy. In *How to Spot a Dangerous Man Before You Get Involved,* Sandra Brown explains why such a panicked pursuit of relationships is leading another generation of women into the "dance of victimization." No wonder women of all ages, cultures, socioeconomic backgrounds, and education levels grow "numb from bad choices," ready to embrace another dangerous man.

If you want details about the man who "done her wrong," listen to blues music. In this book, Sandy goes the next step. She shows women how to recognize different types of dangerous men, and then she shows them how to avoid being drawn into their sometimes deadly web of deceit. Using the skill she's honed as a therapist for victims of violence, Sandy gives simple, hard-hitting explanations that expose a dangerous man as not just the guy who hits women or spends his paycheck on crack while the children go hungry. This book shows emphatically that a dangerous man is any man who is harmful to a woman's "emotional, physical, financial, sexual, or spiritual health." The book also offers a glimpse into what psychologists know about psychopathology by revealing dangerousness as a pervasive—or, in lay terms, permanent—pattern of behaviors. It may be a wake-up call to women of all ages to learn that they have a right to refuse to compromise their safety and well-being by wasting time trying to change in a man what is unchangeable even with the help of highly trained professionals.

Women who are bold enough to take this information to heart and examine their own dating patterns have a chance to break free and find a satisfactory, life-affirming relationship with a man who values his mate. Yes, says Sandra Brown, there are men like that. Those men will be the first to applaud this book, because they don't want their mothers, sisters, aunts, friends, or female coworkers to fall prey to dangerous men.

Sandy leaves readers with hope by showing them how to identify their own red flags and then how to use these intuitive warnings to flee before it's too late. As she cautions, "You can't avoid what you don't see." Hopefully reading this book will stop the pain from getting worse and will prevent the loss of another woman's dignity, sanity, the contents of her bank account, and possibly her life to a dangerous man.

— *Kathie T. Erwin, Ed.D.*
National Certified Psychologist
Florida Licensed Mental Health Counselor
National Certified Counselor

Preface

I have looked at the issue of dangerous men from the various perspectives of woman, mother, therapist to victims, and therapist to dangerous men. Over time, I have gathered some thoughts from the enlightening experiences I have had with both victims and perpetrators. *How to Spot a Dangerous Man Before You Get Involved* is a natural outgrowth of the sociological concerns, the experience-based awareness, the professional knowledge, the parental fright, and the feminist perspectives I have gained from my dealings with dangerous men.

I came to my knowledge about dangerous men through my profession. I have been a psychotherapist for fifteen years and have treated female victims of violent crime. These women have lived through interactions and relationships with dangerous men that included assaults, stalking, rapes, emotional devastation, financial ruin, and child abductions. From their stories I learned what women have survived at the hands of dangerous men (and, tragically, sometimes not survived, since some were murdered), and I learned what dangerous men do to trusting women.

On the other hand, I have also studied and have extensive experience in the treatment of psychopathology, which is the study and treatment of those who are and will remain permanently mentally ill. I have treated both women and men in private practice, in community mental-health systems, in lockdown psychiatric hospitals, in churches, and in residential treatment programs. From pathologically ill individuals, I learned how they seek out others, what they do once they have them, the context of their relationships, how their personalities are structured against change, and why they are successful at what they do. I have treated those who have abused others, domestic-violence offenders, sexually addicted men, men who have raped—and those who have probably done more but did not say so.

As I continued to treat both the victims and the dangerous, my interests expanded to the study of the most extreme levels of pathology and dangerousness. I studied serial killers and serial rapists. As I immersed myself in understanding psychopathology and victimization, a growing portrait of dangerous men and the women they select began to grow in my mind. Since I had one foot in treating victims and the other in listening to the dangerous men's stories, a cause-and-effect rationale began to form in my ideology. I began to see patterns, connections, and links. I saw who sought whom and why. And who responded to whom and possibly why. I watched women ignore red flags and plunge headlong into their fourth and fifth relationships with dangerous men. I watched women's selection patterns and how they overlapped with men's seeking patterns. It was a fascinating concoction of victimology and pathology. But it was also a very dangerous one.

I was disappointed with what women were learning and not learning while getting help for their dangerous men. "Support and encouragement-based therapy" seemed merely to consist of mutual whining between victim and counselor. These same counselors were telling their clients to "contact me again when you're ready to leave him." Women's cycles of selecting dangerous men showed few signs of being broken by this type of intervention. By the time the women were referred to me they had suffered years of damage from various dangerous men, to the point where they perceived dangerous men as being just "everyday guys." They no longer recognized their men's patterns as dangerous. They were numb from years of making bad choices.

What did these women need to hear that they weren't being taught? What was missing in this dynamic that might have been the key to helping them get out—for good? Not just help them get out of a current relationship with a dangerous man, but help them avoid all such relationships in the future? What was missing from the information that was routinely being given to women?

I began to teach women what I knew about pathology. Helping them understand *why* these men were dangerous and *what* would never change in these men because of their pathology was the only thing that made sense. Women began to "get it." They learned to spot dangerous men earlier and earlier in their interactions with them, so that finally their lives were becoming more free of disasters and danger.

My frustration also led me to write this book. The outdated programs we were using to reach women apparently weren't working. Since the 1970s, we professionals have watched women cycle in and out through our doors, constantly reentering potentially deadly relationships. It appeared that women needed better tools for identifying dangerous men. You can't avoid what you don't see. This book is designed to do the same thing for you that my work with my clients did for them. It is designed to help you be able to spot dangerous men. With any luck this book will help you and other women recognize these men as well as listen to your inner cues and hunches—two skills that will allow you to make better decisions about who to date and have relationships with.

The names and identifying characteristics of all the individuals mentioned in this book have been changed in order to protect their identities.

> — *Sandra L. Brown, M.A.*
> *January 2005*

Introduction

Dangerous men exist in all of our lives. As a woman, I recognize this as a factor that affects all women. But as a mother, I saw a dating future for my own daughters that was full of young dangerous men, and as a psychotherapist who treated female victims of violent crime I saw the women who kept picking these types of men. As a psychopathologist I also saw the dangerous men themselves in therapy. It is what people do not understand about pathology that puts them at risk for choosing pathological individuals to date and marry. Therefore, my goal is to make pathology understandable for the layperson so that any woman can know when a man is dangerous and pathological. I hope that focus will distinguish this book from others on violence, unhealthy relationships, and women's issues.

Every chapter in this book contains stories from one or more real-life women who got involved with a dangerous man or men. Some of these stories come from my psychotherapy sessions either with women or with dangerous men themselves. Exactly how many women these stories represent is hard to estimate. I know I have heard hundreds of stories in my fifteen years of practice. Other stories in the book come from women I have known in my personal life, women whom I have watched engage in a dance of victimization with the dangerous men they have dated.

1

My women friends also sent to me their friends, who had their own stories of dating dangerous men. Some of those stories are also included here.

I obtained still other stories from a posting I placed on the Internet asking for women to tell me their dangerous-men stories. I received about fifty responses to my posting, from the United States, Canada, England, Australia, Israel, and Indonesia. Some of those stories are included here.

All the women I interviewed, whether face-to-face or over the Internet, were asked specific questions that examined their own mental-health issues, the childhood messages they received from their families of origin, and their beliefs about society, culture and women. The questions also covered the women's dating histories, including how many men in total they had dated, how many were dangerous men, what categories of dangerous men they had dated, how the women's red flags had made themselves known, why the women had ignored their red flags, what it had cost the women to ignore them, and what the outcome was.

To the degree I can show each woman's demographic profile in her story, I try to do so. It is important that we understand that dangerous men come to us all—to women of all ages and all educational backgrounds; to single, married, and divorced women; to women of all races and all religions; to the childless woman and the mother; to the urban and the suburban woman; to women in all careers (even careers that train them to recognize at least some of the symptoms of dangerousness); to the poor, the middle-class, and the wealthy woman; to the virgin and the woman "at the well." Getting involved with dangerous men is a universal experience.

The stories and the demographics of the women also helped me to see women's patterns of selection and assisted me in grouping together similiar experiences that might help us understand women's reactions to different types of dangerous men. Finding yourself among the stories should not be difficult. We all have a scary time in our own dating history as well as a future that could potentially include a dangerous man.

The best way to use a book like this is to be open and receptive to honestly evaluating your own previous dating selections. No one wants to feel "gullible" for dating or marrying a dangerous man. But there is no way to work through the process of recognizing and changing your patterns without brutal honesty regarding your personal history. The women who were brave enough to share their stories want you to look for the similarities between their stories and yours. They want you to resist using loophole issues that you think make you different from them and thus more likely to disregard the fact that you, too, are vulnerable. It is not important how your man is *different* from the men portrayed in these pages, but it *is* important to determine how he is *like* these men.

These are the eyes we want you to develop—eyes that can see potential similarities between your story and those of these women. Doing so may save you from getting involved with a dangerous man. Instead of looking for ways to say your man is not like these men, how about, just for a moment, really allowing yourself to see if he *is* like them? How about letting yourself live with the uncertainty raised by this question? Live with the fact that you may not know right now if he is or is not dangerous. Do not rush to say he definitely "isn't," because once you have labeled him safe in your mind, you will stop looking further for any signs of dangerousness. The stories can offer you insights if you make yourself open to reading, thinking, and listening to your inner self about the men in your past and the men in your life now. As a woman who attended one of our workshops said, "I didn't think my husband was like these men. I was there for general information. But I took this information home and just became more aware. What I became aware of and suspicious of led me to uncover the fact that he was a pedophile who was abusing our child. I turned him in. But this would never have happened if I'd refused to even 'see' if he was in any of these categories. Ladies, just be open."

To this end, the middle chapters of this book (Chapters 3 through 10) are devoted to describing dangerous men and how they seek women, date them, and marry them. These chapters also offer defense strategies for identifying such men before getting too deeply involved with them. First, however, in Chapters 1 and 2 I lay the foundation for this understanding. In Chapter 1 I offer a working definition of what I mean by the term "dangerous man," and I outline the various categories of dangerous men. I also discuss which of these men have clinically pathological disorders. In Chapter 2 I show how women have a biologically built-in "red-alert" system that warns them against danger of all kinds, and I discuss how and why many women have allowed this internal alarm mechanism to become dismantled.

Chapters 11 and 12 are devoted to discussing warning signs that indicate a bad dating choice, elements of healthy boundaries and relationships, and women's own self-sabotaging behaviors and thought patterns. In addition, Chapter 11 contains a questionnaire titled "Am I in Danger of Dating More Dangerous Men?" Take this quiz to see if you are at risk for repeating dangerous dating choices.

The book's final chapter, Chapter 13, contains women's success stories and offers a vision for your own success. You *can* succeed in changing your choices so that in the future you select healthy men to have rewarding relationships with. The chapter shows how other women have done so. And finally, at the back of the book, the Resources section suggests other books to read and websites to visit, and it also lists sources for obtaining help. *If you are in an abusive or potentially abusive relationship, please avail yourself of one or more of the resources listed there for victims of domestic violence.* This book is geared toward helping you to recognize, label, choose, and change—but whether or not you do so is entirely up to you. Your ability to call yourself on your own behavior will largely determine how many more times you will date dangerous men. If you see yourself in a story, let yourself see it. It doesn't mean you are "bad"; it only means you made a dangerous choice in the past. The best use of that experience is to learn from it. To refuse to learn from pain and experience is incredibly fruitless.

Who in the world *wants* pain? But if we happen into it, we might as well get something out of it.

Let the lessons learned from experiencing this pain teach you so you don't repeat the same choice again. The only difference between a woman who has dated only one dangerous man and a woman who ends up dating five is that the first woman was open to learning immediately following her bad choice. The second woman refused the lesson, made excuses, or otherwise failed to make herself available for the learning curve. As a therapist, I'm saddened when I see a woman in her fifties or sixties whose life has been one long series of involvements with dangerous men. She might have started as a young woman by getting involved with a married man, then followed that up by spending ten years with an addict, then fifteen years with a violent man, five more with a mentally ill man, and another five with a predator. Now in her late middle-age, she looks back on a life lacking even a moment of relationship happiness or serenity. She wonders if in her remaining years she might actually find someone different from the men who've made up her past. She is angry that she wasted the only life she had on waiting and hoping that these dangerous men would change. Now she knows: Such men do not change. Only her choices can change. Pain has finally taught her, but it took her thirty years to pay attention.

A note about the title of the book: Although the title talks about spotting a dangerous man *before* you get involved, nearly all of the stories in the book are about women who *did* get involved. Furthermore, a quick look at the red-alert behavioral checklists contained in the chapters on types of dangerous men will make it clear that in most cases you will at least have to engage in a few conversations with a man in order to identify him as dangerous or not. In some cases, you may recognize him as dangerous based on information you have received from others that you take into consideration. You may decide that what you've learned about him is worrisome enough that you can't even contemplate dating him. Hopefully, as you become better at quickly identifying dangerous men, the amount of time it takes to gather the necessary insights will decrease. Likewise, as you become better at doing your homework about a man, responding to your red flags, and listening to the input of other wise women, you will learn to make an accurate judgment more quickly and will be able to eliminate dangerous men from your life.

Chapter 1

Understanding the Face of Dangerousness

Dangerous men come in all shapes and forms. They slip into our lives by appearing, at least initially, incredibly normal. There are no overt, flashing neon signs. There is no one-size-fits-all description of how they look or act. There isn't a telltale career type, eye color, or face shape. Most of the time they blend into society, looking like any other man we might consider dating. This means detection is entirely up to us. But too many women have stories that begin with "I didn't know he was like that. I didn't recognize the early signs. I believed his story."

We know that women are battered, stalked, raped, abused, and killed every day in this country, mostly by dangerous men. We know that each day domestic-violence shelters take women in to shield them from dangerous men and from behaviors the women did not recognize in time as dangerous. Just today I was notified that one of my previous clients from a domestic-violence center was shot in the head by her dangerous man. In every town across America, women are being counseled or helped because of dangerous men—and not just men who are violent. As this book will show, "dangerousness" comes in many types of packages.

But we must be missing something if millions of women continue to end up with men who could be classified as dangerous.

There must be something in many women's personal detection system that is offtrack. Our most well-tuned detection system often seems to exist only for other women. We ask incredulously, "Doesn't she know he beats women? ... has a drinking problem? ... has a criminal history?" We seem to be all ears, eyes, and antennas when another woman's life is at stake. But when it comes to our own life, our antennas are often short-circuited. We claim to know the reality about what happens between dangerous men and the women who get involved with them, but still we date or marry dangerous men.

Dangerous men have always lived among us, and they always will. It's unrealistic to imagine waiting for a "dating and marriage utopia" where all choices will be safe choices. Therefore, it is up to us to learn what can and will keep us safe. It is up to us to know the signs of dangerous men and then to heed those signs. Understanding what dangerous men look and act like—what professionals call their "presentation"—is a life skill that might just keep these men out or get them out of our lives. You cannot avoid what you do not see. This book is designed to help you see, and then to help you choose differently.

Why Women Choose Dangerous Men

Let me define what I have come to understand the term *dangerous man* to mean. I use the word *dangerous* to describe any man who causes damage to his partner's emotional, physical, financial, sexual, or spiritual health. The damage that can be inflicted on a woman by her partner is not limited to the physical or sexual. Women tend to overlook this truth about dangerous men. They don't understand, beyond violence, what makes a man dangerous. These men harm in a multitude of ways that we need to recognize. This definition gives us a wide base from which to examine men whose presence in our lives has caused us or could cause us an emotional meltdown that might take months or years to recover from—or even worse, whose presence may cost us our lives. I purposefully leave the definition wide in order to include marginal men who are living so close to the edge of dangerousness and pathology that at any time they could become harmful in one or more of the ways listed above.

Women want to know why we pick such men. Throughout my research women consistently asked this question. Is it because women are overcome with loneliness? Is it because of our past habits of choosing poorly? Are we programmed to believe that anyone will do? Do we like the thrill of being involved with a dysfunctional man? Do painful divorces open us up afterward to an increased risk of selecting dangerous men? Does a dysfunctional family upbringing contribute in any way to these choices? Why are we a society of women who date dangerous men? Why aren't crimes of domestic violence against women declining significantly? Surely, since the development in the 1970s of violence-intervention programs and women's services, we have learned a few things about this epidemic.

All this raises the following questions: Have we learned to *personally* recognize dangerous men and how they enter our lives? Or do we merely look for dangerous men in other women's lives? Do we intimately understand this phenomenon for ourselves, and have we applied the knowledge to making meaningful change in our lives?

The answer to these questions must be "No." The awareness that dangerous men really do exist appears to be knowledge many women don't apply to their own lives. Yet most of us claim to know something about "bad boyz." We've heard rape-prevention lectures and other women's-oriented safety information. We've grown up learning physical defense strategies but apparently not emotional ones.

The universal awareness of the existence of dangerous men has failed to keep women safe. Could this be because the knowledge usually comes to us in the form of watered-down, naïve-sounding warnings about "bad men" from our mothers and other elders? Have we talked in mythical-seeming generalities that have failed to help women sense, see, and avoid choosing dangerous men when they show up in our lives? Whatever the reasons, the truth is we have *not* succeeded as families, as a feminist movement, or as a society to help women define and identify, in an understandable way, dangerous men. If we had, women would be responding to these men differently.

It would be far easier if we could define one "type" of woman who is attracted to dangerous men. Then, all the women who match that description could be identified and educated about dangerous men. But responding to and selecting dangerous men is a pervasive epidemic that bypasses any group of stereotypically defined women. All types of women choose dangerous men. Yes, there are some childhood experiences, some family structures and behaviors, some abuse histories, some disorders that increase the possibility that a woman will respond to and date dangerous men. (Some of these specific issues affecting women are discussed in more detail in Chapter 2, on red flags, and in the chapters on the various categories of dangerous men.) But, again, we must understand that *all types* of women choose and respond to dangerous men.

Minimizing and Glamorizing

An issue that seems to affect our ability to get a handle on dangerous men is our society's inadequate language for them. Depending on the era, we nickname them "bad boyz," "cowboys," "hoods," or "thugs." The 1920s' "gangster" has evolved into the early twenty-first century's "gangsta." We have renamed dangerous men in ways that gloss over their destructive, sometimes criminal behavior. We say, "He's a little rough" or "He's had some tough times" or "He's a man's man." We talk in generalities that avoid the specifics of his character by focusing on other things: who his family is, what possessions he owns, where he lives, or what he does for a living. We avoid describing and defining the characteristics that have caused him trouble in the past and that make him a danger to women today. We minimize his past, his negative personality traits, or the absence of strong character. We dismiss these things as old history, as though they have no relevance to his current and future potential or behavior.

We tend to see dangerous characteristics as being "normal" for men. This was by far the most prevalent defense mechanism used by women in my research. Many women who have attended my workshops lament that "there would be no one left to date" if they took my descriptions of dangerous men seriously. This implies that many women accept dangerous behaviors as a normal blueprint for how men should act. I often see women identify behavioral problems and mental-health issues in their men, but then turn around and focus only on other aspects of the relationship, such as his "availability," his "attractiveness," his capacity for "distracting" them, or maybe his helpfulness. Women repackage men's problems and call them something else.

But why? What has society taught us about dangerous men? MTV and movies treat thugs as acceptable dating choices by portraying their romantic relationships with girls and young women as standard fare. Normal girls are often shown hooking up with abnormal guys who pose as normal guys. No wonder our culture cannot differentiate between the dangerous and the healthy. Dangerous is being made to look like the only choice, the likely choice, the popular choice for teenage girls from middle-class suburbia. Depict these "bad boyz" as financially well off—from God knows what kind of income sources—and you have an even more enticing picture.

Of course, none of this is new. Movies from all eras have embraced the same theme: The dangerous man gets the "normal" women. *West Side Story* portrays Maria with a street thug. *Dirty Dancing* did the same in the 1980s. Humphrey Bogart frequently played a guy on the edge. We have been fed romanticized images of dangerous men for decades. Today's TV, film, and MTV images are more frequent, more suggestive, and stronger than ever. We see Britney Spears, originally a Disney Mouseketeer, slithering around on the floor surrounded by thugs who have her on a dog leash. Some Eminem videos depict young women hanging on his arm as he threatens to kill people. On the TV show *The Gilmore*

Girls, the kids are students at Yale, but Rory keeps hooking up with a school dropout and drifter. And what about Whitney Houston, who can win music awards but can't disentangle herself from the abusive and very dangerous Bobby Brown? Or Pamela Anderson, the blonde cutie who tolerated too many years of Tommy Lee's abuse before ditching him? These are among our culture's female role models, and since they end up with dangerous guys, it makes it seem like an acceptable choice for women. We know that this type of propaganda is effective. All we have to do is turn on daytime TV to see Jerry Springer or Maury Povich portraying pathological relationships as normal and packaging them as entertainment. Is it any wonder we are confused about what and who is really dangerous?

Developing Your Own Language for Dangerous

One reason why a woman might date four or five dangerous men before she begins to make safer choices is that we as women do not use our own language to define *dangerous* in terms we understand or have experienced. Perhaps we have been living by someone else's definition of *dangerous,* be it a man's, our mother's, our culture's, or the media's. Whatever the source of our understanding about what makes a man dangerous, we often fail to own the description in a way that will keep us safe. Developing a personalized language based on our own experiences is key to changing our patterns. We must define what is dangerous in order to defy our earlier choices.

We may have been told about "bad men" as we were growing up, but in order to remain safe in our dating lives we must develop a personal "knowing" that comes from our history. By "history" I mean how we developed specific traits that led us to make certain dating choices, the language we've always used to define and describe men, and our dating patterns. We need to recognize that knowing *about* dangerous men is not the same as knowing how to spot them before we get involved. Only by examining our history closely will we personalize the concept of what a dangerous man is and perhaps use that information to impact our future choices. This is how the information provided in this book can help women change their choices in ways that some women's programs and services have failed to do. An even wiser approach would be if we could develop a knowledge based on other women's experiences with dangerous men without having to live the experience ourselves.

To this end, Chapters 11 and 12 will help you compare and contrast dysfunctional behaviors in relationships with healthy ones. These chapters discuss the necessity of good boundaries and show how establishing strong boundaries can insure a lifetime of better and safer choices. Chapter 11 also contains an important questionnaire, "Am I in Danger of Dating More Dangerous Men?" Once you're equipped with the information provided in the first ten chapters of the book, taking the quiz will tell you whether you're at a low, moderate, or high risk of continuing your pattern of selecting dangerous men. Finally, Chapter 13 shares some success stories from women who changed their lives and are now heeding the lessons learned from their past to avoid getting involved with dangerous men. They are living happy, fulfilling lives. These women's stories are proof that the goal of having healthier relationships is within your reach!

As a companion to this book, I have written a workbook designed to help you go deeper into the process of identifying and avoiding dangerous men. The exercises contained in the workbook will guide you to an understanding of your specific patterns of selecting men. They will also give you an opportunity to reconnect with the red flags you've ignored in the past. The good news is you can still glean the lessons those red flags have for you, even today. Finally, the workbook will guide you through a process of creating your own personalized "do-not-date" list. When actively explored and utilized in this way, your past is your best teacher. In the future, you will compare and contrast new relationships with previous ones. By doing so, it becomes *your* language that teaches you how to make wiser choices, based on men *you* have dated and learned from.

Categories of Dangerous Men

My years of working with dangerous men and the women who get involved with them have led me to observe that dangerous men generally fall into certain categories. Let me introduce you to eight hotties who are dying to meet you:

1. The permanent clinger: He is a needy, victim-based man who will give a woman a lot of attention in return for all of his needs being met all of the time. He fears rejection above all else, so he is jealous of other people in your life. He asks you to give up your outside life and make him your only life. He convinces women that he has been wounded and that the woman can love him into wellness if she will focus only on him. He may even threaten to harm himself or "never get over" being wounded if you don't do what he asks of you. Women have the overwhelming sensation of "having the life sucked out of them" by these men.

2. The parental seeker: He wants a parent, not a partner. He needs you so much. In fact, he needs you to run his entire life for him. It is hard for him to do adult things like go to work, make decisions, be consistent, or act grown-up. He will shower you with lots of adoration, but he has very low functioning capabilities.

3. The emotionally unavailable man: He is married, separated, engaged, or dating someone else. He usually presents himself as "unhappy with" or "not quite out of" a relationship, and he is more than willing to keep you on the side. Another type of emotionally unavailable man is the man who is preoccupied with his career, educational goals, hobbies, or other interests, to the exclusion of ever having a true interest in a long-term relationship. With the emotionally unavailable man, there is always a reason why he can't fully commit to you, but he's usually happy to keep stringing you along. After all, the situation is still convenient for him as long as you're willing to keep seeing him or sleeping with him on a "casual" basis despite the fact that he can't or won't get involved in a serious relationship with you.

4. The man with the hidden life: He has undisclosed other lives that might include women, children, jobs, life-threatening addictions, criminal behavior, disease, or other histories that remain unrevealed to you. You only find out about these hidden lives way too late in the relationship, at which time you are already at risk.

5. The mentally ill man: He can look normal on the outside, but after dating him for a while it becomes obvious that "something is amiss." Most women lack the training to know exactly what is wrong, but depending on his diagnosis he may be able to convince you to stay, seeming healthy enough to deflect attention away from his mental illness. He may hold you emotionally hostage by saying that "everyone" abandons him, or he may wreak such havoc and create such instability in your life that you can't find a way to get out.

6. The addict: Most women do not recognize up front that he has an addiction problem. Some women never see the addiction, or they mistake it for his being a "fun-seeking kind of guy." This "fun" can include sex, pornography, drugs, alcohol, thrill-seeking behavior, gambling, food, or relationships.

7. The abusive or violent man: He starts out as very attentive and giving. But then Mr. Hyde appears—controlling, blaming, shaming, harming, perhaps hitting. Women who think abuse comes only in the form of a physical assault may miss warning signs of other kinds of abuse. Abuse can be verbal, emotional, spiritual, financial, physical, or sexual, or it can be abuse of the system to get his way. (Each of these is described in Chapter 9.) With an abusive or violent man, anything goes when he decides he's in control, and he will always be in control. And abusive or violent behavior always gets worse over time. What may have started out in the first months of your relationship as occasional name-calling may eventually escalate into a life-threatening assault. Men who kill their partners don't usually do so on the first date. It happens after months or years of a woman putting up with violence that grows worse and worse. How far his abuse and violence goes is dictated only by his imagination and your continued presence.

8. The emotional predator: This pathological man has a sixth sense about women and knows how to play to a woman's woundedness. Although his motives might be to prey on a woman's financial or sexual vulnerabilities (to name just a couple), he's called the "emotional" predator because he hunts for his victims by targeting their emotional vulnerabilities. He can sense women who have recently been dumped, who are lonely, or who are emotionally or sexually needy. He is a chameleon and can be whatever any woman needs him to be. He is very tuned in to women's body and eye language as well as to the subtle messages behind their words. He can pick up on hints about a woman's life and turn himself into what she needs in the moment. These men can turn out to be lethal.

There's also a type of dangerous man that I refer to as the **combo-pack man.** This is any man who fits the criteria for more than one of the categories listed above. For instance, an addict may also be violent, or a man with a hidden life may also be an addict. Addicts are almost always emotionally unavailable. Clingers and seekers almost always have interwoven mental-illness issues. Emotional predators always have a hidden life, because hiding what they do is half the fun. Many combinations are possible, and some are fairly predictable. Women need to understand that the more categories a man falls into, the more dangerous he is. Each category brings its own pitfalls and symptoms that make that type of man a bad dating choice. But add another category, another pitfall, and another list of symptoms, and you have a man unlikely to ever get it together. The deck is stacked against him.

Bottom line: If after reading the above list you see your man in one or more categories, that is a red flag. (I talk a lot about red flags in this book, starting in the very next chapter.) Know that anyone who makes it onto this list will most likely end up causing you heartbreak.

A Few Words about Pathology and Personality Disorders

Throughout this book I use the word *dangerous* loosely interchangeably with the terms *pathological* and *personality disordered.* Let me explain why. As a psychotherapist for fifteen years, I have spent much time face-to-face with people suffering from severe disorders. This is how I first came to understand the field known as "pathology." I did not set out in my career to be a "pathologist." It wasn't even a concept I believed in. I came from the optimistic branch of psychology and spiritual beliefs that valued "self-help" and the ability to "transform one's life through growth and insight." And yet there I sat, year after year, staring into the faces of individuals who were incredibly dangerous and pathological, and also into the faces of the people who kept picking them as dating or marriage partners, over and over again. In those faces there was a lesson for me to learn about psychopathology.

Much of dating dangerously could be eliminated if women really "got" what pathology is all about. Probably the most important fact to learn, from the perspective of women who are at risk for selecting pathological men as dating partners, is that individuals who are clinically pathological, which also includes people who have a personality disorder of any kind, can usually never be made well. Most experts agree that there is very little permanent change that can occur to make such individuals "less pathological." For our purposes, this is one of the functional definitions of the term *pathology*. There are just some things about certain people that are so hardwired into their psyches—characteristics that are genetically and biologically embedded—that they are for all practical purposes rendered "unfixable." They are so "bent" in an abnormal direction that no degree of counseling, medication, or love will make them well, ever. To help you grasp what this means in practical terms, I urge you to understand that if your man is diagnosed with something called a "personality disorder," you should think of it and refer to it as a "permanent disorder." The only difference among dangerous men is that each dangerous man harms women in ways that are reflections of his own pathology and specific disorders. What makes a man dangerous is the fact that he is pathological and unfixable. And what could be more dangerous than someone who cannot be made well?

I've included this discussion of pathology for a couple of important reasons: First, most women don't get the chance to learn what pathology is. They don't know what the signs and symptoms of pathological men are. These women remain in the dark about what pathology looks like, and they remain unaware of the guaranteed outcomes of dating someone this sick. They assume that a clinically pathological individual would exhibit some "obvious" sign of mental illness or dangerousness that would be notable to anyone. Yet pathology is usually not that blunt—not even to a therapist.

Second, many women who learn what pathology is seem to believe that they and their man are the exceptions to the rule. This belief is manifested in their attempts to change the dangerous man or some aspect of him. They choose not to accept years of psychological research. They refuse to understand that their man has a disorder embedded within his personality structure that cannot be removed. Since the pathological man will never change, the next step the woman takes is to try to change herself to make the pathological relationship easier to cope with. Disaster can be the only outcome when a woman tries to conform to a pathological and abnormal relationship. As you read this book, remember that you have the choice of believing and acting in accordance with what the professionals have already learned about pathology and are warning you about here.

"But My Man Isn't Pathological!"

Before you rush to convince yourself that you are not dating a man who could be considered clinically pathological and that therefore you are safe from danger, it is important to remember that many pathological individuals are in the early, formative stages of their careers as dangerous men. A forgery, a couple of tickets for reckless driving, or an incident of breaking and entering could be laying the groundwork for an emerging criminal career. It's also important to remember that individuals who have symptoms of various personality disorders (which will be explained later) occupy all walks of life. The ones who are higher-functioning and have higher IQ's often end up as corporate executives, doctors, or lawyers who perpetrate so-called white-collar crimes like fraud, extortion, embezzlement, or Enron-style financial misconduct. The lower-functioning ones usually end up as career criminals who perpetrate less imaginative crimes. The worst—whether high-functioning, white-collar types or low-functioning "common criminals"—are capable of theft, criminal fraud, assault, rape, pedophilia, and homicide. When it comes to pathological individuals, predicting outcomes is very hard to do. Even the less violent ones are unpredictable; furthermore, they often don't fit our mental images of someone who is "pathological." Be open to the possibility that at this point in your life you might not have all the information you need to immediately determine who is pathological and who is not. If you did, you probably would not have picked up this book or ever gotten involved with a dangerous man. There is some learning that can still be done, and this book can help you do it.

Ted Bundy, one of the nation's most infamous serial killers and rapists, had boyish good looks, a high IQ, and clever ways of drawing women to him. He also had antisocial personality disorder. He'd studied psychology in college and attended law school. He'd volunteered at a crisis hotline, worked on a governor's political campaign, and even saved a boy from drowning. Besides being strikingly handsome, he was incredibly verbal, which is our society's primary measure of intelligence. Bundy's early criminal career consisted of minor thefts and brushes with the law. Ultimately, during the early to mid-1970s, he murdered thirty-six young women across several states.

Ted Bundy illustrates the fact that pathological individuals can come from all sorts of backgrounds and are often successful by society's standards. It is a mistake to think that antisocials or other pathologicals are always society's lowlifes. Many of them have a higher than normal IQ. Bundy's intelligence helped him to escape prison—twice! Again, before you say to yourself, "The worst I'm attracted to is the occasional married man, and here she's talking about Ted Bundy—I guess this discussion doesn't apply to me," be aware of two things: 1) Bundy had two normal, high-functioning girlfriends (unbeknownst to each other), neither of whom had any clue that he would turn out to be a serial killer and 2) if you think the worst choice you've made is picking a married man, remember that you have no idea what *else* he may be besides married. Dismissing someone's petty misdeeds can be a deadly mistake. CrimeLibrary.com says about Bundy, "His psychopathic nature was being revealed, but most people that witnessed it didn't realize what they were experiencing." They didn't realize it because they dismissed his smaller acts of crime and failed to recognize what he was building up to.

Some women want to split hairs over whether a man is merely "dangerous" but not totally "pathological." Let me make it easy for you. If he is in my book he is either definably pathological and therefore unfixable, or his behaviors veer so close to pathological that for all practical purposes his dangerousness mimics full-blown pathology. I use the words *dangerous* and *pathological* interchangeably because they are so closely aligned. Let's not dicker and look for a loophole so you can keep this man. If you see him in this book, he is dangerous and probably pathological. And anyone who is pathological is unlikely ever to be different.

What Causes Pathology?

Along with wanting to know why women choose dangerous or pathological men, this is the other question any woman who has dated or loved such a man wants to know the answer to. And, as pathologists, so do we. Theories vary. My study of serial killers and rapists has revealed several common factors that affected their early emotional development: severe early-childhood abuse (often sexual); terrible neglect; or parents or other family members with chronic addictions, mental illness, or chaotic lifestyle patterns. Some had endured severe, blunt head trauma. (Yet, as an illustration of how confusing pathology can be, Ted Bundy did not claim childhood physical or sexual abuse, head trauma, or any other reason for his pathology.)

Other pathologists believe that the brain of the pathological individual suffers from a chemical or biological "impairment." Many studies of brain function in these populations have led some experts to conclude that such people are, in fact, "wired differently" from normal populations. Traumatologists focus on the childhood events—such as abuse or neglect—that shaped early development. Neuropsychiatrists focus on head traumas and neurological impairments that affect emotional regulation, unbridled rage, and a lack of conscience. Other specialists look at social learning: how the individual "learned" his pathological behavior through family patterns and dysfunctional role modeling.

I have come to believe some aspects of all of these theories, depending on the individual's personal history. *But the most important thing I've learned is that the "why" of his disease is less important to you than "what" you are going to do about your situation.* Why he has a sad story of a chronic and unrelenting disorder is not the question that will keep you safe. You will never change the history of how he acquired his disorder. You will never change his physiology or his bad wiring. You will never love him into safety, sanity, or sanctity. The only thing that should concern you is deciding what to do when you face a man who you figure out is dangerous or pathologically ill.

To shed some light on the language and the diagnostic criteria used by professionals to define pathology, I've included an Appendix at the back of the book that describes most of the clinically recognized pathological or personality disorders. The Appendix also lists and describes other types of mental disorders that may be seen in dangerous men.

I include this information with a warning: Don't get too caught up in trying to diagnose your man. As I said above, figuring out which clinical diagnosis best fits him is less important than deciding what you're going to do about your own life. My main purpose in including this information is to drive home the following points. First, each of these pathological disturbances carries the same outcome: very little possibility of change in his core self or level of dangerousness. And second, to repeat a point made earlier, if he qualifies as one (or more) of the eight types of dangerous men, then he either is pathological or is dangerous in other ways.

The fact that these impairments are called "personality disorders" is very important. They are given this name because the personality was forced to develop around environmental or emotional deficits. Another way to look at it is that because of the deficits, the personality failed to develop. If you have completed your childhood, your personality has already developed, for the good or the bad. There is no going back and changing how it developed or failed to develop. Areas that did not develop in childhood create pathology.

Most of the eight categories of dangerous men include those who could be diagnosed as pathological. It is, in part, because they have personality disorders that I consider them dangerous. Some women have tried to persuade me that violent men, addicts, and emotionally unavailable men are certainly dangerous but not necessary pathological. The truth is, in many cases they are both. Still, if you think he is merely dangerous rather than pathological, I must ask why you would consider dating even a "merely dangerous" man.

The line that separates "dangerous" from "pathological" is very thin. In some cases, the two are indistinguishable from each other. For instance, the violent man almost always has an undiagnosed pathological disorder, or his violence is often fueled by drugs and alcohol. Addicts are known for specific types of personality disorders that are seen in higher frequency in them than in other populations. Additionally, mental illness is seen in higher numbers in addicts than in normal populations. And what about the poor, misunderstood married man? What in the world could be pathological about him? Just about anything! Simply because someone else chose to marry him doesn't mean he isn't pathological. Individuals with certain types of personality disorders are more prone to sexual acting out than are other populations. Remember that Ted Bundy had two "normal" girlfriends in the early stages of his criminal career. Just because you may be normal and selected him doesn't mean he's normal.

Here's another way of looking at pathology and personality disorders. They indicate that the person is "too much" of something. This means he's unbalanced in terms of his personality or his behaviors. For instance, a borderline personality disorder indicates too much emotionality, too many unstable relationships, too much anger. An antisocial personality disorder means too much of a lack of conscience, too much daredevil behavior, too much instability. A narcissistic personality disorder indicates too much self-focus, too much interest in his own abilities. Pathology, as you will soon learn, means too much of a lot!

What You Can Expect from a Pathological Man

Dating a pathological man means the following:

* Pathology usually implies some type of personality disorder, diagnosed or undiagnosed.

* Pathology is forever. He isn't going to change. Everything in him is wired against change.

* Pathological symptoms often increase with time and age.

* Pathology implies very little ability to have insight into one's own problems.

* Pathology often results in noncompliance with medication or therapy.

* Pathology often results in lower functioning in various areas of life (depending on the diagnosis).

* Pathology results in dysfunctional interpersonal relationships.

 * Pathology often means an inability to experience authentic emotional intimacy with you or anyone else.

 * Some pathological diagnoses can endanger you or your children.

 * Some pathological diagnoses often go hand in hand with severe and long-term addictions.

 * Some pathological men are or can become violent.

I can't stress the following enough: Your experience with a pathological man will *not* be the exception to the rule. A personality disorder is a virtual guarantee against any possibility for long-term change in an individual's core self. The pathologically dangerous man will never be able to step up to the plate and to the challenges of real life the way a normal man will be able to.

Pathological vs. Chronic Disorders

As we have seen, there is a tendency for some women to consider men "dangerous" only if they're violent or if they're pathologically ill/personality disordered. These are the descriptors of men that women find most threatening. Yet men who have other types of mental illness can also do great damage to a woman's emotional health. Men who suffer from what are known as "chronic" mental disorders are not pathological, but they are often dangerous.

Chronic disorders are mental problems for which some limited treatment choices are available. Note that these are treatments—*not* cures. Some forms of treatment can assist the patient in managing his symptoms and improving quality of life. But he will most likely have the disorder for life. Such disorders are labeled "chronic" as opposed to "pathological" because they are not part of how the individual's personality developed. This is what separates a chronic disorder from a pathological one. Most chronic disorders occurred *after* the patient's childhood development.

Any chronic disorder implies—

* the individual will probably *always* have the disorder

* he will most likely always need medication

* the disorder could (and often does) worsen over time or with stress.

Chronic disorders include the following:

* Bipolar disorder (formerly called manic-depression)

* Posttraumatic stress disorder

* Major depression

* Schizophrenia or any other delusional disorder

* Obsessive-compulsive disorder

(See the Appendix for descriptions of these illnesses.)

Besides being described in the Appendix, some of the disorders discussed in this chapter will be illustrated in more detail in later chapters, especially in the chapters on mental illness and on the emotional predator. Note that the disorders discussed here *do not* represent every diagnosis that could be dangerous in a relationship. I recommend that you talk with a mental-health professional for information about other disorders that are potentially disruptive and dangerous to relationships.

As previously discussed, there are lots of ways to be dangerous. Remember from earlier in the chapter that a dangerous man is any man who harms his partner's emotional, physical, sexual, spiritual, or financial health. These are the issues women must keep foremost in their mind when meeting men and considering whom to date. Bear in mind as well that dangerous men, even those who technically might not qualify as pathological, are similar to each other in their ability to cause great harm. Their approaches and characteristics don't vary greatly from one to the other since they're all based on dangerous behaviors. Using this book to find out how "unhealthy men" behave will help you in any relationship. Furthermore, all women need to know the signs and symptoms of dangerous men in order to be able to educate other women about them. More specifics about what to look for are covered in Chapters 3 through 10 and also in Chapter 11, "Signs of a Bad Dating Choice."

In the meantime, trust the fact that there is a reason why you picked up this book. Something in the title drew you to explore how and why you have chosen, dated, or married dangerous men in the past. Something inside of you desired to choose a healthier path. The most intuitive part of you is looking for answers. In the next chapter you will be rewarded for your search by learning how to tune back in to your own red flags. Doing so will give you the best possible chance of keeping yourself safe.

What Should You Do If You're Already Involved with a Dangerous Man?

Perhaps you picked up this book because you are already involved with a man whom you suspect or know is dangerous. Let me remind you again, if you see him described in this book, he meets the criteria for dangerousness. This book isn't about guys who are just sort of close to dangerous. If he's in here, you need to be concerned about your safety, your future, and your choices. Dangerous doesn't just mean violent. I want to remind you again that there are lots of ways to be harmed by dangerousness.

Women who have made a pattern of choosing dangerous men are often women who look for loopholes to justify staying with a dangerous man. Up until this page, you have probably tried to find a way in which this book *isn't* about your relationship, right? "He isn't *exactly* like that." "Nobody's perfect—I mean there are things about me too." "He's not *always* like that—just sometimes." Whatever mental gymnastics you have performed to be able to stay with him or to justify why he isn't dangerous, now is the time to start challenging your thinking on this issue. Maybe you're thinking, "But I've been with him for fifteen years!" If so, I would ask you the following questions:

How many *more* years are you willing to invest, now that you know he is unfixable?

What is it that you are investing in?

What will the next fifteen years look like?

What will *you* be like by then?

Why do you want a dangerous man?

These are important questions to ask yourself. Honest answers may help point the way to choices for your future. Examining such choices often takes outside insight from a professional. I recommend contacting human services in your area. Perhaps a mental-health counselor, a counselor at a domestic-violence agency, or a professional from another human-services agency can help you look at your situation and your own pattern of behavior.

If you come to the conclusion that you are going to end the relationship, professionals can advise you on safety considerations, safe housing (if need be), further counseling, and legal referrals. Leaving someone who is pathological is not something to be done by yourself. You need guidance, support, and someone to oversee your safety.

Not All Men Are Dangerous

Readers are probably now wondering, "Are there any healthy men on the planet?" Yes, there are—if you are! And you will be able to engage with them if you are willing to identify and eliminate from your life all the men who are not healthy in order to have the time, energy, and emotional health to focus on the healthy ones. The whole purpose of *How to Spot a Dangerous Man Before You Get Involved* is to help you free up your emotional resources so that you know what is dangerous and can begin focusing on healthier selections. That is the good news. This book can give you the ability to choose a healthier man.

I count it a great blessing that my first boyfriend, Michael, was a healthy young man. It did a lot for me later to be able to compare and contrast my less healthy choices with Michael. I had a template for what healthy behavior in a relationship looked like. Once I realized I had drifted in my selecting, the memory and experiences from that early relationship helped me to focus on what had worked and why it worked. In Chapter 11, we look at some examples of healthy versus unhealthy patterns in relationships. This material should offer a good testing ground for your new relationships to see which patterns line up with healthy interactions. Inevitably, all relationships will have issues, but it is important for you to realize which issues point to an unhealthy relationship and which are struggles typical of otherwise healthy relationships.

A healthy dating relationship can be a restorative experience. It can help you see that not all men are dangerous. There are some loving and wonderful men out there who are just waiting to meet you. But first, you've got to clear out the dysfunctional ones so you can make a beeline to the healthy ones. The best way to do this is to stop wasting time and energy with unfixable, dangerous men.

Meet Tori

Let's meet Tori, our first example of a woman who got involved with a dangerous man. We will revisit Tori in several places throughout the book.

Who could resist a Vietnam vet who had served his country well? Who voluntarily went to Ireland to fight the civil unrest there and was imprisoned for his beliefs? Who made mercenary work look like missionary work? Who called himself a poet and read classic literature to "soothe his soul"? Who rode out West on his Harley to find himself? Who worked the Alaskan pipeline and forewent creature comforts in order to make an honorable living to send home to his child? Who lived his blue-collar life as a badge of honor and only wanted for "home, hearth, and happiness"? Not my friend Tori. She couldn't resist Jay, his self-reported history, or the lines he used.

Her tale, so typical of women who pick dangerous men, begins with a woman of higher than normal intelligence but with a heart bigger than her knowledge of pathology. Tori was no novice to the subject of psychology. She had gone to therapy and had even been married to a psychotherapist. She prided herself on having read almost every self-help book published. Based on these reasons, she never counted herself as a woman who would attract pathologically dangerous men, so she never worried. Because she never worried, she never learned about dangerous men or even knew to be on guard against them. Add to this a big heart, an abundance of patience, and an ever optimistic attitude that everyone will grow into their full potential, and Tori was a sitting duck for dating a dangerous man.

Too many women are convinced that they will not attract or be attracted to pathological, violent, mentally ill, or other dangerous men. But that hasn't proven to be true. Tori, even with her knowledge about therapy and psychology, resisted the idea that her man was pathological when I suggested it to her. Jay didn't "look like" he was disturbed. Where was the drooling, foot-dragging, medicated, glassy-eyed appearance of the extremely deranged? Since those symptoms were absent, she stayed with him for another year, scrutinizing him as if he were under a microscope but failing to see the symptoms that *were* present. She was waiting to see the third eye in the middle of his forehead before she would pronounce him an "undoable" date. She sought an overt sign to show that he should be relegated to the "unfixable" pile. And yet, pathology is usually quite subtle, at least in the beginning.

Once Tori decided that Jay was probably indeed dangerous, she spent another chunk of time toying with the belief that "if he only went to therapy he could get better." Tori chose to believe that decades of psychological research on predatory men was inconclusive in his case. She, like too many women, refused to believe that someone with Jay's nature was permanently disordered. You can read more about Tori in Chapters 2 and 10.

Each woman has to decide for herself what she will do when she comes face-to-face with a dangerous man. Will you be like Tori? Will you

* take too long to recognize the signs and symptoms of a dangerous man?

* recognize them but keep dating him anyway?

* become aware of his probems, then wish and hope he would get well?

* spend your energy trying to get him into therapy?

* date him while he sucks the emotional life out of you?

Or will you choose to do it differently?

In case you're wondering, I do still believe it's possible for many people to change and grow. Otherwise, I wouldn't have written this book. I wrote it because I believe women who have a history of dating dangerous men can usually learn to make different, healthier choices. I've seen many women who have gone on to create better lives for themselves through change and growth!

For this book to have any lasting impact on your ability to spot dangerous men before you get involved, you will have to wrestle with your own belief system about such men. You will have to become aware of any tendency within yourself to minimize or glamorize unacceptable behavior on the part of the men you date. You will have to reconnect with and heed your red flags. You will have to embrace what experts know about pathological individuals—people for whom there exists no real possibility of positive, long-term change.

Will you accept the challenge?

2

Red Flags and Red Alerts: Knowing, Sensing, Being Aware —and Following Through

Chapter 1 introduced you to the different categories of dangerous men and offered some general insights about why women get involved with such men. My hope is that you will be able to use that information to help you identify men who are not and never will become good dating material.

This chapter turns the focus back onto you: a woman at risk for choosing dangerous men. The point I want to emphasize in this chapter is that you are the only one who can change your behavior and make different choices. Yes, dangerous men exist and are more than willing to draw you into a frustrating, unhealthy, destructive, or potentially deadly dynamic. But the responsibility lies entirely with you for your choices—past, present, and future. It is up to you alone to see how you ignored warning signs in the past and to relearn how to pay attention to and act on those same warning signs, starting now.

It is tempting for many women to blame "him" for all their problems. It may be true that he is an alcoholic/a workaholic/ mentally ill/a womanizer/a career criminal ... or whatever his baggage is. But in order for you to change your pattern of selecting dangerous men, it is crucial that you accept responsilibity for the fact that you chose to get involved with him. It was a mutual decision, made between two consenting adults. Refusing to see this will keep you repeating the same behaviors you are seeking to stop.

Too many programs that aim to help women focus on just the man, as if we women were blind, wandering idiots who "fall" into relationships and don't recognize any part of what's happening. My research, which you will read about later in this chapter, indicates the opposite. We aren't blind and helpless. We know and we choose. What I'm saying here is not "victim bashing"; it's about accountability. In the beginning of a relationship you may not have seen all of the things about him that added up to dangerousness. But there came a time when those things became clear. Understanding why you ignored your red flags and stayed with him anyway is the first step toward changing. While it may seem easier to believe that you were solely his "victim," in fact, it is much more empowering to realize that dating is based on mutuality, not on hostage-taking. Grasping this truth can change your life.

Your Built-In Danger-Alert System

We each have a system of red flags and red alerts that can act as a personalized internal monitor for dangerous men. In fact, when interviewing women about red flags, never once did I have to define what a red flag was. There was a universal knowledge of the existence of red flags, even when I interviewed women from as far away as Indonesia.

This red-alert system is sort of a cross between womanly intuition, a biological sensory response system, and a spiritually whispered warning. Each woman has to become aware of how she most often receives her red flags and warnings. Some women have very real physical sensations, others notice mental or emotional symptoms, and others sense it spiritually when their red-alert system fires off warnings. Some women experience a combination of these. How you sense these warnings is not as important as what you do with what you sense.

Let's take a look at the different ways red flags present themselves to us.

PHYSICAL RED FLAGS

A sensory response system is something that all humans are born with; it is called the *autonomic nervous system* or *fight-or-flight response*. You can think of it like a home burglary alarm. At birth, normal, healthy babies have a sensory-based warning system. They know automatically when they are hungry, scared, or otherwise in need. They don't need to be told when to cry or how to respond if they feel threatened. Their alarm system responds automatically by causing them to be startled, to raise their hands into the air, and to start crying. Over time, they learn what danger is through conditioning. But before they could "learn" it, they just "knew" it because of the biological adaptations they were born with.

Conditioned learning in babies eventually picks up where biology leaves off. Babies begin to learn through trial and error what is safe and what is harmful. Unless they have been abused, they don't ignore or reframe these trial-and-error messages. The reframing of warning messages seems to be an adult, maladaptive, learned process rather than a natural childlike state steered by biology. Children pay attention to the truth their bodies tell them. Adults learn to allow their defense mechanisms to alter the truth.

As adults we are alerted to danger by bodily sensations that we need to pay attention to. These could include a flash of fear, sweating, a tight stomach, a pounding heart, the hair standing up on the neck, or a general feeling of discomfort that we may be unable to name. But sometimes we adults ignore these sensations. We do not respond the way we automatically did as children. We don't stop to recognize what our bodily reactions are telling us.

The bodily reactions we experience when we're with a dangerous man hold a lot of the information we need to know about him. Women who want to avoid dangerous men focus on the physical messages their biological system is sending them. One of my workshop attendees put it this way: "I had a constant stomachache when I was with this guy. I also started having symptoms of TMJ [temporomandibular joint] syndrome. That's when I realized I was having stress reactions to him. In a real sense I couldn't 'stomach' him or his lines! I also was jamming my mouth shut so as not to respond to the things he was saying that were pushing my buttons. Luckily, when my jaw really started to hurt, I got the big picture."

SPIRITUAL RED FLAGS

Our spiritual red flags come from what we refer to as "knowing," "intuition," or "sensing." This system has all the wonderful makings of a free bodyguard service—if only we will listen *and* respond to it. Spiritual intuition alerts us when we sense that something is not right or when we just "know" this isn't the person for us or the place for us to be in. We know these things without any overt knowledge or concrete information as to why we know them. Trying to specifically name "why" we sense something is not always necessary, but responding to it is. Women everywhere have stories about their intuition and how it diverted some disaster when they really listened to it.

Knowing, intuition, and sensing can give women an opportunity to respond to clues they get about dangerous men. For women to ignore the clues and wait until the clues have become facts places them in extreme danger. Many adults sense, but not all respond. It is okay to respond to a clue without having or ever getting the hard facts. By the time the event is a fact, it could be too late. Sensing without responding only gives us the opportunity to regret what we failed to respond to.

Spiritually tuned-in women do not ignore their sensing and intuition. Marla can attest to that. She couldn't shake an unprovable feeling that a guy she was on a date with was dangerous or in some way unsafe. Outwardly, he was so polite; he did all the things her mother told her were signs of a "good" dating choice, like opening her car door. But deep inside it was like God was whispering into her ear to avoid being alone with him. He said he forgot his wallet and had to go home to get it before they could go out. Marla waited in the car while he went inside. When he appeared at the front door on the telephone with a worried look and motioned for her to come to the door, she thought something terrible had happened. She went to the door and he continued to pretend to be getting bad news. He motioned her in and calmy closed the door behind her. He ended the call, pushed her to the couch, and attempted to rape her. She fled successfully but was left astounded by how she'd ignored what, on some level, she already "knew" about him.

MENTAL AND EMOTIONAL RED FLAGS

Mentally and emotionally we are also given plenty of clues about our true feelings in a relationship. This red-alert system is another avenue for our protection if we will tune in. Sometimes this information is best gathered from people who know us well.

Think about the following questions in regard to a current or past relationship: How are you since you've met this man? Are you balanced and grounded, or from an emotional perspective are you swinging wildly all over the place? Do your friends tell you that you are different in a negative way? Are you more anxious than normal, awaiting the call or worrying about where he is? Are you melancholy without knowing why? Do you feel confused about the relationship? Do you feel a general unease without knowing why? Are you having difficulty sleeping, eating, or concentrating? (Contrary to what folklore might tell you, this doesn't mean you're in love!) Are you keeping up with the rest of your scheduled life, or have you abandoned your normal activities for him or for the promise of him? Have you acquired some of his bad habits? What kind of things are you thinking about now that you are dating him? Are they healthy and realistic things, or are you off track somewhere?

The answers to these questions can indicate red flags in a relationship. Wise women are aware of their emotional condition in a new relationship, and they honor their instincts by getting out when their emotional or psychological distress—even if it's "inexplicable"—signals a warning. When Sierra began dating Chase she ignored her growing need to help, fix, and stabilize him. On a rational level she "knew" she couldn't fix anyone, but that didn't stop her from indulging every whim to fixate on Chase's mounting problems and his mental illness. His out-of-control life quickly became a diversion for her, and soon all of her emotional energies were being sucked up by her growing anxiety over "what will happen next?" Unfortunately, she didn't respond to her early red flags by ending the relationship, and the outcome was nothing short of disasterous. You can read Sierra's whole story in Chapter 7, "The Mentally Ill Man."

Why Do Women Ignore Their Red Flags?

If our red flags can provide protective insights into relationships and into potentially dangerous men, why don't we listen to them? We women have an uncanny ability to ignore our red flags. Our dating patterns reveal that we often ignore all the warning systems that we are born with and that would keep us safe. Many of us have successfully ignored physical sensations, spiritual intuitions, and emotional reactions for years. Somewhere between childhood and adulthood we have allowed many of our built-in alarm systems to become dismantled. Years of overriding internal warnings with reasons to move ahead anyway, combined with the ability to numb the feelings triggered by our own system's messages, have deadened many women to the symptoms of being in a dangerous relationship. This perilous cycle can lead women to date four or five dangerous men before they begin to notice the spiritual, emotional, and physical messages they have been ignoring. Another workshop attendee said, "If I had just clued in for a second, I would have realized that I was getting the same red flags over and over. My red-alert system was consistent!

I had the same sensations emotionally and physically with each guy who turned out to be dangerous. I didn't have them when I chose healthier guys. In the end, it was good to know that my system was accurate if I'd just listen! And how many dangerous men could I have avoided?"

There are all sorts of reasons why women ignore red flags despite their obvious usefulness. Some of these include

* unspoken societal rules

* cultural gender roles that assign women's behaviors

* generational family traditions and early conditioning regarding male behavior in a woman's family of origin

* a woman's own mental-health history and/or abuse history

Each of these is explored below. As you read on, bear in mind that in many cases the explanation lies in a combination of these factors.

UNSPOKEN SOCIETAL RULES

Exploring women's historical and traditional roles has helped us to understand women's patterns of development, women's values, and women's life choices. The unfolding field of women's studies helps us to ask questions about where we have come from and where we are going in the context of a mostly male-defined world.

From this perspective it is helpful to think about whether our patriarchal society has taught girls and women certain behaviors and rewarded us for ignoring or "overlooking" certain dangerous character flaws. Has society reinforced the idea that for women and girls it is more important to be polite than it is to question men's behaviors that might concern us? That it is more important to accept everyone unconditionally than it is to see who proves trustworthy over time? That it is more important to embrace a supposed Judeo-Christian ethic of loving the unlovable than it is to realize that it's not safe to love everyone? That it is more important to turn the other cheek than it is to know when boundaries are being violated? Has society taught women that it is more important to believe that everyone can change than it is to accept the fact that psychopathology has taught us this isn't true?

Have we failed to challenge society's unspoken rules for women and girls, thus placing ourselves at risk? Have we embraced a message that says ignoring our red flags for the sake of fulfilling these rules in our interactions with men is more important than staying alive and healthy? We have to ask why we still ignore our red flags in order to meet these mandates. Do women who date dangerous men do so because they challenge these rules less often than other women? Following these prescribed roles can certainly lead to the dismantling of our red-alert system. Tori counts this as part of what led to her bad dating choices. Her mother taught her to trust everyone and to play with the kids whom other children wouldn't play with. Tori became overly tolerant of society's castaways because her upbringing had desensitized her to what in their behavior made them undesirable as playmates. Once Tori was an adult, it became easy for her to overlook a lot of undesirable behavior in just about anyone.

CULTURAL GENDER ROLES

The argument for gender equality begins with the argument that women should have the right to be safe and to question anything that threatens their safety. For this reason, the fact that we women have learned to ignore many of our sensory-based responses to red flags raises some questions about women's and men's gender roles. Why have we come to believe that we "should" ignore red flags? And why is the behavior of dangerous men acceptable?

Our gender roles play a part in causing us to expect certain types of behavior from men. This can occur at both the cultural level and the family level. The attitude that says "boys will be boys" tells us that even men's behaviors that are less desirable are just to be "expected." By contrast, women are expected to be put up with all sorts of unacceptable behavior for long periods of time. Women are expected to be tolerant of poor character in men. We are expected to turn a blind eye to inappropriate behavior. We are expected to remain hopeful and vigilant for change in men who probably will never change.

Unfortunately, this means women have learned to ignore what we feel, what bothers us, and what makes us uneasy. We have learned to be "the rock" within the relationship, the family, the community. We remain defined by our gender roles. Tori's strict Catholic-Italian background prescribed entrenched roles for males and females. Her mother was a Polish immigrant who waited on her Italian Mafia husband like a house servant. If Tori's mother was unhappy, it never occurred to her to even think about it. Tori watched a subserviant, passive women live her life being disrespected by and fearful of her own husband. Tori grew up thinking these were normal marriage dynamics.

In my research, women who dated dangerous men told me they had an underlying belief that men choose women and women respond to the choosing. On the one hand, we are progressive women who can ask men out on dates, yet at the same time, in the eyes of these women, the whole dynamic of dating, courtship, and marriage involves women's responding to men's choosing them as partners. This message may be enhanced by family training that teaches girls and women to always respond favorably to men's approaches. One has to wonder if other women—those who don't date dangerous men—see the dynamic the same way.

Some women who have been involved with dangerous men told me they waited to be "released" from relationships and did not initiate breakups even when they no longer wanted to see the man. Even when they feared a man, they hoped he would break up with them. Other women admitted to marrying men they did not love because they didn't think they "could" or "should" say no to a marriage proposal. A man had chosen them for this honored position, and they did not know how to turn him down. Willow fell into that trap with Garrett. She pitied him more than she had passion for him. She didn't want to marry him, but she had never learned the skills to help her say no and back it up with fortitude when he pressured her to marry him anyway. In Willow's family of origin, when her dad wanted something—anything—he got it. Women's desires and needs were secondary. No wonder she didn't know if she had "the right" to not want a marriage.

FAMILY TRAINING AND TRADITIONS

Our families, good or bad, are the largest training grounds for our red-alert systems. Home is where we internalize our families' beliefs about women, men, relationships, boundaries, safety, verbalizing needs, or sucking it up and keeping quiet. All of these values and behaviors are taught, and most of them are unspoken. It is at home where girls and women learn what generations before them believed about women's behaviors, men's behaviors, marriage, dating, and dangerousness. It is at home where we may have learned the lesson "just get the man and later you can change him." It is at home where we may have learned to excuse dangerous behaviors like violence ("He's had a hard day at work") or addictions ("He likes his beer at night") or unavailability ("He's almost divorced, and besides he hates his wife; she's such a witch").

Women have normalized generations of negative behaviors by reframing them with messages like "The Smiths always have tempers—that's the Irish in them" or "You know the Schultzes are big beer drinkers—they're German; it's in their blood" or "The Brown men have always had a roving eye for other women, but they always come back." Earlier generations of women trained the next ones to discount dangerous behavior, minimize unmet needs, and basically ignore inner alarms that might be sounding loudly. Young girls' early conditioning to disregard, reframe, and rename dangerous behavior and to attempt to make relationships work at any cost is just one more way they learn to dismantle the red-alert system.

Soon, whatever your autonomic nervous system is trying to tell you, you no longer hear it over the mantra you've adopted: "He isn't *that* bad." "He's a nice guy, I guess." "At least he's a hard worker." But your jaw is clenched, your stomach is tight, the hair on the back of your neck is standing up. The still, small voice is saying, "Something doesn't feel right," but the mantra continues. "He isn't *that* bad." "He's a nice guy, I guess." "At least he's a hard worker."

Eventually, when he says something that is scary, appalling, or inappropriate, you excuse the behavior without wondering where it came from or whether there will be more of it. You see his temper revealed when he is rough with his language, with an animal, or with a child, and you remember another time when you saw a similar behavior from someone else and how it did *not* turn out well. But you "don't want to compare" him to someone else, so you move on without having the foresight to pay attention to your fears.

You find clues to his character through your discovery of a lie, an undisclosed past, or other red flags, but you repeatedly give him the benefit of the doubt, all the while increasing your risk for personal harm. You hear the family messages that taught you to give everyone repeated chances, to avoid being suspicious, to expect men to be like this.

Now, contrast these responses to how a baby would naturally respond to something that scared or bothered it. There would be no calling it something else, no ignoring it, no toughing it out. The baby would be crying, shaking, or acting startled—all normal reactions to an act of violation.

We must wonder why the women in our family didn't teach us that we should be keeping a mental file of character traits of the men we get involved with. Why didn't we learn that we should heed the moments that reveal who he really is, even when he doesn't mean for us to notice? Why don't we automatically know to keep tabs on how we feel when we experience these things? Why didn't our mothers teach us that we should pay attention to our jaw, our stomach, and any other place where we hold tension and truth? Why don't women teach girls about dangerous men in terms they can understand, which include bodily sensations of fear?

Tori says:

> My mother didn't speak English until she was in her teens. She was married before she realized men had pubic hair! How in the world could she have helped me as a young woman understand the complexities of relationships? Instead she taught me that "this is just the way Italian men are." When my father took mistresses and they even came to our front door, my mother said this was just what men did. When he drank and was violent, she said, "At least he provides well for us." She was always teaching me in some way that women are supposed to just passively accept whatever karmic outcomes end up in their lives. I was shown in many ways over and over that I was powerless. Society had rules about how women were expected to be, gender roles were entrenched and unbreakable, and my mother's excuses for a violent, alcoholic, and abusive husband taught me that this is what families were all about.

Families who display black-and-white thinking train children to see the world in overly simplistic ways. Women who were taught in their families to see people's behaviors as either good or bad usually end up choosing to see people as all good. But most of real life is lived in the gray areas. Gray areas are like holding tanks for ambiguity, wait-and-see rooms for testing out character. This is especially true until we know a person well enough to recognize the stark realities of his character. Women who were trained to trust unconditionally believe that trust should come first, even before he's proven himself. If she "trusts" someone, he must be "good," even if she knows nothing about him. If she is dating him, he is good. If he is a police officer, he must be good. If he's a minister, he is certainly good.

This line of thought is especially dangerous when a woman thinks that if his behaviors are "good," then he is good. If he opens a door, pays for a meal, or gives her a compliment, it simply means his manners are good. It does *not* mean his character is good. Good manners do not equal good character. But because of their familial culture, some women do not know how to process dichotomous information like this. They don't know how to see that a man's behaviors can be good even while his character is bad. (In postmodern terms, we call this "posing.") In these women's eyes, a man has to be either good or bad. He cannot have both good and bad characteristics. This contradiction places pressure on a woman to label any man she comes into contact with as either good or bad. She must internally make a decision. Families who train children in black-and-white thinking are thus setting them up to erroneously equate behaviors with character, conditioning that can lead to the dismantling of a woman's built-in red-alert system.

External gestures and career titles tend to carry more weight with certain women than character issues. If he is a polite teacher who acts kindly toward children, then he is "good"—even though he may have a lengthy history of shoplifting or lying. Marla, whom we met earlier in the chapter, says the only training she got about men was based on what kind of jobs they had and what kind of manners they displayed. Her mother told her if men had good manners then they were good. But the same guy who opened the car door for her later attempted to rape her! Marla didn't know how to choose when she was presented with a dichotomy between the training she received from her mother and what her red flags were telling her about this guy. Marla's mother also put a heavy emphasis on careers. Firefighters were "good and brave men" even if they beat their wives. "Men of the cloth" were to be respected "just because." Marla grew up believing that certain jobs automatically commanded respect and indicated that a person was safe.

A WOMAN'S MENTAL HEALTH

Another area that may give clues as to why women ignore red flags is their own mental health. Family systems that teach young girls to ignore their own needs set up a lifetime of unhealthy psychology. Families that discount violence, excuse inappropriate behavior, hold different standards for males and females, and violate personal boundaries more than likely will produce adult women with mental-health issues.

These problems can include low self-esteem, a pattern of accepting any kind of treatment in a relationship, fear of abandonment, trust issues, addictions, codependency, eating disorders, depression, anxiety, sexual issues, and chronic loneliness. They can also include other disorders, diagnosed or undiagnosed.

A woman's early childhood may have taught her erroneous and unhealthy messages, leading to dysfunction, destruction, and desperation, that may then set her up to accept dangerous men later in life. Women who were physically or sexually abused as children, who were raped as adults, who came from homes where one or both parents were addicts, whose parent or parents had a serious mental illness, or who had traumatic foster care experiences are at particular risk for getting involved with dangerous men. A woman with her own history of abuse may unknowingly remain numb and not pick up on the signals of her own red flags. She may need counseling to help her reconnect with her feelings so she can recognize the red flags in the future. Maybe you are already aware of your own psychological issues. Either way, be aware that depression, loneliness, and a history of childhood abuse can condition women to ignore red flags. As a previous client of mine said, "If I had known that my own mental-health issues were helping to lead me to the lousy men I kept picking, I'd have gone into counseling a lot earlier or gotten on medication—anything to stop the cycle. I didn't know that my own disorder was fueling some of my crazy behavior and choices."

Let me emphasize that dangerous and pathological men are not attracted only to women with mental-health issues. Stories you will read later involve women from stable and normal families who dated dangerous men. A woman's mental-health history is only one reason why she might date a dangerous man.

Tori's Red Flags

No one in Tori's family taught her that her body could tell her more truth than her mind could. When she was with Jay, she would say on a weekly basis, "He's a pain in my behind." She regularly told her friends that she wished he'd move out (although she didn't tell him). Soon Tori was sporting a huge abscess on her behind. Her red-alert system had been trying to send her a message all along, but she'd ignored it. Now she realized that her red-alert system had moved into emergency mode, manifesting visibly for her what she had been saying with her lips but failing to take care of in her life.

For almost a year, Tori suffered from the abscess despite undergoing medical treatment. I told her, "Get rid of Jay, and it will go away." A month after Jay left, the abscess was gone.

Sometimes our red-alert system is less dramatic than Tori's. It is a whisper in our hearts when we can't sleep at night. It's a disconcerting comment about him from a friend that keeps replaying in our mind. It's the knot in our stomach that won't go away. It's the nagging question we know the answer to but choose to ignore. Maybe it's the laissez-faire attitude we try to project when we pretend to be dating him "just for fun"—even while our clenched jaw feels like anything but fun.

Underneath the lies we tell ourselves is the truth of our red-alert system. It wants to get your attention, but years spent ignoring, denying, rationalizing, minimizing, and lying to yourself have muffled the inner alarm that is trying to warn you that someone unsafe is invading your life.

Your Own Red Flags

You probably already have a good idea of how most of your red flags operate, even if you have trained yourself to stop paying attention to them. The good news is that you can retrain yourself to listen to them. You can bring back into your awareness the inner alarm system that you've been ignoring, and you can learn to use it for your protection. Whether you've ignored your red flags because of society's unspoken rules, gender roles, family conditioning, your own mental-health issues, or any other reason, starting now you can make better decisions about what to do with the information they provide to you.

Your past, including your dating history, holds enormous information that can help you change your pattern of selecting dangerous men. For this reason, the exercises in the accompanying workbook were designed to help you systematically examine your past and extract every opportunity to learn from your own experiences. This detailed journey into your personal history will allow you to explore childhood messages and adult choices to obtain new insights into what may have fueled your decisions to get involved with dangerous men.

But it isn't only our own experiences that can teach us. Wise women are willing to learn wherever they can and from whomever they can. We can learn what other women are willing to teach us about their histories and their red flags. We can learn how other women ignored and dishonored their red flags, and we can learn the consequences of those decisions. We can choose to take these lessons to heart and allow them to influence our decisions. In this way, we don't have to date every type of dangerous man in order to learn about each of them. That's why women's stories of their involvement with dangerous men form an integral part of this book. Read each story in the next several chapters with an open mind that will allow you to sense the particular message each one holds for you.

What Other Women's Red Flags Can Teach You

As I did the research for this book, I wanted to know about women's red flags and how women did or did not respond to them. I wanted to know the outcomes of women's decisions to ignore or to heed their red flags. Women consistently told me the following:

1. Yes, there were indeed red flags as early as their first date with a dangerous man.

2. They knowingly ignored the red flags.

3. The red flags were related to the eventual breakup of the relationship. (In essence, this means women's red flags were good predictors of probable relationship outcomes.)

In fact, not a single woman told me there weren't any red flags. Women indicated that after they broke up with the dangerous man and spent some time examining the relationship, they recognized that there were red flags early on, and these flags were indeed related to the reasons why the relationship ended. Women also wondered why they'd waited until the relationship was over to even notice the red flags. Why hadn't they responded to them all along? As you've learned by now, there are many possible issues that might explain why women tend to ignore their inner alarm systems.

The women I spoke to seemed to universally recognize certain sensations as red flags and to know what they meant. And yet they still ignored them or did not speak about them with others. Fortunately, this implies that we have control over what we do with the information we get from our red-alert systems. In the long run, ignoring our red flags only seems to postpone what we already know in our heart of hearts will be the inevitable outcome of a relationship with a dangerous man.

The following are some examples of how women's experiences with red flags played out over time:

1. Often their red flags were confirmed by others (family members, a friend, or an ex-girlfriend of the dangerous man). Not only did women ignore their own red flags; but they also ignored the confirmation from others, thereby missing more than one opportunity to avoid a broken heart.

2. Even when there were red flags, women preferred to focus on the man's good points and to diminish, ignore,

deny, or reframe his negative, dangerous, or dissatisfying character traits or behaviors. It was more important to find something positive in him to relate to than it was to be aware of his dangerous behaviors. To this end, women also preferred to focus on "why" he was ill or on the sad story about his disorder or his life rather than on how these issues could harm them. His sad story distracted the women from asking themselves, "What do I need to do for *me*, now that I know this?"

3. Women tended to believe they were going to be the exception to what their red flags were telling them. They believed the red flags would prove to be wrong this time, with this man—for some miraculous reason they couldn't explain logically. These women already had experiences with red flags and knew that red flags were good predictors of outcomes, yet still the women overrode them. Fantasy thinking overrode fact.

4. Women were willing to accept some attention (usually a physical or sexual relationship along with some semblance of an emotional connection) in exhange for flaws in the relationship. Most women recognized early on some of the dangerous man's limitations but chose to accept what he brought to the relationship despite their own dissatisfaction with and, often, concern over his negative behaviors. This is related to how women diminished, ignored, denied, or reframed their man's behaviors (see #2 above). They recognized those behaviors yet still became willing to accept what he brought to the relationship.

5. Once women began to accept the man's flawed behaviors, they would tell themselves they could "change" the parts of him they were dissatisfied with or concerned about. However, these behaviors were often related to what made him dangerous to begin with, and thus, in the

end, the women were consistently unsuccessful in changing these aspects of him.

6. Not knowing how to be alone or being uncomfortable with being alone led many women to accept frustrating and dangerous relationships despite their red flags. Issues that seemed to play a role in whether a woman was inclined to get involved and stay involved with dangerous men included being recently divorced or in the middle of a divorce, dysfunctional early family relationships, or a history of childhood abuse. Some women cited loneliness, an intention of not "really" getting involved with him, or wanting to avoid boredom as reasons why they ignored red flags and dated men whom they found dangerous or dissatisfying, or who were married or involved with another woman.

7. Most women I interviewed did not bother to glean information from their own previously failed relationships. Many could not cite the similarities among all the unsuccessful relationships they'd had. Most did not stop their dating sprees long enough to examine character flaws that kept being repeated in the dangerous men they'd dated. Nor had the women looked at their own issues, including mental-health issues, that might have led them to choose these types of men. While they did acknowledge that they'd ignored their red flags, they did not recognize the similarities in the types of men they'd dated over and over.

8. Of those few who could define the types of dangerous men they had dated, many believed it was unlikely to happen again. Even without counseling, almost all of these women judged themselves "enlightened" and felt assured it would never happen again, simply because they "had been hurt." Having been hurt gave them an unrealistic confidence that they would never choose dangerously again. Sadly, however, the facts often tell a different story.

Even some of the women who contributed stories for this book and who were zealously confident they had learned from their pain are reportedly once again in dangerous relationships.

9. A large portion of women wanted to blame the dangerous men they'd been involved with. They continued to see themselves as "victims" and "targets" of men who wanted easy prey. While this is often true, especially with men who qualify as emotional predators, what these women failed to see was that, as women who said yes to the first date and to every date thereafter, they were equal partners in the choosing. Women who did not stop long enough to evaluate why they had dated two, three, four, or more dangerous men and to examine what their patterns of mutual selection were saying about them were at extremely high risk of repeating the behavior by getting involved with more dangerous men. These were women who were also likely to wait for him to "release" them from the relationship instead of ending it themselves.

Most of the women I interviewed were professionals. They were intelligent and successful in their fields. Therefore, the natural inclination to link dangerous-man choices with the young, the less intelligent, the poor, or the less educated did not bear out in my research, in most cases. Likewise, the younger women who were included in my research (ages sixteen to nineteen) were good students and came from upper-middle-class families.

Implications

It was shocking to see how some women chose to get involved with dangerous or pathological men out of boredom. Equally disconcerting was seeing how women continued to date dangerous men because they refused to evaluate their own histories. What was most noteworthy was the overwhelming need of most of the women to not be alone. There was almost an unspoken fear of long-term "abandonment," which turned out for most women to equate to "not currently dating." How is it that women would come to equate a status of not dating with the prospect of never again being in an intimate relationship?

For the women I interviewed, the idea of dating someone casually for a lengthy period was fairly obsolete. Women seemed in a hurry to "hook up." This was true for women in varying age categories, not just the young. Although most seemed to want to imply that they were above "dating for mere attention" and did not want to admit that they feared loneliness, abandonment, or a status of not dating, they still very much fit that profile. They verbalized these fears in the same disguised language they used to reframe and downplay men's dangerous behaviors.

Women who got involved with dangerous men usually dated quickly and intensely, allowed the relationship to become sexual within the first few months, and moved in with the man within months of meeting him or married him impulsively during the first twelve months of the relationship. Others were knowingly and willingly available for married men.

All of this is great news for a dangerous man looking for another willing partner, but it is decidedly *not* good news for women who want to find healthy, meaningful relationships but who still exhibit these sorts of relationship patterns. Too many women embrace a flawed approach, a broken belief system, or a tendency toward casual complacency when seeking someone to date. Too often we women ignore our own awareness of red flags, dissociate ourselves from the reality of a man's character, and accept unacceptable behavior on his part—all to avoid facing loneliness or boredom. Such attitudes serve to place dangerous men squarely in women's radars, and vice versa.

Telling Yourself the Truth

If we aren't going to tell our dates the truth about our belief system as it pertains to relationships, then let's at least start telling *ourselves* the truth. Being honest with yourself about what you *think* versus what you *do* could save your emotional health or even your life. This includes the things women tell themselves about "why" they are dating a certain man.

Most of the women I interviewed did not tell themselves the truth about what they were doing or why. The untruths they told themselves seemed to be a variation on the theme "I'm dating him for entertainment purposes." They translated this as meaning "I am not going to really get involved." Yet they were dating men who were mentally ill, violent, or otherwise dangerous. Other women told themselves, "I am well aware of what I am doing. I've been down this road before. I've been hurt, so I am alert to what's going on here"—while dating men who had hidden lives or were emotionally unavailable or married. Having "been down this road before" made women believe they would avoid becoming ensnared, and yet the very fact that a woman is willingly dating a dangerous man means she is already ensnared. Just what do women consider "entertainment"?

The lies women told themselves ranged from outright denial to a sort of narcissism. They seemed to think they were above the inevitable and natural consequences of their bad choices. Or they convinced themselves they could not be harmed by "casually" playing with dangerous men. Their inability to identify their real motives, admit what they were doing, and predict the likely outcomes of their behaviors placed them in jeopardy. These women lacked the basic life skills of being able to recognize cause and effect, choices and consequences.

Women's Self-Sabotaging Behaviors

What I said early in the chapter bears repeating: As much as we would like to blame our involvement with a dangerous man solely on the fact that he chose us, the fact is that women contribute to this dynamic through acts of dissociation and denial. We are not victims; we are volunteers. And the good news in that is that if we are volunteering, we can quit! We can "unvolunteer."

We can take ourselves out of the loop once we recognize our own sabotaging behaviors—those that increase the likelihood of our choosing poorly. Let's take a look at some of these self-sabotaging behaviors.

CHOOSING TO IGNORE RED FLAGS

In order to avoid dating dangerous and pathological men, women must come to understand that ignoring red flags leads to the dismantling of a woman's red-flag system. If you've noticed a red flag, then you are aware that your red-alert system is working. If you make a conscious decision to date this guy anyway, and you minimize the red flag by saying, "He's no one I would get serious with—just someone to do things with," then you are not listening to your inner safety system. But as you continue seeing him, and as you become more aware of his limitations, you're forced to focus on only the "good things about him." You try to make the relationship "more fun" so that dating him is about "distraction." Meanwhile, you are actively dismantling your red-alert system. You, the person who should care the most about your own safety, are unplugging your inner alarm. No one is doing it to you. You are doing it to yourself.

Following your slow but methodical dismantling of your safety system, your standards begin to drop. You wouldn't knowingly date someone mentally ill, so you ignore the signs that he has chronic mood swings. Your boundaries shift, too. You don't advocate that anyone date an addict, but your man is not really an addict—he's just a fun, party-loving kind of guy. He's had a lot of good reasons to celebrate lately. And who would knowingly stay with a violent man? But punching a wall is not the same thing as hitting you, so he isn't *really* violent. Your family would never approve of you dating a married man, but he's "going to be out of that relationship any day," which in your mind makes him available. Soon those alarms buzzing inside of you are just a numbed vibration.

LACK OF PERSONAL BOUNDARIES

An equally dangerous behavior on the part of women who get involved with dangerous men is a lack of standards and boundaries. According to the women I interviewed (as well as women I've treated in private practice), if they are bored or lonely, anything will do to rectify those feelings. This ties in with the lies they are telling themselves—that they aren't going to get involved if they are merely "playing," and if they are "just playing," then they aren't at emotional or physical risk. But since when does "only playing" help a woman avoid a rape?

Women have repeatedly demonstrated that the longer they violate their own standards and boundaries, the easier it is to do it the next time. More information on boundaries will be covered in Chapter 11, but for now it is important to know that we train ourselves about what behaviors to accept from others. This means pathological behavior starts to look pretty normal if the only kinds of men you have dated are pathological or dangerous ones. The longer you embrace a certain belief system, the more normalized it becomes within your worldview. Women are consistently shocked to realize they have dated four or five dangerous men. They all want to know how they fell into such a destructive and possibly deadly pattern. They did it by having low standards in their personal boundaries and by ignoring red flags in every relationship, until they had a history of several dangerous relationships and dangerous men began to be "just the kind of men they date."

This is not hard to fathom. If we continue to ignore the emotional, spiritual, and physical red flags that our body and psyche faithfully send us, then we will eventually train ourselves to ignore any and all incoming messages. That is why women who think they are consciously choosing to "just play" or "just hang out" with someone who fits one of the categories of dangerous men are really playing with more than just mere amusement and distraction. They are training themselves to accept the next dangerous man who will be all too happy to distract them. And as I mentioned earlier, the longer women date pathological men, the more they conform themselves to the pathological relationship to make it easier to be in. This reminds me of the Stockholm syndrome, wherein people held in captivity begin to empathize and identify with their captors as a way of adapting to their situation. It is too incongruous to be in a relationship with someone whose thinking and behavior are disturbing. Something has to line up, so women accept the pathological thinking and behavior to eliminate the disturbance they feel.

Some women in a hospital program where I worked "sounded pathological" during group therapy sessions. It was later confirmed through psychological testing that they weren't pathological. They were what we came to call "pseudopathologicals." Each of them had been in relationships with various pathological men for so long they began to "act" pathological even though they wouldn't have been technically diagnosed as such.

LACK OF INSIGHT

Women want to credit themselves with having far more insight than they actually use. They may have insight, but somewhere in the dating game the insight gets shelved and the women continue to end up in dead-end relationships with dangerous men. These women have not gleaned what their past relationship failures could teach them. They ignore their own histories and patterns. They make excuses for not examining their own lives. They act based on impulse and on the intensity of emotional or sexual attraction.

Their lack of insight has been replaced with "magical thinking." Magical thinking ignores reality and replaces it with fantasy. It tosses out logic and inserts wishful thinking. It hopes for all things, but from the wrong person. It clings to fairytales and folklore in which Sleeping Beauty is kissed by a prince and awakens to a new life, and Cinderella escapes a dysfunctional family by dancing with a prince.

Conclusions

We each have the following basic tools at our disposal to help keep us safe—if only we choose to use them:

* the ability to sense and respond to our red flags

* the ability to read our past experiences and learn from them

* the ability to tell ourselves the truth about our own thinking, motives, and behaviors

* the ability to choose differently by conscious decision

Acknowledging this list places all of the responsibility for choosing safe, healthy relationships on us. To make use of these tools we must listen intuitively, look at the hard truths our previous choices show us, be tough with ourselves about our hidden motives and our intentional departures from reality, consciously make different choices, and remain accountable for those choices.

Before you decide that you've learned all you need to learn because you've "been hurt" in the past, read the next few chapters about the categories of dangerous men, and then take a look at the quiz in Chapter 11 titled "Am I in Danger of Dating More Dangerous Men?" Allow yourself to see just how at risk you might be of getting involved in yet another frustrating, unhealthy, dangerous relationship. The workbook has a section that helps you identify and examine your loopholes and what you say and do to talk yourself into staying in dangerous relationships.

In addition, as a way of reminding yourself how much the wisdom of your red flags can teach you, remember the following acronym. I like to think of staying tuned in to our red-alert system as keeping our WITS about us:

Women's

Intuition

Training

System

And finally, remember that our sisters in humanity have much to teach us if we will learn from their mistakes. If we heed our red flags, embrace the lessons offered us by what we have lived and learned, and listen to what other women tell us about their history with dangerous relationships, then we can enjoy safe, healthy relationships.

A Gift from Your Sisters

From here, we will examine in detail the different types of dangerous men. Each of the next eight chapters is devoted to one of the categories introduced in Chapter 1. But first, a few of the women who tell their stories in this book wanted to share with you some of their insights about opportunities they missed to recognize their red flags:

> I ignored early reports that he had physically fought with other girlfriends. Why should I think it would be different with me? He even told me a former girlfriend had used a knife to get away from him. Why would she need a knife? I found it odd that he hated his parents and most of the people in his family. But then, he also told me his father beat his mother regularly. Don't we always say that the apple doesn't fall far from the tree? Why didn't I believe that? He told me he had tried to get a "mail-order bride" so he could find a submissive woman. How did I contort that into something I could find okay?
>
> I knew early on that he reminded me of my father, who used to beat on women. He lied like my father, and they were both alcoholics. The red flags were screaming, and I wasn't listening. That he was so much like my father should have been a big-enough clue, but because he was rich and famous, I wanted to believe he would marry me. But I had to learn to listen not to the words he said but to what his behavior kept saying and what my red flags were screaming.
>
> — **Amy**
>
> *(Amy's story appears in Chapter 9)*

I shouldn't have allowed myself to be too attracted to really glib conversationalists who have a lot of superficial charm. Too charming is definitely a red flag. If someone now ever exhibits a behavior that makes me uncomfortable, I'm out of there—not just out of his presence but out of the relationship. I now know there is a reason why I'm uncomfortable in those situations. I've learned to keep my ears very, very open—to do research with a guy's friends and family and to learn all about a guy early on to avoid surprises. If you research and go slow, you can always bail out easier if you aren't in too deep, too soon. Also, guys' patterns of employment have proven to show a lot about them.

— **Jenna**

(Jenna's story appears in Chapters 10 and 13)

Most of all, the women who shared their stories for this book want you to know the following: Do not focus excessively on what is different between their relationships with dangerous men and yours. Do not look for loopholes in these stories so you can stay in a dangerous relationship and make an excuse about why he is "different" from the men depicted here. Instead, affirm what is similar between these women's stories and yours. Learn from what so many women have lived, so that you will be safe and will have the ability and opportunity to make better choices.

Chapter 3

The Permanent Clinger

Looking for a love that will never leave you? Well, here he is! But remember, the operative word is "never." When you pick Alan Adoration, he wants it to be forever.

Alan Adoration-Turned-to-Suffocation

The permanent clinger naturally attracts women who have spent too much time with other types of dangerous men. Emotional predators, violent men, and emotionally unavailable men (all of whom you will meet in the next few chapters) make the permanent clinger look like a gift from heaven ... initially. It is not uncommon for women to swing from relationships with other types of dangerous men into the arms of an attention-giving clinger. However, although predators, violent men, addicts, and emotionally unavailable men may seem more overtly dangerous, clingers harm their partners via a hidden agenda of incredible neediness—a neediness so extreme it can become abusive.

This is a problem shared by women who get involved with either permanent clingers or their cousins, parental seekers (discussed in the next chapter). Both of these men initially look so much less pathological than other types of dangerous men that women get caught off guard. They aren't looking for "dangerous" under the guise of "meek and mild." Women who have been burned by involvement with more frightening types of dangerous men feel they are relatively safe if they date a guy with the consistency of limp spaghetti. But make no mistake: Clingers are pathological.

Clingers appear to be emotionally sensitive, a quality women find irresistible. Almost like one of your girlfriends, they can empathize, sympathize, and cry over past hurtful experiences. Too many women step up to the plate to try to "mend" the injury caused to these men by their sisters in the dating game.

In reality, the sensitivity that initially attracts women repels them in the end. It merely masks severe neurotic problems in the clinger. Unmet needs from his early childhood are the most likely culprit for his extreme need for attachment to you. But what starts out as mere desire for attachment turns into suffocation. His clinging eventually begins to obstruct the airways of the woman he's involved with. And what she continues to pour into him in terms of reciprocated attention only satisfies him for brief periods of time.

Whereas the parental seeker wants motherly attention from you (he wants to be waited on and pampered), the permanent clinger is willing to do that part for you. Frantic in his need for you not to leave him alone even for a moment, he will exhaust you with personalized attention. He will willingly breathe your exhaled air. He is (too) willing and (too) able to supply every bit of attention you ever would want or could stand.

Clingers are emotionally needy men. Many of them could qualify for a diagnosis of avoidant personality disorder (see Appendix). When you begin to set limits with them, they melt into victims and act as if you were asking for something that would kill them. But most women are merely asking for a little space or time with friends. A clinger's relationship toolbox is filled with guilt and demands for time and attention that he uses on a woman to keep her to himself because he has few friends or interests. Because of his own lack of a life, he doesn't see his demands on you as unreasonable. But giving up your interests, your friends, your family, and your life is just the beginning of what it takes to keep a clinger from pouting, throwing temper tantrums, or becoming paranoid. The more you give up, the more secure he feels initially. But then comes the next request for you to surrender your needs—and the next, and the next. The bar keeps getting lifted higher until it is beyond any woman's capabilities.

His wanting to be the center of your attention soon turns to "needing you completely." Likewise, the attention he gives you turns into jealousy and paranoia in attempts to prevent you from having an outside life. A clinger's paranoia is a hidden tool. He will act paranoid (whether he really feels that way or not) to control you into giving up the parts of your life that he is afraid for you to experience. His paranoia can be about your girlfriends, job, family, or male friendships. Basically, any outside life you have can cause paranoia in a clinger. Neurotic and dependent, he can only find his sense of self in relationships. Therefore, *anyone* will do to keep his awareness focused away from his lack of self-identity. The women he dates are not truly important to him in and of themselves. They are only important to the extent that they help him avoid feeling his fears.

Clingers are preoccupied with criticism (real or perceived) and rejection. They are hypersensitive to the smallest correction of their behaviors. A clinger views himself as inept in most situations and feels incredibly inferior. His demeanor can be described as shy, quiet, fearful, and sometimes intense.

Clingers avoid responsibility at work. They fear the criticism that may go with a job promotion, so they tend to be low-functioning in their careers. A clinger fears the disapproval of coworkers, his boss, just about anyone. This keeps him the low man on the totem pole when it comes time for promotions because he doesn't step forward. He is just as awkward in social situations as he is at work, so he doesn't want to hang out with your friends. He sees many ordinary activities as threatening.

As a man with avoidant personality disorder, which is a form of pathology, he finds in every relationship some reinforcement of his view of himself as limp and impotent. As women leave him, how that self-perception is reinforced is forever changing with the next woman who arrives. He never feels secure because his self-concept is based on the woman he is with at any given time. He becomes frantic at the end of a relationship. He tries to prevent it from ending as he feels his sense of self slipping away. His lack of an identity causes women to be the primary focus of his life so he can avoid loneliness and feelings of rejection.

Clingers get left because women get exhausted. Clingers have histories of women fleeing their death-grip clutches. Women give more to them than they do to newborns. Clingers cost more than the national debt in emotional resources—but still their needs remain unfulfilled. What clingers want and need is beyond the abilities of any woman to provide. You cannot and will not ever meet the needs of a clinger. It's a black hole that sucks women's souls into it but remains unsatisfied. Whatever their childhood deficits were, it is clear that draining the life out of their adult relationships will never fulfill what they failed to get as children.

Clingers are difficult to break up with. They will cry, cling, threaten to harm themselves, call repeatedly, and verge on stalking you in order to avoid being "left" or "rejected." Although all this drama may feel flattering to some women, be aware it isn't about you. It's not about your personality, your dreams together, or the uniqueness of your relationship. It is merely that you are a breathing object whose presence helps him forget what he fears most: rejection. Women frequently make the mistake of thinking that if they "beef up'" his self-esteem, they can quickly slip out of his life. They put off breaking up with him in order to build up his sagging self-esteem. One problem here: His esteem never gets built up, so there is never a good time to end it.

Who They Seek

Since permanent clingers appear to swoop in to mend the wounds left by other dangerous men, women with recent histories of devastating breakups or dirty divorces are good targets for them. Women who have consistently chosen men who are narcissistic, self-focused, or emotionally unavailable provide just the right feeding ground for clingers. Because clingers particularly like "sensitive" women and can talk their language, it is music to women's ears to hear a man express exactly what she is feeling since he has been there too. Women find an immediate connection with men who speak the language of having been dumped and misused by past partners.

Women tend to call clingers "good guys" or "the last really nice man" because their true status as perpetual victims is cloaked in mutual wound-licking based on a shared history of poor relationships. He seems to her more like a "friend" who is recovering from his own heartbreak than he does a pathological individual. Clingers count on being considered cordial, supportive, and like-minded to women who want nothing more than to share stories about their painful pasts.

Clingers fantasize about idealized relationships, especially since they've never had one. Women who share these fantasies will be drawn into his "concept" of relationships. It all sounds good to the ear—the only problem is he's never lived it before.

Women who grew up in families with neurotic men might have their guard down against this type of dangerous man. Women who don't want to be seen as rejecting and critical end up with clingers because even though their red flags may start waving soon after meeting him, they don't want to "hurt his feelings" by ending the relationship. This is just the type of woman a clinger banks on! Knowing that, like him, sensitive women might have been wounded makes these women likely candidates to want to avoid hurting someone else. It's a theory that has paid off over and over again in his dating history.

Women who think they can love a man out of his devastating history are particularly attracted to permanent clingers (as well as to the mentally ill and parental seekers). Women who believe that the clinger "just needs the love of a good woman" should stick to singing country and western songs at karaoke clubs instead of dating this type of dangerous man, because it can take years to rebuild yourself and your life following involvement with a clinger.

Why They Are Successful

Clingers are successful because of their effective salesmanship of themselves at your time of need. They are obviously the opposite of the men who previously harmed you, so they get to become the hero you will never leave.

Their attention is excessive, yet in the beginning it seems like the attention you have looked for all your life. For once football does not come ahead of you. Neither do his buddies (there aren't any!) or even his career. There aren't other women hanging around him that you have to worry about. For some women this is so radically different from their previous relationships that they wonder if it's "how relationships were supposed to be all along."

Clingers can verbalize what sound like healthy ideas about relationships. This is because such a relationship exists so naturally in their fantasies. Their fantasies include never being rejected and embrace visions of living a full and active life. To be able to talk about these dreams as if they were real can be appealing to women who either are shy themselves or want a man who is willing to "put himself out there." However, with these avoidant-based men, these dreams and concepts never seem to materialize in the real world.

A clinger moves quickly to usher you into the center of his world. He naturally expects full and total reciprocation because he also wants to be the center of your world. The courtship is fast-paced and intimacy feels immediate. Involvement is almost 24/7. His biggest fear is to be rejected by you, so he kicks up the pace of your courtship to ensure a solid connection before too much reality creeps in. Soon, being the center of his world means foregoing your involvement with anyone or anything else.

It is important to note that one of the primary reasons why clingers—and, indeed, any of the dangerous men described in this book—are successful is because pathological men in general are gifted in their abilities to attract women, at least initially. Some are more gifted than others. But one more reason why pathological men are dangerous is because people who *aren't* pathological fail to pick up on their crafty approaches until they've learned the hard way.

Women's Stories

See if you can identify with Willow's and Patrina's suffocation as you read about their clingers and the women's attempts to flee them.

WILLOW'S STORY

Willow doesn't understand where she went wrong. Her first love was Michael, who was a giving and balanced young man. She started out well by dating someone who was moral, conscientious, and healthy, but her next selection, Dane, was a ladies' man. His unspoken philosophy was "nonmonogamy at any cost." He had a narcissistic side to him that chewed up the women in his path. His interests were himself and his needs. Willow became engaged to him, and when it ended mutually, she counted her blessings that the union never took place.

She wasn't paying attention when Garrett waltzed in. She was in college and was working part-time for a temporary agency. She was placed in an office where Garrett worked. Her heart was fried from too many go-rounds with Dane, and she just wanted some downtime from dating. Garrett asked her to go to lunch with a group from the office. It seemed harmless enough and like a good way to meet the staff.

Garrett was the opposite of Dane. Willow, twenty years old, felt that if Dane was bad, then good would be finding someone with opposite traits. Garrett was all of the things that were unlike Dane. Dane was focused on himself, his career, his friends, and other women. Garrett was completely focused on Willow, her loss of her relationship, and anything else she wanted to talk about.

After a few group lunches, Garrett and Willow began having lunch on their own. It was then that Garrett said he was separated and had a two-year-old daughter. Willow wasn't sure how she felt about that. He was still married and had such a small child. Shouldn't he try to work it out? But he said they had been separated for a year now and that his wife had had an affair prior to their separation. He felt victimized by her, and he was certain it would end in divorce.

It was Willow's goal to just "see what happens" and to move slowly. After all, Dane had done an emotional number on her. But it seemed Garrett was moving in fast-forward. He was sort of overwhelming to her. He paid her so much attention, and she wasn't sure if this was healthy or not, especially since she was coming out of a relationship with Dane, where attention was a rarity.

Garrett wanted to spend every second of every day with Willow. He seemed to swallow her up in his own need to move on. Soon, Willow found it wasn't okay to talk about her previous relationships or about how she was working through things. Garrett began acting wounded and jealous whenever she talked about Dane or even her male friends. Then he started acting suspicious of her girlfriends. For Garrett, there seemed to be no safe place for Willow to have any friendships other than within her immediate family.

Although Willow felt red flags about Garrett's jealousy over any of her friends, she reconfigured her red flags into something she could accept. She decided he was "just wounded because he is coming out of a divorce, has lost his child, and his wife had an affair. He needs a little attention now, and then he will stabilize." But month after month, Willow remained the primary object of his attention. Likewise, he insisted on being hers, to the exclusion of anything else she might have wanted to do.

School was becoming an issue. When she graduated, Garrett asked, did she really want to become a paralegal? He seemed uncomfortable with the idea of her spending as much time around attorneys as the position would require. He suggested maybe she should become a legal secretary instead.

Willow had stopped working at the temp agency. With any job she took, Garrett wanted to come to her office to "pick her up for lunch," when really he was scoping out how many other men were in the office. He told her he did it because Willow was so attractive and "all men were scum" that couldn't be trusted.

Willow's girlfriends began to complain that she never came out for a girl's night or went shopping with them. Willow found it was just too much work to go through to get Garrett to allow her to get out at night and then have to reconfirm with Garrett for weeks afterwards that she had been "good." Willow's family began to tell her they thought Garrett was a "wimp" and was too needy, clingy, and dependent. But Willow always went back to comparing him to Dane. "At least he isn't running around," she thought. Still, there was much more to be concerned about in Garrett's behavior than Willow let herself see. Instead of comparing Garrett's behavior to that of Michael, who had been a fairly emotionally healthy young man, she compared him to Dane, who had been awful. Clingers have a way of looking much better than other types of dangerous men when their behaviors are viewed side by side.

Garrett had only one friend. But he never wanted to do anything with the friend except go by his house with Willow in tow. Garrett had very few outside hobbies. Most of the things he enjoyed he could do in the garage while Willow was home. He needed constant reassurance that he would "never be left" and said he felt abandoned if Willow so much as wanted to play tennis with a girlfriend.

Unfortunately, Willow married Garrett, and the obsessive suspicion continued. Immediately after the wedding, Garrett wanted to move to another state. Willow missed the red flag that he wanted to isolate her from her family. Once they were settled in, Garrett did not want Willow to work as a paralegal. All of her hard work in college was not going to pay off. She took a job in another industry, and soon he was monitoring what she was wearing, what time she left for work, and when she got there.

Problems flourished in the marriage, and Willow realized that Garrett's obsessions and neediness probably had ruined his first marriage. The night Willow decided she could no longer stay in the marriage, Garrett got into a fetal position on the floor, crying and rocking and threatening to kill himself "if one more woman ever left him." More attempts to leave him resulted in more threats to harm himself. Willow did leave, and Garrett was placed in a psychiatric hospital until he stabilized. By the time he was released, Willow had relocated back to her family. Garrett began to drink heavily, blaming his drinking on "women who continued to abandon him." He went from one relationship to another, using his neediness and dependency, as Willow put it, "to hold emotional hostages."

PATRINA'S STORY

Patrina met Isaac in college. She was a journalism major and he was an art major. This was Patrina's first long-term relationship. Her high school years had been spent casually dating and avoiding big romances. She felt she wasn't old enough to really fall in love during high school. Isaac, on the other hand, had already been "madly in love" with a dozen women, all of whom had left him "brokenhearted," to hear him tell it.

Patrina says:

> Isaac's first clinging behaviors started about three months after we met, when he became insanely clingy and needy following my receiving a Christmas card from a previous boyfriend. Still, we lasted three years, which isn't a credit to me.
>
> His neediness following any interaction I had with men was pathetic. He couldn't even stand my going into the next room if I had talked to a man that day. He would chase me down and accuse me of not caring for him because I went into the other room! He'd drill me each and every day about any man I had talked to—the gas station attendant, the dry cleaner, anyone! It was pitiful, and I was getting sadder and sadder as I watched this shell of a man try to have a relationship with a woman.
>
> Isaac's fear of my interaction with men escalated. If I had had any conversation with a male, Isaac's sexual pursuits of me became unbearable. He had a compulsive need for physical closeness as a part of his obsession to control me and to validate his own need for attention. Sex with him felt like it was

reparation. He was trying to repair his soul by using a sexual connection with me. I felt like the object a dog lifts his leg on to mark that it "belongs" to him. It was my first introduction into the concept that dependency is not love.

This jealous, needy, clingy, possessive, and controlling behavior eventually drove me away from Dr. Jekyll/Mr. Hyde, as it had done to a dozen women before me. What kept me tied in for three years was the fact that I thought I loved his tender and sensitive side. He acted like he adored me. On good days he treated me like no one ever had, and I was convinced (at least in the beginning) that his exceptionally clingy behavior was just that—an exception. But over time I experienced it on a regular and daily basis. I realized it wasn't me he loved. He feared being alone more than he felt the need to love someone else. I distracted him from a lot of emotional work he needed to do.

We had many go-rounds with counseling and couple's therapy, but the issues were never resolved because he never truly addressed them. His denial about his behavior was so strong that we were never able to unearth, much less resolve, what had damaged his psyche badly enough to make him like this. And certainly my caring for him in no way made him feel secure. In fact, his caring for me actually pushed him over the edge. He couldn't balance caring about someone in a mutual way without obsessing and making her miserable.

Red-Alert Behavioral Checklist

The permanent clinger

✳ needs you so much and can't stand to be without you

✳ pleads, begs, cries, pouts, and guilts you into being with him, into changing your plans for him, into not leaving him

✳ threatens to hurt himself if you ever leave

✳ blames you for his neediness by saying his love for you produced his vulnerability

✳ wants constant reassurance about his desirability

* wants constant reassurance that you are not interested in other men and wants promises that you won't reject him

* puts himself down so you will build him up

* evokes pity from you to keep you in a relationship with him

* has very few close friends

* has very few, if any, outside interests

* sees himself as a victim—has had multiple "discouragements" in life

* has had multiple unsuccessful relationships

* may have an unusual relationship with his mother

* produces a feeling of suffocation in you when you spend prolonged time with him

Your Defense Strategy

Clingers seem to adore you early in the relationship. They appear loyal and faithful to the point of having an old-world charm about them. They act chivalrous and honorable. They give you the attention that was probably lacking in some of your previous relationships. But they are a little too interested; they want to see you a little too frequently; they are a tad too loyal and faithful before they have a track record with you.

It's always a good defense strategy to put the brakes on in a relationship. Slow down and see how a man reacts to your change of pace. If he reacts by moving in closer or appearing to "need" you more than what you're comfortable with—pay attention! He's more interested in alleviating his impending sense of rejection or abandonment than he is in honoring your boundaries. If he begins to show up where he thinks you will be when you have asked to pace the relationship differently, notice the red flags! His adoration is only a cloak for neurotic behaviors.

These are men with patterns of failed relationships due to their suffocation of their partners. To hear them tell it, no one has ever been faithful or loyal to them. They are victims at the hands of heartless women. If you find yourself feeling sorry for a man or dating him because your primary feeling toward him is pity, you are probably with a clinger. Save your pity for charity work; it should not be a primary feeling in a dating relationship.

Clingers are prone to depression and anxiety, so be sure to look for those symptoms as well. Social phobias are high among clingers, which explains why they don't enjoy your friends or desire social activities. Additionally, clingers can have qualities that are similar to and overlap with those of the parental seeker (see next chapter), making them excessively needy and dependent.

Clingers often have unusual relationships with their mothers. As adults they may be too close and enmeshed with their mothers, or they may have elusive or controlling mothers. Any of these mothering styles will not be repaired by a relationship with you. You just can't fix what is wrong with a clinger. Underneath all that devotion lies pathology.

Remember, the best way to guard against clingers is to take charge of the pace of the relationship and to notice his reaction. Women need to resist being cajoled by his adoration and instead need to listen and watch carefully when he talks about his perceptions of relationships, rejection, loneliness, and betrayal. Dependency is not love.

Women's Insights

In retrospect, Willow now says this about her relationship with Garrett:

> Now that I look back on it, I guess it *is* an issue when no one in your family thinks a guy is okay and when your friends are talking about why he needs you so much. It's not a compliment to be needed that way, because he doesn't really need "you" per se; he just needs to not be alone. I could have been a cardboard cutout and that would have sufficed for him to avoid having to

face himself. As adults, should we really "need" someone else in order to be complete? That's sort of scary now. If he isn't complete in himself, I am sure not going to do that for him. There's a reason *why* he isn't complete. Another person will never make you be something you aren't already.

He was so verbal about my being everything to him—but I wasn't gone two months before he had another, older woman living with him. He just needed anyone in order to avoid being alone. That's all I was, too. He was getting divorced when I met him and he didn't want to face himself, so I filled up his time.

The woman who came right after me didn't last long. Then there was a really young woman, but she didn't last. Then he got involved with someone who was very ill with a chronic disease, probably thinking she wouldn't dare go elsewhere, but she did. His unrelenting adoration caught my attention after Dane had hardly paid attention to me. But even too much attention is now a red flag for me.

Chapter *4*

The Parental Seeker

A distinguishing feature about this category of dangerous man is that you quickly learn that his child*like*ness is really child*ish*ness. And how attractive can that be after a while?

Tommy Teenager

How could a benign-seeming mama's boy break anyone's heart? What in the world could make this perpetual little boy pathological? Like his cousin the clinger, he's not necessarily violent, addicted, or predatory. He isn't scouting for other women or hiding his life behind closed doors. His only sin is that he's around, constantly ... like a toddler around your knees. Yes, he's available—*always* available, way *too* available.

Like permanent clingers, parental seekers are natural selections for women who have dated the more frightening types of dangerous men. Selecting more passive men seems a safer choice in their mind. The loyalty of a parental seeker seems refreshing after dating a few guys who display too much "testosterone."

This type of dangerous man is best thought of in terms of age brackets. Many of these men failed to develop adult personality structures. Instead, they were stunted in their early development, which, as discussed in Chapter 1, ends up producing a full-blown personality disorder. Women who date parental seekers immediately want to know why he is the way he is. Their hearts bleed over the sad story of his stunted growth. They wonder how their love might "fix" his yearnings for a mama. But remember, pathological men are not fixable—even those who "need" a mother.

According to personality-development theory, seekers look for women who'll be mother-replacements because they were wounded in childhood by their own mothers—or the lack thereof. (This can apply even to gay men whose personalities failed to develop adequately in childhood. They may not seek women to date, but they seek motherly figures as close friends.) The parental seeker's stunted early development could have been caused by any number of factors, including childhood abuse; parents who were nonsupportive, nonnurturing, or noninteractive; addicted parents; or a chronic childhood illness, to name a few.

Parental seekers are looking for the eternally absent parent. Maybe it was the father who was never around when they were growing up or the mother who was never emotionally present for them. Many seekers have complicated abandonment and separation issues with their mothers. But the clue is that they are always seeking an ever-elusive parent figure. This means that even when someone else is trying to parent them, for example a woman whom they are dating, the parent of their youth is forever absent. The hole in their soul is shaped like the absent parent. More importantly from your perspective, that hole can *never* be filled by something with your shape.

Some parental seekers' stunted and unfulfilled emotional growth results in their acting like ten-year-olds, while others resemble mouthy, rebellious fourteen- to sixteen-year-olds. To spot these types of pathological men, look for the behavior of a ten- to sixteen-year-old boy. This allows you to see childish behavior for what it is and provides you with a reality check when you hear their sad story.

Parental seekers' egos are small, as is befitting the emotional age bracket they fall into. They need constant reassurance about their choices, decisions, and actions. Many could fit the diagnosis of dependent personality disorder (see Appendix). Although their symptoms are similar to those of their cousins, the permanent clingers, their motives, the ways in which they were wounded, and the type of woman they seek are somewhat different. Still, the end results are the same for women who get involved with them. In much the same way as you would encourage a fourteen-year-old boy to ask a girl to the dance, you will live your life boosting the parental seeker's sagging self-esteem and compensating for his low level of functioning. It takes him forever to make a decision, and even then he can only do so after lots of assistance in weighing the pros and cons. Whether or not he stays with his decision is another issue. Because of his deficient decision-making skills, there isn't much action in his life. It is spent in suspense—thinking, weighing options, choosing, but *doing* very little.

Because the parental seeker is still trying to get his little-boy needs met, he wants to be waited on hand and foot. The mama-maid role adopted by women who get involved with him fits nicely with his attempts to get some nurturing. He's trying to fill the hole in his soul that was left by neglect that occurred early in his life. When you take care of him, he says he feels "good" or "special." In truth, however, your stepping into the role of his waitress does *not* repair the damage from his childhood.

The parental seeker does not participate in many adult chores. You will find him lacking in interest, ability, or willingness to help with routine adult tasks. Painting the house is probably out, along with paying the bills, driving the kids to school, or anything else a grown man could be expected to do. But he will be Johnny-on-the-spot when it comes time to play sports with the kids, watch cartoons, or imitate pro wrestling in your living room. His biggest contribution to family life will be playing with the children.

Shayla, who was married to a seeker, explains it this way:

Dan was emotionally thirteen years old. I also have a teenage son, and the two of them hung out together and played basketball. It's good for a dad to hang out with his son, but this wasn't parental guidance we are talking about here. At the end of the day I had to call both of them to dinner, tell both to wash their hands, tell both not to bring the basketball to the table, ask both if they had taken their vitamins, and ask both if they had gone to their jobs that day. Eventually, I had to take Dan's paycheck each week because of his overspending on sporting equipment and music—just like I had to make sure my son was depositing his money each week and not spending it on videos. There was no difference between Dan and my son except I was having sex with one of them.

Task delegation is another battleground. Much like a thirteen-year-old, he doesn't initiate anything on his own, so you assign a task and he engages you in a power struggle. Although he likes for you to direct him to do the things he can't manage to do for himself, he still has control issues surrounding his inability to initiate anything.

Job hunts, chores, hobbies, and adult male friendships do not happen for the parental seeker without prodding and threatening and guidance from you. Consequently, he has few outside interests, so he is always around you, like a small child with a death grip on your knees. He needs constant reassurance that all will be well before he responds to the prodding and the threats.

Like an eleven-year-old, the parental seeker will lie in bed and want special nursing care for a sore throat. And during episodes of other minor illness, you can expect that his pain tolerance will be low and his pampering needs high. If he doesn't get waited on, sick or not, he will pout. Shayla says, "Both my son and my husband had the flu, and it was a competition between them to see how many times I would help each of them. They would tally points and high-five each other if they got their medication given to them in bed."

It isn't long until the seeker's partner is limp from carrying the load of another person's life on her shoulders. But he is full of reminders for you about all the females who've previously failed him. The burden of proof that the women in his life can redeem themselves lies solely with you. If you are a good codependent and hell-bent on loving him into wellness, this dynamic will hold you hostage in the relationship—well into burnout.

Who They Seek

Parental seekers are the number-one hottie selection for some women. Women with personality structures that are overly nurturing choose these boy-men to date. These aren't women who merely like to pamper others a little bit. They are women who find meaning for their existence in the rescuing and raising of emotionally dependent men. It's a symbiotic relationship based on the man needing a mom and the woman needing a child. Somewhere along the way the man's childhood needs and the woman's parenting needs got twisted—and instead of each of them finding a therapist, they found a relationship with each other. Women with histories of childhood abuse are likely candidates for these types of men. A woman who was abused may attach herself to a mama's boy so she can replicate the type of nurturing she needed and failed to get in childhood by giving it to a man in adulthood. However, when a woman tries to get her own needs met through the excessive nurturing of a partner, it usually fails to pay off for her. Instead, she ends up saddled with one more person who does not nurture and value her.

Some women confuse their professions with their private lives. Women working in the caregiving fields—such as nurses and other medical workers, social workers, clergywomen, and teachers—are at risk for dating and marrying parental seekers, permanent clingers, addicts, mentally ill men, or men who are some combination of these. Likewise, women who regularly volunteer at church or as long-term caregivers for family members and friends may fail to be on guard against men whose needs feel so natural to them. The saying "Charity begins at home" finds new meaning with women who literally think this means marrying the type of person they serve in their profession or through their volunteer work. On the contrary, charity work needs to remain at the mission, at the church, at the hospital, or at the social-service building; it should *not* enter your dating and marrying life.

Women who want more children often subconsciously look for seekers to fill some of that need. This does not mean that women who want children or who love to care for the elderly or the infirm are pathological nurturers and that there is something wrong with them. But there *are* personality types that will be drawn to this type of pathologically disordered man. This is because his needs for nurturing, guidance, direction, and overall assistance fall right in line with her pattern of giving, and giving, and giving.

Oddly enough, some strong-willed and controlling women also like parental seekers. Women who are high-powered executives are not immune to selecting seekers. These dangerous men enjoy the structure and control such women bring to the relationship. And they will take the structure and control any way they can get it—in the form of either the gentle, nurturing mother figure, or the decisive taskmistress. Anyone who will organize and steer his life is a target for the parental seeker.

Parental seekers' fear of abandonment causes them to move quickly from relationship to relationship, urgently seeking another source of care when one ends. They have difficulty being alone and want or need people around them constantly in their attempts to ward off feelings of loneliness and abandonment. Women who are indiscriminating about how many partners a man has had are attractive to a seeker.

Women who date parental seekers have to go above and beyond the call of duty for these men. A seeker creates a scenario in which a woman will willingly go to great lengths to prove she will not be like the mother who left him so unloved and wounded. These men manipulate their sad stories and a woman's soft heart to set up a double bind that leaves the woman in a no-win situation. In order for her to prove herself and for him to "feel loved," she has to show Herculean effort in sustaining ongoing attention and adoration. There is no allowance for her being tired or taking care of her own needs. Proving her love to this wounded man-child is a 24-hour-a-day job that will never end.

Why They Are Successful

Parental seekers are often playful and childlike. They come in under women's radars because they're like "big kids." There is nothing overtly threatening about them. Indeed, there is something "sweet" about a parental seeker's harmless disorganization that reminds you of your brother. You see his sensitive side as he talks about his dysfunctional family life. He needs a woman to spruce up his house, his wardrobe, his life. He's just a big dorky guy, sort of like all of your brother's friends. He's like the kid next door you remember from childhood.

Seekers like women who call them "my baby" or "just a big kid at heart." They won't balk at any of your references to their juvenile demeanor and behavior. They look for women who take the lead, who seem organized, and who have children. Single or divorced women with a big caretaking streak are especially drawn to these men. Women with their own unresolved mother issues might not be on guard against this type of dangerous man; both of them will spend time lamenting their inadequate mothers.

Before long, however, all of his issues with women will begin to reveal themselves. He places the responsibility for "feeling loved" on his partner. It's her job to somehow overcome his years of abuse, loneliness, and unmet needs for mothering. Fulfilling these needs for him is impossible, but she doesn't know it yet. She must continually perform extraordinary feats of devotion to prove that she is the one who will love him, unlike the women who have failed him. This is emotional hostage-taking at its highest form.

But the parental seeker is a bottomless pit of pathological need. He is a cracked vessel that cannot hold what is poured in. All the love given to him merely runs out of the fractures in his wounded psyche. He wears out the relationship by needing so much love that it can never be enough. A woman who loves a parental seeker ends up feeling inadequate in her attempts at loving him. She feels exhausted from having given more to him than to anyone else in her life, and yet, according to him, she has still failed.

Parental seekers take low responsibility for their own emotional or physical needs and place high responsibility on their partners to meet those needs. It's a full-time job with no benefits for the woman.

And yet, parental seekers are very hard to leave. For a woman with a big heart, children of her own, or her own mother issues, leaving him feels like nothing less than abandoning a child. She worries and wonders, "How in the world will he ever get by on his own?" As is the case with his cousin the clinger, you must remember that dependency is not love.

Women's Stories

Laura attempted to babysit an ongoing parade of parental seekers. Shayla luckily learned her lesson the first time around. In both cases, see how coddling their men failed to pay off for these two women.

LAURA'S STORY

Laura was only sixteen when she began dating parental seekers. She came from an upper-middle-class family. She was the youngest child and received all the doting attention reserved for the baby of the family. Her father was in the construction business and her mother was a social worker. She lived a stable and comfortable life. By watching her mother's work, she had learned all about showing compassion to those who struggled and reaching out to the downcast. But Laura ended up confusing social work as a profession with a life of dating parental seekers.

Laura completed training for her certified nursing assistant's license while she was still in high school. Soon thereafter she began collecting wimps like other adolescent girls collected stuffed

animals. The boys' sad stories, strangely similar to each other, tugged at her heart. Most of them had sad mother stories—moms who'd had them too young and couldn't emotionally meet their needs. Their early problems had left holes in their souls the size of Texas that Laura felt only she could fill.

Each boy's story was sadder than the last: foster homes, addicted mothers, unknown fathers, neglect, bedtime hunger. It was enough to land them on *Montel*. Instead, they landed in Laura's life. The sadder the story, the more intent she seemed on getting involved. One right after another they came and went, with Laura footing the bill for dates, subsidizing their chronic unemployment, and attempting to pay their way out of a lifetime of problems. They took advantage of her heart, her pocketbook, and her trust.

Laura's upbringing had encouraged her to believe that if only *she* were stable enough, he would "morph" into someone like her. So she surrounded each man with her family members, hoping against hope that their stability would rub off on him. Laura, like other women in caregiving professions, found that being a certified nursing assistant was compatible with adopting the role of caretaker in her relationships. She used her skills to try to nurse each sad parental seeker back to emotional health.

It began with David, a skinny, underfed adolescent who had lived on the streets since his early teens. He never knew his dad, and his mother was very young when she had him and then lapsed into addiction. He had been sexually abused by one of his mother's boyfriends. His mother wouldn't come home for weeks on end, so finally he just left and trusted the streets with his life. Soon it was Laura to the rescue! In came her family—her social-worker mother, who listened to David's sad stories; her father, who tried to help find him work; her sister, who drove him back and forth to jobs. But in the end, David just wanted to lie in bed in a fetal position and wait for his mom to come home.

Then there was Charleton. His mother, too, was an addict, and he had been handed over to his grandparents to be raised. Now his mother was in prison and dying of AIDS. Again, it was

Laura to the rescue. She gave him lots of support while he wasn't able to work due to being depressed about his mother. She funded their dates, including the prom, and anything else. She transported him back and forth to the prison to see his mother, and finally to his mother's bedside when she died.

Next was James. His father abandoned the family to leave the country following criminal charges. The mother bounced around between alcoholism, drug addiction, chronic poverty, and unemployment. James, too, had made a living by engaging in petty criminal activity. He said that no one in his family had ever worked and that he "didn't know how to" because he did not have a role model. Laura to the rescue! She got an apartment, worked two jobs, and moved James right in with her. He was going to "learn how" to work and be productive. Laura's father had long conversations with him about the work ethic. Mom, the social worker, developed financial budgets for them to live by. James played video games and hung out with friends but never found full-time or permanent work. He committed more crimes and landed back in jail. At that point the relationship between James and Laura ended.

Laura had spent several years on the search and rescue squad for Sad Young Men. And all of the men she'd gotten involved with were willing to be rescued. Still, Laura never acquired a hero's status or won the Silver Star medal.

SHAYLA'S STORY

Shayla was a stunning woman. Manicured and professional, she worked as a psychiatric nurse. Surely she was trained well enough to recognize Dan's emotional issues. But he slipped under her red-flag radar and planted himself in her life, undetected. They married and had three children. Shayla counted him as the fourth child. She often talked about lining up the kids for nose wipes, vitamins, and lunchboxes. Dan was right there in line with them.

She met him in college while she was a psychiatric nurse intern. He was a handsome football player. She noted early on that he was somewhat disorganized and unmotivated. Luckily, football carried him where his studies never would. Lots of excuses were made about his lack of success in real life for the sake of athletics. Soon that pattern infected his relationship with Shayla. Dan was unmotivated, indecisive, childlike, and irresponsible. Even after the children arrived, he would quit jobs because he simply didn't "feel like going to work." More and more of the responsibility fell on Shayla. Working, organizing the children's activities and his, cooking, cleaning, and paying all the bills were just the beginning of taking care of Dan.

His whimsies included quitting jobs when he was bored or didn't feel like working, spending money on sporting equipment instead of the mortgage, siding with the children against Shayla and arguing a child's point of view, trying get-rich-quick schemes instead of real jobs, and squandering their savings on elaborate fishing trips or novel toys for himself.

Soon Shayla was working two jobs, then three jobs—doing whatever it took to keep her family afloat while Dan played basketball in the backyard with the boys. Evenings would include Shayla writing out elaborate plans and schedules for Dan—jobs to check out, projects to do around the house, and errands to run. But they were never done. He would job hunt for a while and then stop. Start a project and lose interest. Whine if he had to run errands. Shayla was becoming more and more exhausted. Finally her only resolve was to get rid of one of her life stresses, and the biggest one was Dan. Dan panicked at the thought of losing Shayla. Who would help him get organized, take care of his needs, remind him of appointments, be there for him? He feared the loss of a female role model in his life.

Because Dan, the chronic parental seeker, couldn't manage to hold down a job, he had a poor track record of employment. Consequently, he was able to get alimony from Shayla. Soon the children were recruited to help take care of Dan. Their weekends at his house were spent cleaning up and doing dishes that had been dirtied when they weren't even there. Incomes from their part-time jobs paid for things that most dads would normally cover. Even the children began to feel the weight of caring for their dad.

Dan's next conquest was an elementary-school teacher. Like Shayla had done, she ignored Dan's low functioning ability and soon married him. Her salary carried him for a few years before she became exhausted. Still, Dan's primary fear was who would take care of him. Who would fill that mothering role if his second wife left him?

Red-Alert Behavioral Checklist

The parental seeker

* wants constant reassurance

* wants to be waited on and refuses to do basic things for himself

* doesn't help with adult chores

* expects special treatment because he is needy

* pouts if you don't wait on him

* claims he wants you to do things for him because it makes him feel good

* wants to be told what to do and needs direction to get anything done

* wants you to make decisions for his life

* neither has nor wants outside relationships, friends, or interests

* is childlike in his emotional needs

* underachieves as a way of avoiding responsibility

* has a history of being rescued, kept, or sheltered in relationships

* probably has had several failed relationships

* appears to need a mentor in all areas of his life

Your Defense Strategy

Your defense approach with the parental seeker has to begin with a good examination of yourself. What is it in you that would find a pathological man-child a suitable partner for dating or marrying? What is it in his dependency and vulnerability that you find appealing, attractive, or sexy? Asking yourself these questions may jar you into examining your own motives.

On the surface, the dynamic between a woman and a parental seeker may appear to be that of a woman in control of a childlike man. But look again. The two are engaged in a standoff in which the woman controls him via her mothering, and the man controls her via his underfunctioning. They are held in position by a mutual tension that comes from each one controlling the other, one overtly and the other covertly. Neither position represents anything that would be seen in a healthy relationship.

Seekers find their identity in being cared for. It is their attempt to deal with a relentless fear of a lack of a parental figure in their lives. They attempt to get attention by requiring guidance from you.

Women who confuse rescuing for intimacy find parental seekers irresistible. Taking care of this seemingly helpless individual gives them a sense of empowerment. A man who comes across as a victim or as childlike should therefore be a red flag to women. He has plenty of sad stories to go along with his need for mothering, but none of them are your responsibility to heal.

Men who have patterns of being "kept" or "sheltered" in relationships are most likely parental seekers. Those who lack a track record of age-appropriate responsibilities in a relationship, a job, or adult life are probably highly regressed men who also lack the capacity to change and grow. Seekers cannot regulate their own motivational drives. They are disorganized inside, and the result is a disorganized exterior life.

A woman is wise to ask the kind of questions that might reveal a man's level of functioning in life, in work, and in relationships. You might discover the answer to some of these issues from others. Don't discount what other people may tell you about a man you're considering dating, even if it comes from his old girlfriends. Seekers hop from one relationship to another to find caregivers. You might want to find out more about his previous relationships. How long did he go between relationships? How many has he had? And listen to the reasons he gives for why the relationships ended. Read between the lines for messages that may indicate women being overwhelmed by his childlike neediness or needing a break from micromanaging his life. He will most likely perceive this as abandonment.

Determining how well he functions is key. Seekers are at increased risk for depression, anxiety, and adjustment disorders. They may have symptoms of borderline personality disorder, a pathological condition. Chronic illness as a child or a childhood diagnosis of separation anxiety disorder can predispose a seeker to a diagnosis of dependent personality disorder, another permanent condition. (See the Appendix for descriptions of these terms.)

Chronic underachievement can be another sign. These men are not stupid; they just function far below their potential. When IQ, motivation, and potential fail to match up, pay attention. Because of a parental seekers' low motivation, women will find themselves continually trying to pep-talk these men into doing something—*anything*—with their lives. Seekers grew up without any discipline. Their parents probably didn't enforce any kind of boundaries or limits. Their homes were lax, not because of a laid-back parent but because of an uninvolved parent. All of this translates into a lack of discipline in their adult lives.

A seeker perpetually lacks a sense of security about his ability to make everyday decisions because he received no guidance as a child. Therefore, he has no idea about what to do. He has very few social skills, low work motivation, almost nonexistent adult relationship abilities, and very few parenting skills.

Lastly, most "normal" men resist being fixed. By contrast, parental seekers are the original "fixer-uppers." They don't mind a person coming in and trying to fix them or change them. They seem to encourage it and act grateful for it, even though nothing really ever changes. Most people shut down when you try to fix them. But a seeker acts like he will take all the help he can get. He can't see himself as an adult, a parent, or a provider because he had no models for these roles, so he needs the direction that an adult will give him. If he isn't shutting down in the face of someone's attempts to change or fix him, a red flag should be flying high. "Fixing" someone is a sign of codependency. It is not a sign of emotional maturity—for you or for him.

Women's Insights

Laura wonders:

> What in *me* makes me want this type of man? I guess that's what I have to wonder. And why was I drawn to so many of the same type? I now know the end from the beginning. I get a feel for their neediness early on. But I can't say it has stopped me— yet. There's some drive in me that just thinks I can love him and he'll grow into a spectacular guy for me. In the back of my mind I know this isn't going to happen, but I am a sucker for that sad little boy who never had a mom. And pretty soon I am trying to mop up his life and grow him up into a real adult. It's interesting how that *never* happens. I mean there really *is* something about these guys that doesn't grow up. I've had enough of them to know. Maybe I'm getting it—slowly. I am so tired emotionally that I hope I do get it. I don't know how many more times I can go through this. If I want a child, why don't I just have one?

Shayla says:

> There aren't a lot of women who would think these men are dangerous on the surface. But let me tell you, they cost you plenty! I should have paid attention in college when nothing got done in Dan's life. He just bounced around aimlessly. His whole life has been that way. If it weren't for me, we wouldn't own a house, have a car, pay taxes, or have an adult life of any kind.

Women don't realize that these men are exhausting life-suckers who can just drain you. Every resource you have will be lost to them—your emotional life, your finances, your spirituality, your friends, your career quality, everything. They demand your whole life, and yet they are still thirteen years old. I married this child-man and invested a lot of years in my marriage. But I finally got it one day when having sex with him felt "incestuous" because I felt like I had raised him. I knew then that our relationship was sick.

Chapter 5

The Emotionally Unavailable Man

What's the harm of a little extramarital fun between adults? Or how can a guy who really digs his hobbies possibly hurt you? Keep reading. Plenty of women are lining up to tell you just why Donnie is a highly dangerous date.

Donnie Don't-Call-Me-I'll-Call-You

These bad boyz sadly qualify as women's number-one dating choice among the various types of dangerous men. That's because their "dangerousness," when compared to that of the other men described in this book, may not even be apparent to a woman. Women often think the word *dangerous* only applies to men who are violent or abusive. Yet the emotionally unavailable man wreaks more havoc and causes more women to seek counseling than most of the other kinds of dangerous men. Still, many women overlook his dangerousness and fail to see him for what he really is, e.g., a threat to their happiness!

The emotionally unavailable man shouldn't be considered serious dating material because his emotions are connected elsewhere, even if superficially. His attention is directed toward his career, education, or hobbies, or he is married, engaged, seriously dating someone else, or not quite out of a relationship. For whatever set of reasons, he just doesn't have emotional energy for you, and he probably never will.

One type of emotionally unavailable man devotes most of his time and energy to his career, job, educational goals, or hobbies—or to some combination of these. The point is, emotionally unavailable men are fixated on parts of their lives they find much more interesting or important than a relationship. He could be a motivated career climber with his eye on only one thing. And it isn't you; it's the next promotion. Or maybe he's juggling graduate school while holding down two jobs. Perhaps he's getting a pilot's license, working toward a black belt in karate, or pursuing his goal of sailing around the world. Maybe he's a running freak, stamp collector, or chronic camper. He may live for fly-fishing, computers, or rock climbing.

He doesn't have a wife or a girlfriend and doesn't really want one (even if he says he does). Instead, he has interests that are so all-consuming that dating and relating count only as second thoughts. Sure, he'll drop by your house for a quick romp in the sack. But then off he goes to what *really* interests him. He'll squeeze you in once or twice a month, between swap meets, work commitments, or competitions. His finances, weekends, vacation time, and emotional highs are reserved for his other interests. He may swear that just as soon as this training season or this super-hectic period of his life is over, there will be more time for you. Or he may be honest enough to tell you he doesn't want to get involved in a serious relationship because of his other commitments. Yet he's usually more than willing to keep you and your emotions engaged in a friendship or a "casual" dating relationship that leaves you unavailable to pursue relationships with other, more available men.

I am sure this is the dilemma presented by trying to have a relationship with the Lance Armstrongs of the world. You will always remain secondary to his other interests. Add to this the fact that guys who are really into their hobbies tend to have more than one of them. They have varied and wide-ranging interests that perptually keep them tied up. I am *not* saying that being passionate about one's career or hobbies is a negative character trait in a man. It's positive and healthy for a person to be interested in his or her life. Just be aware that there are plenty of men out there who have satisfying and busy careers and hobbies, yet still have time and energy for a healthy, intimate relationship. I *am* saying that some men seem to remain chronically unavailable for a long-term, serious relationship. They will always have a reason or reasons why they can't "get serious" with you; that's what qualifies them as emotionally unavailable. The danger for a woman who gets involved with this type of man is the inevitable frustration, despair, or heartbreak that results from longing for and pursuing a true connection with him. Unfortunately, the two of you do not share the same goal.

The other type of emotionally unavailable man is unavailable due to his relationship (or relationships) with another woman (or women). These guys are never really committed to a woman. They don't see any relationship as necessarily permanent, including marriage—even if they give lip service to being deeply committed to the woman they're with at the moment. In truth, however, they don't truly value their intimate relationships or take them seriously, because they are merely "playing," even though engagement or marriage hardly seems like something to "play" at. They don't take their relationships seriously because on some level—even if subconsciously—they know they can find someone else who will get involved with them if their current affair ends. What else would cause someone to repeatedly play his future like a crapshoot without really fearing the outcome?

With either type of emotionally unavailable man, women often confuse an availability for *sexual* engagement with an availability for *emotional* engagement, intimacy, and commitment. In fact, most emotionally unavailable men will remain sexually available to you. This doesn't change the fact that they are "taken" in other areas of their lives. And these men understand that completely. But women often don't. Thus begins a spiraling pattern of the woman "hoping" and "waiting" for connection and commitment with him. But by definition, someone who is emotionally unavailable doesn't expect or want—or doesn't know how to expect—emotional depth with others. It is probably because women keep attempting to get close to him that causes him to keep moving from partner to partner or to keep adding partners. He is uninterested in experiencing or is unable to experience deep feelings of connection with another.

Men who are wired this way are not open to authentic, deep relationships. A relationship with an emotionally unavailable man will stay on the surface. He can usually talk the intimate lingo, but he can't deliver the real McCoy: true emotional intimacy. A healthy relationship starts with an emotional connection. But the connection two people feel at the beginning is only the very first step in building a relationship. Real intimacy involves an ongoing, mutual commitment to strengthening and deepening that bond. That only happens over time, through sharing experiences, by caring for the other's well-being, and by building trust through openness and honesty. What is dangerous about emotionally unavailable men is that they are not authentically emotionally responsive. They are emotionally avoidant.

For a man who "cheats" on his partner or spouse, although he may have multiple relationships going on at one time, the continuation of the relationships is not what makes him tick. This means when any particular woman catches on to him and ends the relationship, his feathers are not going to be ruffled, even if he pleads with her to stay and tells her she's the one who means the most to him. He simply does not know how to make major changes in how he approaches relationships. Just as he lacks the ability to be monogamous, he lacks all other serious relationship skills.

Some women get involved with married men or other emotionally unavailable men on a serial basis. Although women may say they date these men "just to have fun" and that they themselves "don't want to get serious," their words simply do not stack up in light of what we know about the psychology and sociology of women's approaches to relationships. Perhaps as a way to justify dating married or engaged men, some women seem to find it far easier to say they are "just having fun" than to admit they are repeatedly sabotaging their own deepest desires for intimacy.

Emotionally unavailable men come from widely varied backgrounds. Maybe as a child he lived with a father figure who was emotionally unavailable to him due to alcoholism, workaholism, or other addictions. Early physical or sexual abuse may have numbed his emotions and disconnected him from human warmth, interaction, and trust. As a youngster he may have received messages that he wasn't valued or that marriage wasn't valued. Maybe his father or stepfather was repeatedly unfaithful to his mother.

Some men may struggle with undisclosed homosexuality or bisexuality. This can produce an internal conflict that detracts from a man's emotional connectedness with his women partners. Some men may have a sexual addiction that fuels their pursuit of rapidly revolving, superficial relationships. Perhaps his sexual addiction takes the form of chronic and compulsive pornography use, a pattern that can diminish a man's normal human responsiveness. Maybe he has mental-health issues that cause him to flee intimacy.

These are only a few scenarios. There are many possibilities as to what caused him to be chronically unavailable for an intimate relationship. As with all the other types of dangerous men, there is most likely a sad story from his past to accompany his present-day dysfunction. He may even have enough awareness to be able to connect the dots himself, as in, "I find it hard to trust women because of my mother's alcoholism and the problems it caused in my childhood"—or whatever the case may be. But, again, remember that the *why* behind his unavailablility is less important to you than what you're going to do with this information.

Whatever the cause, these are often men who have a hard time with monogamy, raising children, or anything else that requires an earnest and consistent focus of their commitments. But be aware that if an emotionally unavailable man also has some elements of the emotional predator, he will come across to you as a devoted father or husband or as an upstanding citizen of his community. Remember from Chapter 1 that many dangerous men come as combo packs. Never discount the possiblity that your emotionally unavailable man may have multiple hidden lives (always the case if he's engaging in clandestine extramarital affairs) as well as being an emotional predator. Certain combinations—for example, emotional unavailability, plus a life he keeps hidden from you or from his wife or girlfriend, plus the keen sixth sense of an emotional predator, plus a sexual addiction—help these pathological men thrive at attracting serial superficial relationships.

Who They Seek

A man with outside interests such as hobbies, careers, and educational goals may seek women to date who have their own interests. He may believe she will understand his "full-fledged devotion" to his hobby, when in fact she probably doesn't and won't. Many athletes date other athletes. This usually works only when both parties' outside interests are balanced rather than excessive on either individual's part. But the emotionally unavailable man doesn't know what the word *balance* means. Whatever he is involved in, it's to an extreme degree.

Other men who are absorbed in their work and hobbies like to date women who have no lives. The idea is that the woman will live vicariously through the man's activities. He hopes she'll like being able to say, "My boyfriend is a skydiver," when her own life consists of work, home, and the couch. And still others, as is the case with many types of dangerous men, prefer women who are hypertolerant and nondemanding. They want a woman who won't rock the boat or expect any more from them than how they have represented themselves. To her occasional attempts at complaining, he'll reply, "Hey, you knew from the beginning that I spend my weekends racing cars."

For the man who is unavailable because of his involvement with other women, a woman's availability itself is a deciding factor. There are no affairs if there are no volunteers. Since long-term intimacy is not what he is seeking, "any port in the storm" will provide adequate distraction from the reality of his life.

In addition to finding women who are available, these men have to locate women who are willing to violate their own emotional, sexual, and ethical standards. Our society's Judeo-Christian ethic dictates that a person refrain from dating or sleeping with someone who is married. A man looking for a woman to have an affair with knows this. So his challenge is to find women who with a little encouragement will deny their values and boundaries and partake.

Who are the women who would deny their own standards? Women who themselves are unhappily married make up a significant proportion of those who are attracted to married or engaged men. They think that involvement with a married man is "safe" and that they can bank on his confidentiality. Other women, those who have been wounded in the past and thus have "sworn off love," are looking merely for distraction. They say they don't want a real relationship, so they find someone who won't give them one. Women who battle low self-esteem feel only worthy of "part of a relationship." Many who have been abused cannot fathom a nurturing relationship. They are good candidates to accept a part-time man. Interestingly, when questioned, many women say they "didn't want to date a married man," but still they overrode their own red flags and their values. With each married man, it became easier and easier to enter and stay in these "go-nowhere" relationships.

Womanizers also look for women who will believe their stories about their home life. Very few of them tell women how happy they are at home, how wonderful their wife is, and how they just really want to have extramarital sex with no strings attached. No, that usually isn't the story line. The story line goes, "No one has really ever loved me, and certainly not my wife. She nags ... doesn't appreciate me ... wastes money ... runs around on me ... is unmotivated and won't work ... has let herself go ... hates sex ... doesn't listen or talk to me anymore." Or, best of all, "Our marriage really ended years ago—we just haven't finalized it yet in the courts."

Women unfortunately take this hook too often. They really do believe that these issues are the guy's only problems. They are sure they will be able to provide something that "she never did" and that they will be able to make him "finally feel loved ... listened to ... appreciated." Once he is loved, she believes, he won't run around on her. She is sure she can change this part of him. A woman who buys this also believes that once he turns his attention toward her, the relationship will shift from the wife to her. She doesn't understand that any attention from an emotionally unavailable man is fleeting. His need is not "once and for all to be loved" as much as it is to get laid, be amused, or be distracted. At some point, however, a woman will probably realize that just because he has committed his attention to her for twenty minutes in bed does not mean he's willing to commit.

A man who runs around on his partners may also seek women who are a little naïve or who say they have no expectations. He hopes a naïve woman will believe it when he tells her she is "the only one." While you might be the "only one" he has on the side at the moment, statistics for the long run are *not* on your side. The man who is emotionally unavailable remains that way. The percentage of women who actually marry and stay married to someone they had an affair with is in the single digits. And, of course, even the existence of those few marriages doesn't indicate whether the men remained monogamous, just that they remained married.

Women who tell a womanizer they have "no expectations" about the outcome of the affair are extremely appealing to him. They have just verbalized his core belief system about relationships. But don't try a bait and switch on him. Don't tell him you're not looking for anything serious and then later try to get him to step up to the plate and have a real relationship with you.

His pathological code of ethics says, "If you date me knowing I am not monogamous, you already know what I'm about. To later hold me to a higher standard is unfair."

Why They Are Successful

Men who are absorbed in their work or hobbies are successful at finding women because they initially appear to be well-rounded. They aren't hanging out night after night at the local pub. They have active lives and many interests. For women disenchanted with the daily grind or with an existence they perceive as mediocre, this guy can look pretty interesting. Every day he has some exciting new story about the latest mountain he's climbed or how he beat his own record in a cross-country run. Maybe he's a thrill seeker who participates in sports like race-car driving, bungee jumping, or hot-air ballooning. All the better—her adrenaline gets to rush for free just listening to his stories. I've had patients tell me about their boyfriends' interests in such detail you would think it was their own lives they were describing. Yet some of them had never even accompanied their partner to one of his hobby-related events. If your date's life sounds way more interesting than yours, it's a red flag. It indicates a desire to live vicariously through someone else's achievements and avoid looking at what isn't happening in your own life.

Another reason women are attracted to chronically busy men who don't abuse drugs or alcohol is because they appear wholesome in this day and age when everyone seems to be addicted to something. A woman might ask, "What can be so bad about basketball? At least he's not in the bars." These guys can slip easily under the radar because their career- or hobby-related obsessions seem benign in a culture used to hearing story lines worthy of *The Jerry Springer Show.*

As for men who are unavailable because of their involvement with other women, it should seem obvious why they shouldn't be anyone's dating choice. But the fact remains that women date these serial heartbreakers perhaps more than any other type of dangerous man—and they often do so knowingly. This suggests that such men are successful because women are willing. Here we can honestly say there are no victims, only volunteers.

The emotionally unavailable man can be quite charming. If he has other women or family commitments, whether or not you know about them, his life is probably quite active. Ironically, this quality can capture a woman's attention by making him seem "the man on the go." He comes across as having a lot of energy and outside interests.

A womanizer may be highly verbal about his relationships. He may share personal information in such a way that women mistake his sharing for emotional intimacy. Women believe his story line about his other relationship(s) without realizing they are hearing only one side of the equation. He knows well enough that women are empathic to tales of empty and sad relationships, so he uses phrases such as "currently unhappy," "trying to get out of a relationship," "a mutual understanding that we can date around," or "just a matter of time until it ends." But the current relationship hasn't ended, and as long as she hangs around, he probably will too—with her, with you, or maybe even with your friend. He is successful when he finds a woman who believes that if a man is "unhappy," he is already out of the relationship and available to her.

Such men may also be successful when they find women who are unhappy in their own relationships. Some women in an unhappy relationship, instead of ending it and allowing all parties to move on with their lives, see getting involved with another man as some sort of answer to their problems. Even though they're struggling in a failing relationship, they add another doomed-to-fail liaison on the side. It's the kiss of death for most relationships to be having problems and then to have to recover from the devastation of an affair with an emotionally unavailable person. These men do harm—to you, to your current relationship, and to your future.

Talking about her extramarital affair, Kayla says:

It is the perfect situation for me at the moment because I have two kids and am married. He's married with a baby on the way. I justify it by remembering that we dated years ago and always clicked, but the timing was always off for us. Now it is the perfect situation because we both are "stuck" and there is no risk of being exposed by one or the other of us. We each have something to lose. If one of us were single, there would always be the danger of the single one falling in love, getting possessive, and confronting the other's spouse. While I wish things were different, I know they aren't and can never be. I have no expectations and am free to just enjoy what we have.

One problem here Kayla: Emotionally unavailable men often feel they don't have anything to lose because they are only marginally invested in the permanent relationship they do have. Banking on an emotionally unavailable man to keep his mouth shut is folly. If you start getting on his nerves, he might spill the beans just to be rid of you, even if it means having to face the fallout in his permanent relationship. After all, he can always find another woman who is willing to have an affair with him. History has taught him well.

An interesting point is that almost every woman who told us her story about getting involved with an emotionally unavailable man said it happened at a time when her self-esteem was low. She may not even have recognized that fact when it occurred, but looking back, she realizes that she either had chronically low self-esteem or was coming out of a relationship situation that had damaged her self-esteem (such as being battered or even going through a divorce). Women accept far more during times of low self-esteem than they do when their esteem is sound. A belief that she doesn't deserve a whole, satisfying, and healthy relationship is a reflection of a woman's low esteem level. If a man gives a woman who suffers from low self-esteem a little attention, and if he promises her that at any moment he will become available to her, get divorced, break up completely with his girlfriend, move on, get over someone, finish a demanding work schedule, or quit a hobby, then too often she willingly falls into his arms. Unfortunately, however, too many women can tell you that moment never comes.

For other women, getting involved with a man who is married or is dating someone else is a way to hedge a bet. If she can draw him away from another woman, she reasons, that means it was "meant to be." She may even feel triumphant. This is one of the ways in which women fail to tell themselves the truth about what they're doing, their motives, and the inevitable outcome. And if she isn't successful in drawing him away from his other relationship, then it isn't her fault anyway because he was already spoken for and not really ready for a relationship with her. She can dismiss it fairly easily by thinking he wasn't emotionally ready. The *real* problem, however, isn't that he's not emotionally ready; it's that he's not emotionally available.

A final reason why an emotionally unavailable man might be successful in attracting women is because the arousal effect of the "stolen moment" can be intoxicating to a woman who is drawn to soap opera–style drama in her life. A woman who is bored or who likes to "flip the bird" to society's rules may find dating a married man to be the perfect way to turn her back on the values she was raised with.

Some of the women who shared their stories for this book indicated that from childhood through adulthood many of their male relationships had been with emotionally unavailable men. They'd had fathers, brothers, previous boyfriends, or husbands who were unavailable. For their whole lives they'd engaged with these types of men, so it was hard to tell the difference when a new dangerous man entered their adult lives. They were just repeating what they had grown accustomed to.

Women's Stories

Nothing is sadder than the inevitable Heartbreak Hotel story, especially when you come to understand that it was preventable.

The women who share their stories here are trying to keep you from checking in at all.

JAMIE'S STORY

Jamie, a middle-aged graphic designer, had been married twice. Both of her husbands had been unfaithful and had predator-like characteristics. (See Chapter 10 for more on predators.) She married her first husband shortly after high school, and he began having affairs soon thereafter. Her esteem took a beating. She hoped maybe her first marriage was a fluke and her second one would be different. But it wasn't. She picked predator number two, and soon he began having affairs. But Jamie stayed on for a while and tried to make things work.

Jamie knew what it felt like to be married to an emotionally unavailable man who had affairs with other women. One might think that since Jamie had had husbands who cheated, then she herself would never do that to other women. One might think she would have a natural empathy for other married women. But she says, "I just got sick of the whole relationship cycle because when it comes to picking men, I suck—plain and simple. You get sort of hopeless about whom you pick, and then anything goes. You just let your own standards down. And pretty soon you're the one who is doing it to other women."

Jamie swung from predators to the emotionally unavailable. After her second divorce, Jamie knowingly became involved with married men on two separate occasions. The first time, they began as friends. He offered to help her out of a bad situation, and the affair grew from there, although she suspects it was part of his motivation from the beginning. "It's a danger to be friends with married men," she says. "More often than not, that's *not* how it stays." Before long, the "bad situation" she was getting out of turned into a terrible situation because she was having an affair with this married man. "I couldn't believe I was doing it. It felt awful, but here I was."

The second time, Jamie met a married man online, and they "clicked." They shared similar interests, and he seemed to provide what she thought she needed. He didn't tell her right away that he was married, and it didn't occur to her that the most unsafe way to date is in cyberspace. There is no way to verify in person what he says about himself, and there's no body language to read. Your red-flag system is at a disadvantage because you're not getting vibes based on your physical senses. Cyber-dating is fantasy-based interacting in which people get to imagine far more than what probably exists or ever will exist.

But Jamie found all this out soon enough. When she learned he was married, her emotions were already engaged in the relationship, so Jamie rationalized their involvement by saying she was the one who felt like his wife. She told herself that they were more emotionally connected than he was to his legal wife. She told herself that she and the wife were both getting what they wanted from the relationship. The wife got the money and the legitimacy, while Jamie was sure she was the one getting "his emotions, his time, and him." Of course, most of their involvement consisted merely of e-mail exchanges.

He repeatedly asked her to marry him, while never exiting his marriage. It didn't register with Jamie that this was a fairly ridiculous proposition. He wanted another wife even though he already had one and was doing nothing to get divorced. It was a way of dangling the carrot in front of Jamie to keep her in the relationship while he did nothing to end his marriage. This is a common ploy with these dangerous men. The state of his being "unhappy but still at home" can linger for years.

Reality finally caught up with Jamie and she broke it off. "I began to resent his wife for having him to herself every night, weekends, and holidays," she says. "His constant promises of divorce that never occurred and his inability to follow through were destroying me. In the beginning, I thought she and I both had what we wanted in him, but obviously that wasn't true because I began to resent everything about her, him, and the relationship. I didn't want to admit it to myself, but I wanted more."

Jamie says her reasons for getting involved with two married men had nothing to do with innocence, perceived security, or a good time. She says:

> I didn't enter in because I didn't know what a married man was all about. I knew. I didn't think he was necessarily going to save me from my current life, although with some of the men I hoped there would be more. And it wasn't just for the sexual contact. It was because for a few stolen moments I was important to someone and they loved me and saw me as I have never seen myself—as beautiful and wonderful. Of course, that's what I thought he was saying and meaning at the time. But if I was so beautiful and wonderful, where is he?

TINA'S STORY

Tina also repeatedly dated emotionally unavailable men. A student working on her master's degree, she says her most recent recovery is from a workaholic, career-driven man. Being dumped for someone's career is no easier to take than when a man goes back to his wife. Emotional unavailability of any stripe still boils down to a man who is not present in your life.

Tina has gained some insight into herself and her dating selections. However, her most recent involvement wasn't the first time she had been attracted to this type of dangerous man. Her past was littered with unavailable bachelors.

Tina says:

> I grew up without a dad. He fled to avoid child support, which really hurt me, so I promised to always protect myself and my heart. I sought out men who were safe in my eyes. But to me, what made men safe was if they were in situations where I knew they could not or would not want to get close to me and would probably eventually leave.
>
> As I grew older, I wondered why I kept choosing the same types of men—older men, men in other relationships, those who lived out of state, career-focused men who were gunning

for promotions, or men fresh out of medical school with no time for a relationship.

On the one hand, I sabotaged myself by choosing men who I knew wouldn't get close or didn't even have time to get close, yet I stayed because I wanted to believe they would eventually give me what I had wanted from my dad—the feeling that I truly mattered. I put these men in the position of making up for my dad. I hoped someone who was "busy" would for once put me ahead of his career, his job, his schooling. Someone, somewhere in the universe would step forward and let me be a part of his life that mattered. I needed to see someone step away from what mattered to him and step toward me.

It doesn't make sense. It also didn't happen. Over and over again, they left. They would cheat, break up with me, go back to their girlfriends or wives, take on a new job that would leave them even less time for me, or sign up for more classes. I just kept standing there waiting, empty-handed.

I guess in some ways I was successful in my early goals—I successfully failed at choosing men who could give me what I wanted.

JONALYN'S STORY

Jonalyn, a late-middle-aged, African-American magazine writer, responded to my request for information on emotionally unavailable men by being flip and self-assured. She confidently reported that her late husband had begun dating her while he was still married to someone else. They eventually married, and while his health was failing, she became sexually active with another married man. She thought the fact that they both were married was a guarantee that neither one would disclose the affair. But eventually he let it slip, and they stopped the affair once they were confronted.

Jonalyn went on to have yet another affair that lasted for several years. When her husband eventually died, her lover dumped her immediately because he was afraid of her availability for a more permanent relationship. This is common for emotionally unavailable men. Having an affair is one thing; having a permanent relationship is another. And more likely than not, that is not his goal.

Jonalyn vowed not to make these mistakes again. Assured that she had learned her lesson by being ratted out by one man and being dumped as soon as she was available by another, she felt that whatever had driven her to this type of dangerous man was surely behind her. Certainly her pain and anguish taught her that these men were never going to step up to the plate and "become available."

But Jonalyn fell into yet *another* relationship with a married man, one whom she'd known for years. He claimed his marriage was on the rocks because his wife had just given birth and her attention was totally focused on the new baby rather than on him. Not surprisingly, Jonalyn learned that a man's describing his marriage as being "on the rocks" and his actually leaving it are two different things. Still, their affair lasted for several years, and he never left his wife. Jonalyn had again invested years in a relationship that ended.

Despite this last episode, Jonalyn claimed she felt that being involved with emotionally unavailable men now actually fit her lifestyle and was just what she wanted, rather than anything more serious. Although her previous statements indicated that she'd been injured, she had grown callous from the effects of her involvement with dangerous men and had resigned herself to these types of relationships.

"The rules of relationships aren't for me," she boldly stated. At least, that is what she has had to tell herself in order to survive her string of doomed relationships with any kind of self-esteem still intact. But after some reflection she admitted, "I am the emotionally unavailable one." For some women, this may be true. They are drawn to emotionally unavailable men because they, too, are unavailable due to their own histories or mental-health issues. For Jonalyn, aligning herself with emotionally unavailable men kept her from seeing that she also wasn't up to the tasks of monogamy and intimacy.

Red-Alert Behavioral Checklist

The emotionally unavailable man

* has interests, hobbies, sports, work, educational goals, friends, or some combination of these that always comes ahead of the relationship and your needs

* is preoccupied with his career to the extent that long-term dating, engagement, or marriage is never considered an option

* is preoccupied with himself and his own activities and issues to the exclusion of being truly interested in you, your life, your needs, or your interests

* is still married, engaged, dating, or involved with someone else

* isn't "quite broken up yet" but is "unhappy" in the relationship

* needs someone who "understands" him

* implies immediate connection with you as someone who "understands" him the way "she doesn't"

* doesn't take time between the ending of one relationship and the beginning of the next

* does not seem to be fazed by the ending of a relationship

* promises to end his relationship with someone else, but "reasons" keep coming up as to why he can't

* has a history of affairs or indiscretions

* may have a history of mental illness or a pathological diagnosis

* may be an addict

Your Defense Strategy

Emotionally unavailable men are exciting at the beginning of the relationship. At least initially they are attentive and fun-loving. Those who are driven by their other interests sound sincere when they promise they will make time for you. Those who are in other relationships seem mysterious; your stolen moments together can increase the intrigue. They sound rightfully unhappy when they describe their other relationship and when they talk about how happy and fulfilled you make them. They promise you are next in line. But your turn never comes.

It would seem obvious that of all the categories of dangerous men, getting involved with this type is the most preventable. True, there are always stories about women who did not know that a man was overly committed to his work and hobbies or was "taken" (see Chapter 6, about the man with the hidden life). But that information always comes to light eventually.

Regarding men who are in other relationships, the ball is in your court to make a decision. Psychology 101 teaches us that pain is a primary motivator. We will change our behavior when we have reached our pain threshhold. Dating married men will surely rush you to your pain threshhold. It will teach you to avoid married men for the same reason you don't willingly stick needles in your eye—*pain!* But a second and equally important reason to refuse to date married men is because of your integrity. Whenever it is that you learn of his other relationship, end yours with him. Tell him to stop calling. If necessary, change your phone number or your e-mail—do whatever it takes to end contact with him.

Women need to ask themselves just how emotionally connected a man can be with them when he is spending eighty hours a week at work or absorbed in hobbies, or if he is married, engaged, or seriously dating someone else. If a woman is seeking a man whose affections will be focused on her, dating an emotionally unavailable man is one of the best ways to sabotage herself and her emotions. These men are dangerous because the outcome of getting involved with them is always at least frustrating and painful and, at worst, disastrous. They are also dangerous because they seem to have little regard for the havoc they wreak. Furthermore, some women erroneously think that if a man is married, he can't also have a mental disorder, an addiction, a pathological condition, or be violent. In truth, he has just as much potential to have those issues as anyone else. Don't dismiss this possibility by thinking his only issue is being focused on something besides his relationship with you.

Men who are unfaithful *with* you will be unfaithful *to* you. His issue is not that he is with the wrong woman; it's that he has the wrong character. His character will not be any different when he's with you than it was when he was with her, because it has nothing to do with the woman he's with and everything to do with him. Character is made up of a person's embedded personality traits. It doesn't change when one changes clothes or hairstyles.

Engaging your own integrity can be a viable defense strategy against getting involved with an emotionally unavailable man. If a married man has approached you, obviously his integrity is not intact. But where is yours? Make a commitment simply to not date men who are married, engaged, seriously dating other women, or not totally out of a relationship. For that matter, show integrity to yourself and your own emotional health by making a commitment not to date men who are too absorbed in other goals to have a true interest in a serious relationship.

Integrity also means not even being a casual friend to a man who is married, engaged, or dating someone else. Women with the slightest crack in their boundaries are at risk of ending up having an affair with someone they only meant to be friends with. Women need to ask themselves, "If I were with this guy and we were struggling with our relationship, would I want him sharing information about it with a woman he just met? Or to a female colleague over drinks after work? Would I want my relationship history told as a pick-up line to another woman?" If the answer is no, then ask yourself why you're listening to his tale of woe. Any guy who is sharing way too much personal information about his current relationship has either major boundary issues or big B.S. issues. This is about challenging your character and being willing to face what it is about you that makes you available to a dangerous man. It presents an opportunity for your own growth.

Finally, remember the experiences of countless women who can tell you that even if you are a gambler, odds are slim to none that a man who's involved with someone else will become available to you. Although many of these men see even marriage as impermanent, some will attempt to stay married even while they have affairs on the side because doing so keeps their other flings from getting too serious. They may claim to stay married because of their religious beliefs (even though they're more than happy to hop into your bed), for the sake of the children, or for financial reasons. The most important thing for him is to maintain the status quo: a wife at home and other women or amusements on the side.

Women's Insights

A common theme among the responses of many women who participated in my research and had been involved with emotionally unavailable men is summed up by Ali, a thirty-five-year-old business executive from the Middle East. She says:

> I believed what he told me about how great I was. I hadn't been a big dater, so I didn't have lots and lots of experience. My self-esteem was low, although at the time I didn't think it was low—but it had to be for me to do something like that! It felt good to hear what he was saying. It didn't matter to me that he was married. I wasn't going to get serious with him anyway. I did wonder why his wife would put up with his crap, but I never felt like I was the one hurting her. It was her husband causing the pain. That's what I made myself think.

Unlike some women, Ali came to some realistic conclusions about emotionally unavailable men and the damage they inflict on others. She continues:

At first, I thought it was fun... at other people's expense. Now I think I don't have the right to decide if someone's relationship should end or not. They should decide mutually, and not because I've been inserted into their relationship, but based on the merits of their own relationship. You can't do that in the middle of an affair. Nothing is clear then. I now am sorry for the pain I caused his family. Even if his wife never found out, I hurt her and I played with her marriage, which I had no business even touching. It wasn't mine.

Charla, a fifty-four-year-old Southern belle, says the reason she has stayed available to her emotionally unavailable man is because "I wanted to be *the one* to break through that wall and teach him what it was to truly love someone. Doesn't that sound narcissistic of me? Like I'm a martyr or something. What I've learned is that I can't teach anyone anything. It didn't work with him! Thirty-four years into a relationship with him, I am still here, alone!"

Jamie, whose story appears earlier in the chapter, reminds us of the pain that must be in a woman's heart for her to even tolerate a dangerous man. She says:

We all look for a connection, for some reason not to be alone. That's where they get us. They tug at our heart strings and everything else follows. In the moment, it doesn't matter that they really aren't yours—and never will be. It's hard to have compassion for myself about how much I hurt right now. I did this. What in me makes me think this was okay? Why did I pick someone like that? The red flag was blatant—if he's with someone else, you don't date him. I hate that I did this to womankind. You just want women to stay on a high moral ground on this issue. We can. I know we can.

But being with someone else no matter how unhappy he says he is means that he isn't being up front with his current relationship, so why do I think he's ever going to be up front with me? This is his character that I get to see so clearly up front: He lies to women. And I'm a woman, and he will lie to me—and he did. These men don't leave who they are with. They aren't looking for love; they are looking for a distraction from who *they* really are.

I'm a good person. Or I thought I was—but that I'd jeopardize my own emotional health by doing something that is so *obviously* stupid makes me wonder about me. I know darn well these things never work out. We all know the end to these stories. It's just so preventable. So I took myself to counseling. There is a deeper reason why I did this. Part of me wants to just blow it off and not look at why I did it. But I don't want to do it again, so I am willing to be in pain to look at it. I want to minimize it and say it was for fun, or I didn't know, or something. I don't want to tell it like it is. My therapist has given me hell over this—it's the wake-up call I needed. This says at least as much about *me* as it does about him. Because if I say I want a real relationship that can grow into something permanent, I've got to be fishing in a place where that is even possible. And this wasn't it.

6

The Man with the Hidden Life

Just when you think you know your man, Hank the Hider reminds you that sometimes you don't know him like you really ought to. And it's not necessarily because you haven't tried. It's because you aren't allowed to.

Hank the Hider

Perhaps of all the types of dangerous men, the man with the hidden life leaves women feeling the most "duped" and "fooled." A woman can't decide if a man is inappropriate for her if she doesn't know what he is really up to. She can't make an informed decision about him if she isn't informed. These closet dwellers are tight-lipped men. What you don't know *can* hurt you and probably will. He understands this, which is why you are not privy to any information about his past life, his current issues, or what he may be planning for his future.

These men come with complicated histories. There are no easy answers for why they behave the way they do. Some are saddled with mental-health issues that have caused them to develop a lifestyle of secrecy and lies. Others had difficult childhoods or parents who intentionally lived out of the sight of most people. Maybe he had a parent who was a felon, drug dealer, or prostitute. Or maybe he had a parent who was a successful businessman and who sheltered his wealth from the government's eyes. Whatever the situation, in many cases it was family members who taught him how to keep most of his life out of view. In other cases, these men's problematic behaviors are linked to addictions—sexual, relational, drug and/or alcohol, gambling, or, biggest of all, an addiction to thrill seeking. Whatever his history, the fact that this dangerous man developed into a pathological hider is what women need to be on guard against.

Men with hidden lives don't truly feel connected to people. Their attention is more engaged by excitement, adrenaline, and thrill seeking than by the love of a woman. They desire the high of the moment, the chase, and the challenge of avoiding being caught—by the police, their mothers, or you. Adrenaline is their mistress when you aren't around. Because a lot of their energy is absorbed in covering their tracks while actively seeking the next thrill, men with hidden lives can be involved in a lot of different activities, most of which you would probably be shocked to find out about. Others are engaged in only one illegal, illicit, or immoral activity. Their activities may change frequently, perhaps to cover up past misconduct. Their identities shift with their latest interest.

Women describe men who have hidden lives as aloof and distracted, and they are absolutely correct. There is just too much interesting stuff going on when you aren't there! These men's identities are not tied up in their relationships. Unlike permanent clingers or parental seekers, they aren't trying to find themselves in you. They are trying to keep a lot of balls in the air while keeping you in the dark. It takes a lot of energy to have so much going on at once.

Since I'm describing illicit, illegal, and dangerous behavior, surely I'm talking about society's deadbeats, right? Not necessarily. Men with hidden lives can be police officers, doctors, businessmen, musicians, or clergymen. What they do as their "day job" usually has nothing to do with what they are doing on the side. These men have an uncanny ability to compartmentalize their existences so that their professional lives and their hidden, pathological lives seem to be unrelated—at least in their minds.

All of this almost guarantees that a man with a hidden life is a combo pack. His mental-health issues, addictions, emotional unavailability, and predatory instincts combine to make him someone to be feared. His hide-and-seek games keep women clueless as to what he's really all about.

But that's what he is counting on! He has the luxury of living a complete other life beyond your eyes and your knowledge. The world is an open playground for him. What he is doing and with whom is only limited by his imagination and your lack of information.

He feels very entitled to having his cake and eating it too. After all, it's really no one else's business what he does personally. This is a common belief among men with hidden lives. They really believe that their lives are their own and they are free to do whatever they want as long as they don't do it in front of you. Rules, laws, society's expectations—all are frivolous to the hidden-life man, even if he works in the field of law or law enforcement. Lecturing him about social norms and conventions is about as meaningful as quoting statistics to him. When it comes to any of the aspects of his life that he keeps in his closet, the rules don't apply to him.

Even his family members and closest male friends don't always know what this dangerous man is up to. They can only allude to the secretiveness he has always embraced. He "is a private man," "doesn't like other people in his business," "has always kept his personal life to himself." There are probably reasons why those things are true—reasons you should know about, because a "private life" is usually just a nice way of saying a "closeted life." And we know only too well the kinds of things that are hidden in closets—things like wives, other women, unclaimed children, addictions to drugs or other substances, criminal histories, second homes, aliases, sheltered debt, diseases, undisclosed bisexuality, psychiatric hospitalizations, transgender episodes, warrants for arrests, and criminal sex offenses. And that is just the beginning of the list.

A woman should want to know about these aspects of a man's life and character *before* making a decision to become involved.

Who They Seek

The number-one enemy of the hidden-life man is an inquiring mind followed by persistent questions and a lively intuition. So it stands to reason that the kind of women this dating disaster is interested in are those who do not inquire, question, or follow up.

Men with hidden lives like women who are trusting and, most importantly, who want to continue that trust. Some women are very invested in maintaining trust as a core value in their relationships with men—to the point that they are willing to look the other way to avoid seeing their trust violated. A woman's value system of trust and her desire to trust are key for this dangerous man.

Over and over in my research on women who dated dangerous men, women indicated that they were raised in homes in which their mothers stressed the importance of trusting people freely. Women who ended up with men who had hidden lives showed a pattern of not requiring that people prove their character and trustworthiness up front. Trust was given openly and freely, with little question. Violations of this trust were responded to with second, third, and more chances. This is exactly the woman this type of dangerous man wants: the "little lady" who equates a lack of trust with being impolite. And impolite is the worst thing you could call her. She doesn't seem to think ending up dead, raped, or injured is worse than being impolite.

Women who are distracted run a close second to women who are overly trusting when it comes to their appeal to these men. A woman may be distracted by an impending divorce, children who are acting out, a stressful career, an active life, her own outside interests—basically anything that will keep her from seeing, asking about, and following up on his inconsistencies and her hunches.

Women who are only seeking to date "casually" are also good candidates for this clandestine lover. Women who date nonchalantly aren't always in the habit of digging around for a lot of personal information. If the relationship deepens, she may then pursue that type of information. In the meantime, she is happy to have an occasional dinner out, a vacation together, or a romp in the sack—all of which seem harmless and fun. Little does she know the risk she is taking.

Lastly, what these men are hiding influences who they date. A man who is hiding the fact that he's married, for instance, may date a different kind of woman than a man who is hiding drug dealing.

Why They Are Successful

A man with a hidden life can seem alluring in the beginning. Your lack of information about him may keep you intrigued. Even his unavailability can be exciting for some women. He hopes that you will find something about his tight-lipped demeanor attractive enough to keep you coming back.

A hidden-life man is not stupid. He knows what kinds of things push women's buttons and run them off, which is strong motivation for him to hide any unsavory behaviors. He probably learned to keep his pathological antics a secret because they ran women off in the past. He has learned from his own track record what to make public and what to keep private—and most of it he will choose to keep private.

On the other hand, some hidden lifers don't know what the big deal is about what they do. They think they can compartmentalize their lives. They believe if they are doing "good" over here in this occupation, that offsets the "bad" they are doing somewhere else. He sees his life as a scale, and as long as his "goodness" balances his "mischievousness," then all is well. He is successful when he can find a woman who will also compartmentalize his behaviors. If he is wealthy, famous, or handsome, some women believe, that offsets his being married, or his having a gambling problem or sexually transmitted disease.

Another reason why this dangerous man is successful is because he is vague. He disguises his secret life by calling himself an "intensely private" person. His stoicism and restraint might seem strong and dignified if in the past you have dated men whose lack of boundaries caused them to disclose too much too soon. A little "discretion" on the part of a man is probably an attractive thing to some women.

But look closer and listen better. When conflicting stories begin to emerge, it is always a marker pointing to your need to obtain more information. Maybe his friends mention details about his life that you have never heard. Or his family members allude to people from his past whom he has never told you about. Maybe his history includes names he used that you don't know him by or careers that do not line up with what he does today. Instead of simply buying it when he tells you, "That was in my past and I'm starting over now," you might want to know what he is starting over from and why.

To make matters worse, the man with the hidden life is usually a combo-pack man. The nature of his character typically qualifies him for at least one other category in the dangerous-man lineup. Perhaps he is an emotional predator or an addict. Most often, it is men with mental-health issues who lack any qualms about lying to women. Combo-pack men are the most destructive of all because, by definition, with them you are never dealing with just one kind of dangerousness. Instead, their pathologies weave together to form a tricky and potentially harmful web.

Women's Stories

The horrors of the three stories that follow should motivate us to test, question, and examine every new man in our lives.

NATASHA'S STORY

Natasha, a nurse with four children, comes across as an extremely stable person. She is soulful, insightful, compassionate, and patient when it comes to shortcomings in herself and others. She seems wise beyond her years. But still she failed to avoid Buck.

Buck was a charismatic chameleon who could be whatever she needed him to be. Distraught over her recently ended marriage, she needed a person whom she could confide in. On the scene arrived Buck, a psychiatrist with his own long history of failed marriages. Although that might have been a red flag for some women, Natasha welcomed him as someone she could easily talk to. Buck, with his puppy-dog eyes and his sympathetic demeanor, allowed Natasha all the time she needed for talking.

Soon, the two got married and blended their families. With Natasha's four children and Buck's three, what a family of nine they made!

But Buck had a huge narcissistic streak. His psychiatric practice always came before Natasha's nursing job and her recent return to school for an advanced degree. His constant need for recognition caused him to work extraordinarily long hours. He was always vying for the position of head psychiatrist at his hospital; anything less than that was "not good enough." Natasha worked diligently at her job and as a student, in addition to taking care of their seven children. Buck usually had meetings in the evenings, so the majority of the children's needs during the dinner hour fell on Natasha.

Buck often delivered lectures on the topics of marriage, relationships, addictions, and abuse. Even though he had several failed marriages in his past, he did not see any hypocrisy in the fact that he presented himself as a specialist in relationships.

Buck had never been good with money. His impulsive nature caused him to spend money in order to distract himself from his growing boredom. He was alternately bored with his home life, his marriage, his work, or himself. Actually, Natasha didn't have a real handle on what Buck's boredom was all about. But she eventually discovered a few things about how he dealt with it. A few years into the marriage, she noticed that Buck drank too much. She learned he had a history of drug abuse and had even been let go from previous jobs for inappropriately using drugs or alcohol with patients after they were out of the hospital. Buck's drug and alcohol usage was covert, and Natasha noticed that it waxed and waned with his interest in his family.

Then Natasha learned he'd recently had an affair with a psychiatric intern. As it turned out, interns were always good targets for Buck because they were only around for a year or two and then long gone. Natasha's discovery of this most recent affair turned out to be just the beginning of what turned out to be a Pandora's box.

When she started looking more closely, Natasha found among Buck's belongings lists of numbers for phone-sex services, locked boxes of pornography, sex gadgets (for whom, she wondered), and puzzling credit-card charges. She began to pay attention to his unexplained absences at all hours of the day and night.

When she confronted Buck, he acted remorseful and confessed to a history of sexual addiction dating back to adolescence. He'd frequented adult movie theaters and engaged in unprotected sex. He'd had sex with strangers in public restrooms. He'd used pornography heavily, used drugs and alcohol to drown his guilt, had ongoing affairs and inappropriate relationships with patients—the list went on. Natasha estimated that Buck had engaged in hundreds of acts of unprotected sex with transient people. Because of his behavior, she was at incredibly high risk for contracting AIDS.

Devastation doesn't begin to describe what Natasha felt. Not only had her husband deeply betrayed her, but she was horrified and fearful for her health. And yet, she began marriage therapy with Buck. For several more years she stayed with him. She worked on their marriage in couple's counseling and went to therapy herself to heal the betrayal she felt.

After a few years, Buck announced that all his pathological acting out was in the past. He said Natasha should get over it because he had, and he once again started to complain of mounting feelings of boredom. To battle this round of boredom and to promote himself, Buck wrote a book that awarded him some attention within his field. But even this small amount of fame was not enough to squelch his growing discontent. He became involved with the transcriptionist who typed his book.

Soon, after the pain of trying to mend a marriage to a sex addict, Natasha was told by Buck that he wanted a divorce; he had met another woman. Buck married this new woman. He also relocated to another state where his multiple marriages were unknown and opened a new practice. He eventually became divorced from his latest wife.

Buck was able to get several women to marry him because he was good at hiding most of his pathological behaviors from them. Whenever he needed to he was able to hold it together enough to present a front as a "normal family man" and a successful psychiatrist. But underneath these facades lay another life, one worthy of an acting award in the horror-film genre.

GINA'S STORY

Not all men with hidden lives are hiding histories as sexual deviants. Gina had been divorced for years. She was a consultant in the chiropractic field who helped physicians establish their practices. She lived a fast-paced life of work, friends, and travel. She wasn't particularly looking for a relationship when she met Derrick. But he pursued the relationship and eventually got her to consent to a date. Derrick said he was divorced, too. Handsome, talkative, open—he seemed like a nice enough guy to pass some time with. But Gina didn't want anything too serious. After all, her life was pretty full with travel, business, and her young teenage boys.

It was hard to reach Derrick because his job kept him on the road. This was before pagers and cell phones, so Gina relied on him touching base with her as his job permitted and when she was also in town. Their time together was mostly on weekends. He would spend one night of the weekend at her house, but, oddly, she never spent a single night at his place. In fact, she really didn't know where he lived—she knew the area of town but not where, exactly.

Gina and Derrick lived about forty minutes apart. When Gina suggested they spend some time at his house for a change of pace, Derrick rented an apartment for their weekends together that provided "easier access" for both of them. The forty-minute distance was reduced by their renting a place halfway between their two houses.

One night, Gina got a phone call from a woman who identified herself as Derrick's wife. She confronted Gina about the "affair" Gina was having with her husband. Derrick, it turns out, was married and still living with his wife. One night per weekend was spent at his home. The times when Gina had sent him to the store or on errands for her, Derrick was actually going home and checking in. His traveling job kept him unavailable for both women. He was elusive enough that no one really knew where he was at any specific time. His ploy had worked well with Gina for a year or more.

JOY'S STORY

Meet Joy, a fifty-year-old corporate executive. She was climbing the corporate ladder in a "man's job" following a divorce from a famous musician. That's when she met Bo, a strapping man who owned his own construction company. What a change from the musician, she thought. His brawn and her class made them quite a pair to behold.

They moved in together while "awaiting his divorce," and Joy kept climbing the corporate ladder. But soon, Bo's business wasn't going well. So he sold it, at a loss, he claimed. Each morning, Bo was up and dressed and out the door by 8:00 A.M., "beating the pavement" for new opportunities. But nothing much ever materialized, especially considering how much effort he put into looking for work. He tried his hand at selling insurance; then he bought a bar, and he "lost money" on that, too. But he was determined, so he left the house every morning looking for a job opportunity for a man over fifty.

Joy and Bo married, and he continued to pursue "employment ops." Eventually, however, Joy discovered that what he was really pursuing was a life of gambling (with her money) and engaging in multiple relationships with women who paid him for his company or to "just help him out," without knowing he was married to Joy. Then there were the hidden alcoholic binges, the money withdrawn from her retirement account for wining and dining other women, the gambling debts, the lying about his job search, the failure to pay child support for his mentally retarded daughter, and a network of women that covered the Tri-State area—none of whom knew about the others.

As it turned out, Bo had been married to more than just the woman he had a daughter with. Joy discovered lots of the other women who had been "Mrs. Bo" at some time or another. And most of them never knew exactly how many times he'd been married before.

Like Bo did to Joy, besides potentially running off with your material assets, these dangerous men also wreak havoc with your heart and soul, your self-esteem, and your ability to trust your own instincts.

Red-Alert Behavioral Checklist

The man with the hidden life

* won't answer direct questions about where he goes, what he does, or who he's with

* conceals important information about himself that you only discover later

* goes by aliases

* engages in secretive behaviors

* is often unable to be reached directly—he has no address, just a post office box or voice mail

 * resists disclosing personal information about himself, such as where he was raised, who he is related to, or where he went to school

 * doesn't disclose information about previous (or current) wives or girlfriends

 * tells stories that don't line up with his actions or with what you know about him

 * tells stories that don't line up with what other people tell you about him

 * receives mysterious phone calls, pages, or letters and has mysterious appointments, jobs, or meetings

 * is not forthcoming with information or details about his employment or how he makes money

 * goes periods of time without contacting you

Your Defense Strategy

The best defense against the hidden-life man is to develop a questioning mind. As opposed to what you might have been taught growing up, not everyone is truthful. What he is saying, no matter how convincingly he says it, may or may not be true. Few sex addicts, for example, confess early on that they have engaged in five hundred acts of unprotected sex. Until you truly know a man well, always bear in mind that he may have wives, lives, and dives elsewhere.

These dangerous men are prone to various disorders, so be on the lookout for hidden addictions in multiple areas. And, of course, pathology is always a factor to be considered since these men lie about their lives so easily.

Listen, watch, and dare to compare his stories and his actions. Ask questions and keep asking. If his response is avoidance, it's okay to be suspicious. It's helpful to put any man on "probation" in your mind until your questions are consistently answered—either by his actions or through confirmation you receive elsewhere.

If the facts about his life don't add up, they don't add up! You don't have to make them add up in your mind so you can give yourself permission to date him. Acknowledge to yourself and to a friend that you have concerns, questions, and doubts about his story line. Most of all, don't stop telling yourself the truth about what your red-flag system is telling you.

The longer you date someone and the more slowly you move in the relationship, the more you can watch and see. The more you see, the more you can question. The more you question, the more opportunities you have to find out information. The more information you have, the more power you have. The women's lives you've read about in this chapter were shattered by their discovery of startling information about men they thought they knew well. Two women thought they knew their men well enough to marry them, but in reality they didn't even know enough to keep themselves safe.

Natasha's story reminds us that women are frequently pathologically forgiving of the lies they uncover. One uncovered lie leads to the next, and instead of questioning what else they will uncover, women tend to rationalize everything by telling themselves, "This is it; I'm sure there's no more." Women would be smart to realize that if a relationship starts off with lying, you have an inside view of a significant and perhaps pathological character flaw in a man. Chances are that noteworthy flaw will be the reason for the end of your relationship with him. Without a doubt it is a red flag.

Women's Insights

Joy laments:

> The worst part is feeling so stupid, so foolish. I am a professional businesswoman and am alert to all sorts of issues in business, and yet I missed *loud* clues in my relationship with

Bo. I didn't apply the same kind of rational thinking in my relationship that I am known for in business. My level head did not prevail in my relationship, and that's so stupid! We don't shelve our minds because we are dating! What's wrong with us?

I have to say, there were plenty of warnings all throughout the relationship. It wasn't just in the end. I remember them in the beginning. But there's that rush of emotion. What exactly does that do to our brains? Why can't emotion and logic coexist? I rationalized, ignored, and, most importantly, lied to myself about what his character really was. I got flickers of inconsistencies—hunches that he wasn't where or even *who* he said he was. I didn't ask enough questions or check him out enough all throughout the relationship when my intuition was screaming. If I had, I might have come to the conclusion early on that he was a liar and a con, and I might have made other decisions. This was a costly mistake for me—he stole sixty thousand dollars from me. And then there's my broken heart and my loss of self-esteem. I doubt myself now—will I ever really tune in and listen to my red flags and be safe?

Gina has feelings similar to Joy's. She says:

For crying out loud—I am someone who helps doctors organize their practices, and I can't even apply the same principles to my own personal life! I don't know if I'm that stupid or if he was that good at what he did. Who pays for another apartment to avoid driving twenty more minutes? That's ridiculous, and I probably knew it and ignored it, because if I'd tugged on the end of that string, what would have unraveled? His story, this relationship, my fantasy? All of the above—and it would have been the best possible thing to have happened early on. I only know he had a hidden wife. What other skeletons are in that closet with him?

Chapter 7

The Mentally Ill Man

Chances are good that attempting a relationship with a man like Mike will result in a meltdown—for you! Getting seriously involved with someone who's suffering from mental illness means a lifetime commitment to someone else's pain. Is that really what you want?

Mike the Meltdown

Labeling men who are mentally ill as "dangerous" presents some sociopolitical difficulties. No one wants to be pigeonholed as an undesirable dating choice based on something they cannot help, like a diagnosis of some kind of mental illness. So let me say up front that this is not a judgment of people who are mentally ill. I treat mentally ill people. Many go on to lead honest, nonviolent lives—lives that would seem to disqualify them from being called "dangerous." In addition, many women who are reading this book may be diagnosed with one or more of the conditions that will be discussed in this chapter. It is difficult to talk about mental illness while avoiding the stigmas that mental-health patients try very hard to escape. Futhermore, not everyone who is diagnosed with a mental illness commits acts that qualify them in this book as "dangerous."

At the same time, the reason why the mentally ill man has earned a chapter in this book is because patients who are diagnosed with some of the conditions described here have a tendency toward dangerousness when they are not under the regular care of a psychiatrist, therapist, or community case manager, and/or when they fail to follow their medication regime.

What qualifies as mental illness falls along a broad spectrum. Few women know enough about the symptoms of mental illness to recognize some of the difficult and pervasive disorders that plague these dangerous men. Discussing every type of mental illness that could affect a relationship is beyond the scope of this book, but this chapter will help you sort out a few of the more troublesome disorders to watch for. In addition, the Appendix, at the end of the book, describes in more detail some of the conditions listed in this chapter. Be sure also to review the sections in Chapter 1 that deal with pathology and chronic mental illness. Most importantly, I want to stress that if you see any behaviors in a man that cause you concern, please take the time to discuss them with a professional who can help you put the symptoms into better perspective. It is better to ask and find out there's nothing to be concerned about than it is to avoid asking and later end up being harmed.

In order to adequately understand the issue of mental illness we need to move away from the images of mentally ill individuals we've grown accustomed to from the movies. The portrayals depicted in *One Flew Over the Cuckoo's Nest, Silence of the Lambs,* and *A Beautiful Mind* won't help us detect dangerous men in our own lives. That's because many mental illnesses do not manifest themselves in the dramatic ways portrayed in films. In fact, many men with mental illness may not yet have been diagnosed at all. Many have escaped diagnosis either because they've not sought treatment or because their true condition has escaped detection when they have sought treatment. A man with a clinically diagnosable mental illness may not even know he has one. That means detection, once again, lies with you.

Mental illness finds its origins in many different life circumstances. In Chapter 1, we touched on the issues of psychopathology and chronic mental illnesses. As we saw, some conditions are genetic, meaning the individual is born with a problem hardwired right into their personality structure. These problems will not change. Other individuals have brain-chemistry issues that make them unstable, and still others have endured extreme childhood trauma that, when combined with genetics or brain-chemistry problems, creates a disorder of huge proportions. Because the causes and symptoms of mental illness fall along such a broad spectrum, it is difficult in one chapter to talk about all the identity issues, personality structures, and dangerous behaviors that can be associated with different disorders. Mental illness is a complex tapestry of biochemistry, genetics, and learned behavior that can make a person difficult to treat and even more difficult to live with.

The main thing that makes mentally ill men dangerous is the fact that their problems are long-term. If your goal is to eventually find a life partner or even someone whose company you can enjoy for any length of time, why would a man who is mentally ill fit the bill for you? Why would a life of possible hospitalizations, crime, depression, manic episodes, medication, therapy, or instability at home and at work be appealing to you?

Perhaps for some women, the word *possible* creates a loophole that lets them imagine their man could be the exception. But professionals in the field of psychology know that the best predictor of future behavior is usually past behavior. A man's history of symptoms associated with whatever disorder he may have can shed light on the possibilities for his future. The one thing that is sure is that with mental illness you can never be sure of the patient's future stability. What he looks like, acts like, and functions like today may or may not be true a week, a month, or a year from now. Fluctuations in a patient's mental health are based on numerous factors that often cannot be predicted, including stress, other medical disease processes, reactions to medication, lack of medication, or the patient's own biology, which may change as he ages.

While working in a domestic-violence shelter, I saw repeatedly that a large proportion of the women who sought safety did so from violent men who were also mentally ill. We regularly saw women seeking safety from men who had been diagnosed with antisocial personality disorder, men who were unmedicated schizophrenics, men with untreated bipolar disorder, and men with borderline personality disorder. Add drugs, alcohol, or the stress of unemployment to the mix, and you have a bomb ready to explode.

Mentally ill men cost women a lot. Yet mentally ill men are another type of man that women have a hard time leaving. They evoke great sympathy from women who mistake their own feelings of pity for passion. These women are willing to stay to avoid the stigma and guilt of being thought of as someone who would "abandon" a mentally ill person. They place their own safety and their children's safety second to maintaining a relationship that's emotionally unstable. Such women take a huge gamble. If you cannot predict a man's stability, how will you know that you, your children, or your future will be safe?

Who They Seek

An alarming number of women are attracted to men with rather severe mental illness. Why that's true is an interesting question. I don't think they knowingly seek mentally ill men; still, something in them is drawn to something latent in the potentially pathological man, and a connection is made. Only later (and often too late) do they find out that the man they have been dating is mentally ill.

Women who were raised by mentally ill parents (diagnosed or not) are more at risk for seeing mental illness as a normal pattern of behaviors. Often, women who have dated mentally ill men later realize that their fathers or mothers were also mentally ill but not diagnosed. They begin to understand why the man's behavior failed to feel abnormal to them. For instance, a history in your family of bipolar disorder (formerly called manic depression) can make a man's symptoms associated with that disorder seem less unusual or noteworthy.

The type of woman who crosses boundaries and carries some function of her career into her personal life by dating a man who is similar to a client is often the type of woman who would take a mentally ill man home. Women in caretaking professions rank highest among those who end up getting involved with mentally ill men. This includes nurses, other workers in the medical field, social workers, clergywomen, and even teachers and day-care workers.

Women who date this type of dangerous man tend to fall into two different categories. Either they date those who are more pathologically dependent, like permanent clingers and parental seekers, or they date those who are more pathologically unpredictable, like predators, emotionally unavailable men, or addicts.

Women with a chronic tendency to nurture, fix, or guide will find some mental disorders nonthreatening. Women who have dated clingers or seekers may find personality structures in other mentally ill men similar to those of the clingers and seekers, so they miss their red flags about what could possibly be wrong with these men. This could include men with pathological conditions such as dependent personality disorder, avoidant personality disorder, or paranoid personality disorder. It could also include men who are diagnosed with chronic mental illnesses such as depression, anxiety, or obsessive-compulsive disorder, or even mild-tempered bipolars.

Other women will find some of the behaviors of mentally ill men similar to those of emotional predators, emotionally unavailable men, addicts, or abusive/violent men they may have dated. These are men who could be diagnosed with a pathological disorder such as antisocial personality disorder, borderline personality disorder, or narcissistic personality disorder, or with a chronic disorder such as posttraumatic stress disorder (perhaps related to combat). Some violent bipolars may find their way into the lives of these women. Women who are drawn to these types of men are often women who are themselves thrill seekers, who prefer a high-speed and exciting life, who like the dramatic ups and downs that "keep life interesting," who have a little "edge" to them, or who have their own histories of crime, addiction, or mental-health issues. On the other hand, it isn't totally unusual to find mild-mannered—even passive—women who like these particular "bad boyz." Perhaps it is their way of "taking a walk on the wild side."

Looking at your patterns—and determining whether one or both of the adults who raised you were mentally ill—may help you see which type of mentally ill man you are likely to select in the future or have selected in the past.

The bottom line is that a mentally ill man must find women who will disregard his disruptive and sometimes pathological behaviors and erratic lifestyle. He needs a woman who is hyperpatient or hypertolerant and who is willing to forego normalcy for him. Altenatively, he will find women who *like* the chaos and instability wrought by mental illness. Some seek women with their own mental-health histories, which often makes for a very combustible relationship. (I am not referring here to situations when, for instance, two schizophrenic or developmentally disabled individuals meet and date, perhaps in a day-treatment environment or because they live in the same group home.)

Our research has shown that many women who end up with mentally ill men do not exit the relationship even when they have information about the mental illness. As mentioned above, this is often because they don't want to be the type of woman who "abandons" those "less fortunate." Many women also stay in the relationship even when they learn the mentally ill man is not following his doctor's orders or is not receiving any medical or psychological care. As you will soon read, this is usually a very bad choice.

Why They Are Successful

Dangerous men who are mentally ill successfully attract women because most women do not know what the mental illness will mean for them personally in terms of a man's dangerous or pathological behaviors. Although we are a society raised on self-help books, most people only have fleeting knowledge about mental illness and know even less about pathology. For instance, most women understand the basic dynamics of depression and might even be able to somewhat realistically assess the difficulties this condition could represent in a relationship. But they may not realize that severe depression can result in psychotic behavior. They may not realize that the individuals most likely to attempt suicide are those diagnosed with borderline personality disorder or that those most likely to commit dangerous and illegal behavior are unmedicated bipolars during a manic phase or that those most likely to kill or rape have antisocial personality disorder. How many women truly understand how bizarre a person's behavior can get if he has a delusional disorder such as schizophrenia and doesn't take his medication?

Women end up taking a crash course in Psychology 101 when they date a man who falls into this category. They find out firsthand about instability, the consequences of treatment options foregone and medications untaken, and the ugly face of irrational and scary behavior. Women who ignored or glossed over the red flags about their partners' mental illness eventually learn enough to be able to teach a class on "How to Survive when Your Man Is Mentally Ill." They learn how to read the signs of an impending emotional crash, how to flee quickly, how to try to protect their children, how to get him placed in a hospital against his will so he will receive his medication, how to thwart suicide attempts, how to clean up financial messes, and how to reframe his behavior to others so he looks less mentally ill.

Still, because many women do not want to be perceived as someone who is prejudiced against mental illness, they stay. Some mistake their pity for his potential; others hope the relationship will end for mutual reasons. Some women try to love their men enough to cure them. Many women don't understand his diagnosis, so they are willing to "wait and see."

Mentally ill men are initially successful with women because some of their symptoms can be hidden. It can take a while to become aware of unusual behaviors that are linked to mental illness, especially if the disorder is cyclic. He may be in between some of the more bizarre manifestations of his disorder when you meet him. By the time women realize there is something wrong, many are already hooked into the relationship and either are reluctant to get out or lack the skills to do so. With some types of mental illness, the man's response to a woman who is trying to end the relationship can be frightening. Women who are afraid to end the relationship because of a man's erratic behaviors can end up dating him much longer than they ever wanted to. They remain in the relationship hoping it will mutually end and they will be "released." This, however, can be a dangerous waiting game.

Pathological men in general can be successful because some women lack the skills to proactively and asssertively end a relationship. These women know how to flirt and date, but they don't have a clue about how to end things safely. A woman who can't readily get out when she wants to shouldn't get into *any* relationship until she learns some exiting skills.

Women's Stories

The women whose stories appear below can teach you firsthand about the consequences of failing to take the time to understand what your man's mental illness means for *you*.

SIERRA'S STORY

Sierra was divorced with five girls when she met Chase. She was a medical professional running a hospice unit, and he was caring for his dying mother, who was a hospice patient. He was tender and attentive to his mother's every need. Sierra remembered the old adage, "Watch how a man treats his mother, because that is how he will treat you." She ultimately learned it was an old wives' tale.

Sierra began dating Chase after his mother died. He showed her the same attentiveness he had shown his mother. What she didn't know and what Chase didn't bother to share was that he was diagnosed with bipolar disorder (previously called manic depression). Since then, he has also been diagnosed with antisocial personality disorder. They married, and Sierra eventually came to realize he'd had mental problems—for which he'd probably been diagnosed—as far back as childhood. Chase had extreme mood swings, and he refused to take his medication. Unbeknownst to Sierra, he engaged in criminal activity during his manic phases.

Once Sierra learned of his criminal activities and his affairs with other women, she wanted out of the marriage. She began to make attempts to end it. But during Chase's depressive swings he became needy, clingy, and childlike. Sierra would be prepared to separate from him, and then he would collapse into deep depressions that resulted in suicide attempts and hospitalizations. Then would come a period of rehabilitation. Sierra would wait it out, hoping he would stabilize so she could again attempt to separate from him. But the cycle would start over again. She remained trapped for several years before an opening presented itself.

Chase's arrests for theft and for dealing guns and drugs were beginning to mount up. Women whom Sierra did not know would show up at the jail and post bail for him. Sierra found piles of driver's licenses that revealed he was also dealing in illegal identification and stolen merchandise. Soon, Chase was notified he would be going to jail for a ten-thousand-dollar theft, arms dealing, and drug charges. Sierra hoped it was the perfect time to end the relationship.

She told him to move out and plan not to return when his jail time was up. Chase obliged since there were plenty of women willing to rescue him, women who enjoyed the excitement of his manic phases and the "mothering" he needed during his depressions. Soon, however, Sierra presented him with divorce papers, and he seemed despondent. She worried he had "nothing to live for"; he already had said that if he "lost" Sierra and the girls his life would be "nothing." One day, while Sierra was at work and the girls were at school, he went to the house, locked the children's dog inside, and burned the house to the ground. Not a trace of evidence linked him to the crime—except his mental illness. But no conviction occurred.

He was frantic afterwards, and his mania spurred him on to deal more drugs and arms. Sierra received a phone call from someone alleging that Chase had raped her. He couldn't get to a jail cell soon enough to suit Sierra, but one more criminal episode lay ahead. He led police in a high-speed car chase that resulted in a shooting. Finally, off he went to state prison. But for Sierra and her daughters, the cost of her marriage to him was their house lying in a pile of ashes.

CONSTANCE'S STORY

Constance, a twenty-something elementary-school teacher, tells about her ex-husband, who had chronic posttraumatic stress disorder (PTSD). He had suffered emotional trauma from his work as a cop and then had become chemically dependent, which is often common in sufferers of PTSD. To Constance, he seemed anxious even when they were dating. She didn't know his anxiety was part of his posttraumatic stress. She thought he was probably just going through a period in his life when things were tense. She didn't date him long enough to see if the anxiety ever subsided. They married, and soon she found herself living "on her tiptoes" as she tried to remove every possible stressor from his life so it would not set off his volcano of emotions. He endured flashbacks, panic attacks, depression, and rage. His functioning level fluctuated a lot. He would work for a while and then go through periods of time when he could not work. Constance's life revolved around stabilizing his.

When Constance was raped in 2001 by a stranger, she broke down emotionally. Now she needed her husband's support, but he immediately left her. Her stress and her inability to micromanage his life while she recovered from her own trauma meant the end of the relationship. She says, "It was then that I realized the extent of his illness. Because of what was wrong with him, he couldn't ever really be there for me. He was too damaged in that way. I could be in his life while I was supporting his illness, but there wasn't anything in him that could do that for me. I wish I had known what a diagnosis of posttraumatic stress really meant."

TESSA'S STORY

Tessa was a university professor. She tells about getting involved with someone who turned out to have a personality disorder:

> I dated a man who was brilliant, but I noticed over time that I started to feel "crazy" around him. I thought his behavior was a little odd, but he always made it sound like it was something about *my* behavior that was odd. I didn't have a history of relationship problems, so I wondered what was really up with this man and why I couldn't tolerate him. I constantly felt like he was pushing my buttons.
>
> I began asking my friends if the things he said about my behavior were true from their perspective. I didn't get any feedback that indicated I needed to look at something in my behavior, so I joined a support group to talk about how I felt in his presence. I learned that what was making me crazy was that I was trying to adjust to his pathological illness. The more I tried to be okay with it or placate it, the worse I got!
>
> Everything was focused on him—on *his* interests, *his* job, and *his* neverending need to have his ego supported at any and all costs. It was nauseating to have a conversation with this man—it was all about him! It was a heavy burden to deal with his ego. He finally told me he was diagnosed with narcissistic personality disorder. Because it is a pathological disorder, it means this is simply how his personality is structured. There wasn't much to be done for him. He could learn a few things about how to be less offensive to people, but, basically, this is how he was.
>
> I have learned the hard way that loving a narcissist is the most futile thing you can do. Loving anyone who has a patho-

logical condition that can never be made better and will only get worse is pretty futile. But I did learn the warning signs. If I ever meet another man with this disorder, I will *run!*

GENEVA'S STORY

Geneva, a thirty-year-old paralegal who has never been married, tells her story about a blind date gone weird:

I had a blind date with a man a girlfriend hooked me up with. He was a successful businessman, handsome, highly intelligent. But during dinner he began to tell me about his need to protect himself. He always carried a handgun in his glove box and numerous rifles in his trunk. What kind of business is he in that he needs that kind of protection? Then it became obvious it wasn't his business that was the problem. It was that he had mental problems. He had converted his basement into a fully stocked bunker in case of "attacks by unknown people." He was suspicious of the government, feared every type of person—was afraid of just about everything. He could rattle off a list of fears connected to every occupation known to man. He suspected people of having motivations that he could really have no idea about. I realized during dinner that he had paranoid personality disorder. He finally discussed being in treatment for his condition. From what I could see, he was a *long* way away from getting well, if he ever would. I changed my phone number the next day. I'm one of the lucky ones who actually reacted quickly to what didn't feel right.

KYLA'S STORY

Kyla, a thirty-two-year-old store clerk, talks about being married to a man diagnosed with borderline personality disorder:

I can say how difficult my life has been trying to love a man with this pathological condition. I have lived with his mood instability, coldness, and detachment—and in the next moment his overattachment to me. He lacks any kind of self-awareness of what he is doing, so therapy has been of little help. He just doesn't "get it" about what he does to other people. When he is rude in a social situation, he doesn't see it. No one comes to our home anymore because his behavior is so bad. He denies anything is wrong with him, even though he's been diagnosed and understands the diagnosis.

I feel so insecure about our relationship. I mean, how can I settle down with someone who is all over the place, when chances are good it isn't ever going to be any different from this? I have to make a decision between living like this and finding a real relationship that isn't based on someone's pathological mental illness. I feel unsettled and like the rug is always being pulled out from under me. I never know what I'll come home to or who he has fought with or offended.

I left my marriage and my two kids for this man! He can't manage my kids because he is like a child. He resents them because they require the attention he demands. He knows he can't handle having them around without getting irritable, so I've lost a lot of contact with my kids for this incredibly mentally ill man! They have to spend more and more time with their biological father because this man is so sick and can't have a normal life with children in it.

But I am really at the point where I realize that things are how they are. If I can't accept him like he is *now,* I have no business in this relationship because I will just be waiting for changes that, according to his therapist, are probably *not* going to happen. I now know that that is what pathological means.

LYDIA'S STORY

Lydia, a single twenty-four-year-old who owns a clothing store, says:

I have dated many men with some sort of mental illness. It's something I really need to look at. The one who was the most difficult to handle was a man with obsessive-compulsive disorder. Jack had to spend hours every day in arduous rituals that involved socks, objects in his apartment, etc. It wasn't that he was cleaning up the place, but that he was arranging everything methodically and compulsively. I thought I could be okay with it at first. After all, I liked being an ordered person—but this wasn't the same thing. It was sad to see how everything took him ten times longer than it did other people. He was very

smart and hardworking, but he had a crummy job below his
level of intelligence and earned very little because he couldn't
finish any task in a reasonable amount of time due to his obsessive focus and his mental disorder.

He kept telling me the bizarre things that ran through his
head about me. It scared me. For weeks I kept trying to talk to
him and reason with him about these bizarre fantasies, thinking there might be some end to this process. It became clear it
was just part of his disorder and I was becoming one more object he was obsessed with. So I ended it. He was never unkind.
He was just miserable with himself. But it really did a number
on my head. It took me a long time to get over it. I had to look at
why I took really obvious signals that something was wrong
and relabeled them "orderly." This wasn't orderly; this was disordered! Why did I do that? The whole experience was just so
disconcerting. It took me out of the dating game for quite a
while!

Red-Alert Behavioral Checklist

The mentally ill man

* may be on any kind of psychiatric medication

* has been hospitalized for emotional problems or life-threatening behavior

* is currently being treated for a psychiatric disorder

* has undergone unsuccessful counseling as an adult

* was taken to counseling as a child, but results were unsuccessful

* currently is or in the past was under the supervision of a
  case manager with community mental-health services

* currently is or in the past was on probation or parole

* is on disability for a mental condition

* always brings the conversation around to himself

* engages in black-and-white thinking

* is inflexible and has difficulty being spontaneous

* believes or acts as though rules are for everyone except him

* thinks he is special and unique and wants to be treated as such

* participates in daredevil behaviors

* has been diagnosed with any of the following:

  - Bipolar disorder (previously called manic-depression)
  - Posttraumatic stress disorder or any other anxiety disorder
  - Conduct disorder (as a child)
  - Antisocial personality disorder
  - Narcissistic personality disorder
  - Borderline personality disorder
  - Dependent personality disorder
  - Avoidant personality disorder
  - Paranoid personality disorder
  - Obsessive-compulsive disorder
  - Schizophrenia or any other delusional disorder
  - Chemical abuse or dependence
  - Major depression

  (See Appendix for descriptions of these conditions.)

Your Defense Strategy

Dangerous men who are mentally ill present a good argument for why you need to heed your internal sensors as soon as you get a message that anything is "off." They prove why we have to both trust and *respond to* gut instincts that tell us something is wrong, even if we can't say exactly what it is. Although such information may not come to us as early as our first encounter with a man, it is important that we respond as soon as possible when it does come.

Women need to steer conversations with a date or potential date toward getting information they need. They have to learn to tune in for signs and symptoms of a man's mental illness from the information they receive and from their own gut reactions. Mental illness can present itself in many different ways, because there are many types of mental illness. Not all are obvious initially, which is why finding out a man's family history is often key to understanding if you should be more concerned about his mental health. Some mental illnesses run in families. The same is true of addictions, which are addressed in the next chapter. Take note of family members he talks about who have schizophrenia, bipolar disorder, or other chemical imbalances. Getting information from his family or other people who know him is always wise.

Women often fear discovering information they "really don't want to know." For example, what if his brother is schizophrenic? That doesn't automatically mean you don't date him. But it does mean you date him with "eyes wide open." It means you keep that information in the forefront of your awareness so you can watch for any symptoms in him.

When I was in private practice treating women with tendencies toward dating dangerous men, we had an open-door policy whereby they could bring in any man they were potentially serious about so we could check out the relationship. We hoped our clients had learned enough about dangerous and pathological men in the course of their counseling to avoid choosing them. But in case they were unsure about a man, they could bring him in for two or three couple's sessions. Afterward, we would privately give the woman our feedback and would voice any major concerns. Most of the time the women really had learned about listening—to him, to their red flags, to what felt uncomfortable —and they were making better choices. But one bad choice comes to mind. Theresa, who had spent two years in counseling—both for her previous dangerous-men selections and for early childhood abuse—brought in her new man, Ted. She had met him at church. We voiced our concerns that he was indeed a dangerous man with mental illness. Two weeks later, Ted raped Theresa.

You, too, can check out any concerns you have with a mental-health professional. It may be money well spent to go to an individual session or two so you can talk about signs and symptoms of mental illness in him or even in yourself. If the relationship proceeds, participating in a few sessions of couple's counseling early on is highly recommended for all women with a history of dating dangerous men. A therapist can make you aware of concerns he or she sees in the man or in the relationship. If a man truly cares about you and is interested in getting serious, he will probably be willing to visit a therapist with you for a few sessions. Just be honest. Tell him you have a history of getting involved in unhealthy or destructive relationships, and you want to make sure this one starts out on the right foot. If he is entirely unwilling to go, it may be a red flag. There is a reason why a man tries to avoid a therapist, and it's usually related to his being afraid the therapist will see something in him. That's all the more reason why you want to hear what the therapist has to say!

Another great defense strategy is to know some of the symptoms of mental illness. Taking a Psychology 101 class or even reading self-help books will at least make you aware of some of the disorders you may run into.

Other women are great resources. Talk to women who have dated mentally ill men. How did it start? When did they become aware of his condition? What symptoms did he have? How did they end it?

Have an "accountability friend" whom you are brutally honest with. Doing so can help keep your thinking clear and your eyes wide open. Friends who can confront you about your "less savory" dating selections are priceless. Don't choose for this role a passively dependent friend who is in her own relationship with a dangerous man, but rather a woman who is looking to make healthier choices or is already doing so.

Women's Insights

Sierra's comments are typical. She says:

> I, of all people, since I work in the medical field, should have been able to tell at the very least that something was wrong. When I was dating him I got the confirmation of his long-standing diagnosis of bipolar disorder [from both him and his psychiatrist]. That in itself should have been a significant concern for me. I understand what that diagnosis carries with it. What did I think—that I was going to be his full-time nurse for his whole life? That my medical knowledge was going to somehow make him better? If the one who is mentally ill isn't going to take care of himself, then there is little anyone can do for him. Certainly our marriage did not motivate him to care for his disorder. Even his professed love for my children did not.
>
> But in addition to that, some time passed between when I became aware of his behaviors, when I learned of his diagnosis, and when we married. There was plenty of time for me to have tuned into what was happening if I had admitted to myself that my life was becoming increasingly unmanageable because of his behaviors. I guess that's the thing about mental illness and especially pathology: The normal motivators to change behavior just don't work with these individuals. They are wired with a system that the rest of us don't understand. Reaching out to them seems to be ineffective. Our family offered him a stable, safe, supportive, and loving environment. I don't think he couldn't appreciate it; it's just that he couldn't respond to it. It wasn't enough to help what was wrong with him. Someone who burns your house down, rapes a woman, and has a shootout with the cops is someone few of us can reach. I realize that not all bipolars are this extreme. But their illness, whatever it is, still impacts your life. There is no such thing as a nonimpacted life when you're involved with someone who is mentally ill. I have come to have a new respect for the issues of mental illness and pathology.

Kyla says:

I should have done my homework. When the therapist said he had borderline personality disorder, I could have read up on what that meant. I mean, if she had said he had prostate cancer, I would have been on the Internet reading everything. But with mental illness, it didn't seem like something you check on. It seemed intrusive to read about something that personal. Personal, hell! It's personal when it ruins *your* life.

My red flag was that he was diagnosed with something I did not readily understand; therefore, I should have taken the time to learn about it. When you read about what borderline personality disorder is, it's awful! But it's real. The description of his condition painted the picture I went on to live. If I'm going to live with a man with a pathological mental illness, I should at least know what I signed on for. And if I had read about it, I know myself well enough to know that I wouldn't have married him. The condition is just too severe. It's cost me and my children way too much. I'm sorry he is disordered, but it's not anything I can fix and it's something that has severely impacted my own life. If I had had the information, I might have chosen differently for myself and my children. There are just some disorders—especially the pathological ones—that indicate the person is not meant to be married or to have the responsibility of children. They just can't handle it. This is one of them.

Chapter 8

The Addict

Partyboy may seem to promise a good time, but by the end of the chapter you'll understand why he offers less than a good time— for you or anyone else.

Paul Partyboy

This dangerous man tends to produce a dichotomous reaction in women—we either shiver or shrug. We either fear him for the pain and havoc he can create in our lives, or we think he isn't someone to be feared by us, which leads us to believe that this is not an issue for us. Many women end up with addicts precisely because they are not on the lookout for them. In some cases, women don't even know what addictions are all about.

Addictions can be loosely grouped into two categories, only one of which is widely familiar. The more well-known category includes the obviously harmful addictions to substances such as drugs or alcohol, or to behaviors such as gambling or sex. The other category encompasses what I call "pseudoproductive" addictions. These include behaviors we are not used to thinking of as addictive, such as an addiction to work or productivity. We don't think of them as addictive because most of us embrace the American work ethic. What's more American than hard work?

But when such behavior turns compulsive, it can create a truly destructive pattern.

Pseudoproductive addictions can take several forms. Some people work to an extent that they have no time for their families (classic "workaholism"), some are overachievers for whom nothing is ever enough in terms of their own accomplishments, some expect perfection from self and others, and some constantly seek approval. An even more insidious pseudoproductive addiction is one in which a person works extremely hard to "rescue" loved ones or family members—who are often other addicts—by never allowing them to face the consequences of their own behavior. It's common for several different types of pseudoproductive addictions to overlap in a person. Of course, both men and women can be addicts of any type.

On the surface, pseudoproductive addictions do not look like the dangerous behaviors that come to mind when we discuss addictions. They may even seem somewhat satisfying to the addict and his family members. After all, they can result in the addict getting ahead, making lots of money, or acquiring attention and approval. By contrast, the other category of addictions—which we might call "unproductive" addictions—seems so fruitless. These addicts may lose everything. They often can't hold down a job. They spend money on gambling, drugs, alcohol, pornography, or thrill-seeking behaviors. But anyone who has lived with someone who has a pseudoproductive addiction knows very well these types of addictions take the same toll on the addict and the family as the unproductive ones.

You might think addictions would be easily identifiable. But sometimes certain behaviors have been normalized by entire generations within a family. Children and grandchildren grow up and adopt the lifestyle, making it "just what this family does." The identities of individuals and of entire families may be tied to various addictions. This can be seen in families who have worked in their own businesses day and night to the exclusion of any kind of family life. It can be seen in families whose members have worked in casinos, horse-racing, family-owned bars, strip joints, or other businesses whose success may rely on the addictions of customers and owners. To opt for something besides working in the family business or participating in the addiction is to deny your family heritage.

Sometimes we miss addictions in individuals who seem unlikely candidates for them. Who would suspect an eighty-year-old woman who occasionally bartends at the local VFW to be a binge alcoholic and gambler? She bet the dogs, the horses, the sports, bingo, every raffle known to man—basically anything that had odds attached to it. On Friday afternoons she went to the VFW, and she wouldn't return home until Monday. While she was there she danced and partied, played poker, gambled, and worked a shift or two. Everyone marveled at the busy life she led for her age. In reality, however, she was busy indulging her addictions. But many others in her family have served at the VFW hall in much the same way she did. Addictions get overlooked because they become part of the family fabric or history.

I make this point to emphasize the fact that the issue of addiction is important in a woman's life, not only in terms of the addicts she might date but also in terms of the hidden addictions that might lurk in herself or in her family. Women who have family histories of overt or covert addictions are more likely to date addicts. And getting involved with an addict guarantees a boomerang effect in your life.

Addiction 101 teaches us that a person's addiction impacts everyone around him or her. Even if you are only "casually" dating an addict, you will eventually be affected by his lifestyle, because all addictions are life-disrupting. Addicts battle lifelong urges. Even some in recovery have continual relapses, no matter what they use as their agent of addiction (the substance or behavior that serves as their "drug of choice"). It is common for addicts to flip back and forth between periods of actively using and periods of "sobriety" (when the addict isn't engaging in the addictive behavior). Having a period of sobriety does *not* mean the problem is over. Relapses can happen after twenty years of sobriety. Switching addictions—for example, giving up alcohol, then starting a daily marijuana habit—is also common. Furthermore, an addict's dysfunctional, destructive, or low-functioning behaviors can continue even if he or she is not using. A lengthy period of sobriety does not automatically mean an addict has worked on the issues connected with his addiction. And it certainly doesn't mean the addict has developed any relationship skills. This is called "dry-drunk" behavior (even if the addiction is not to alcohol). An addict can be "clean and sober" and still be emotionally and relationally messed up.

If you are looking for a man who's active in his addiction to sweep you off to Barbados for a weekend, think again. Addictions rob individuals and families of financial resources (or of time, in the case of pseudoproductive addictions). It is not uncommon for addicts to have financial difficulties they don't disclose to you. Gambling, pornography, sex, drugs, and alcohol are expensive, and the amount they cost continues to go up. That's because the addict always uses more and more. All addictions are progressive. There are no "regressive" addictions.

If occasional "out-of-control" usage does not concern you, consider this: It is estimated that 80 percent of all domestic violence is committed under the influence of drugs or alcohol. An addict's problem means the deck is stacked against his consistently treating you with respect.

People with certain mental illnesses are especially prone to addiction. Individuals with this combination are the least likely to maintain sobriety. The combo pack of mental illness and addiction is especially seen in individuals with bipolar disorder, posttraumatic stress disorder, major depression, or borderline personality disorder. (See the Appendix for descriptions of these conditions.) It is also seen in other disorders besides those listed here. Check with a mental-health professional for more information about addictions and mental illnesses.

Types of Addictions

Here is a short list of the many forms addictions can take. A person can become addicted to one or more of the following substances or behaviors:

* Drugs

* Alcohol

* Food

* Gambling

* Relationships

* Sex, pornography, masturbation

* Achievement, work

* Approval, perfectionism

* Thrill seeking, crisis, chaos, drama

* Religion

Who They Seek

It may seem like an anomaly that some women, especially those who abuse substances themselves or who were raised in homes where one or both parents abused substances, are not particularly "on alert" against addicts. They tend to fall prey to addicts because this type of behavior now seems normal to them. To hear them tell it, women who were raised in homes where addiction was present often "swear" they will never date anyone who has an addiction. Yet time and again they end up with someone who has an addiction, "hidden" or otherwise.

For an addict, finding another addict who will not "nag" or "complain" about his usage is primary. This means women who have their own addictions (even if the addiction doesn't "match" his) are his number-one dating choice. Running a close second will be the woman who was raised in a home where addiction was present, even if she does not use. She knows the addict's games and cover-ups, and she is familiar with what is expected of her in order to be with someone who uses. The two share a mutual history and understanding.

Addicts seek women who are long-suffering and who nurse a belief that the addict is going to quit. Many addicts say they are going to quit or are actively quitting, and they may be sincere even while they remain unsuccessful. If someone is actively using or has just recently quit, any significant improvement in behavior, employment status, finances, and relationship skills could still be years away. When an addict stops engaging in the addictive behavior or partaking of the addictive substance, real change is not immediate. This means women who have an overdeveloped tolerance for a partner's underemployment and mood swings and who tend to minimize their own needs will rate high with an addict.

Women who suffered abuse as a child or assaults as an adult seem particularly drawn to addicts. The aftereffects of any kind of violence leave women vulnerable to selecting relationships that replay their earlier emotional, physical, or sexual trauma. Being involved in a relationship with an addict that leaves you with your needs unfulfilled bears a strong resemblance to the emotional trauma of earlier episodes of abuse.

Why They Are Successful

The reasons why addicts are dangerous and successful are not always obvious. This is especially true if a person doesn't understand the field of addictions. Some women do not know the signs of addictions and thus fall prey by ignorance. But there are plenty of women who have knowingly dated addicts because they didn't believe a man's addiction presented danger "to them," even if they realized he was playing with things that could harm him personally. Again, if women do not tell themselves the truth about their real motives for dating ("I am just dating him for the fun of it"), chances are good that sooner or later they will wind up seriously involved with an addict. Naïvete is not a life skill. And let's not overlook the woman who thinks it's her lot in life to "change" the addict or sober him up. Her belief that she can love him into straightness is an all too common one.

Men who remain active in their addictions are often successful at keeping women in relationships because they promise to
quit. Either they never follow through with the promise, or they
simply switch addictive agents. Many addicts have multiple addictions that take turns surfacing and going underground.
Women often think their partners are clean because they aren't
looking for the signs and symptoms of different addictions. And
it's not only the addict's partner who is fooled by this; often the
unrecovered addict is, too. If he was a drug addict and merely
drinks beer now, to him he is no longer "using." Common
switches include replacing drugs and/or alcohol with sex or food,
replacing thrill-seeking behavior with unprotected sex, and replacing work addictions with serial relationships or gambling.

Cycles of multiple addictions can take years to play out. A
woman may ride a wave of hopefulness when she sees her partner
not drinking, only to find out he is using cocaine. Each go-round
can hook her in for extended lengths of time while she "thinks"
she is seeing a period of sobriety, only for her to find out he has
switched addictions. Maybe what *she* is addicted to is hope. Since
many addictions are kept private, if you're involved with an addict, unfortunately you will not always know when or if you are
at risk financially, sexually, physically, or emotionally. As we saw
from Natasha's story (Chapter 6, "The Man with the Hidden
Life"), this pattern can have devastating and lifelong effects on
your personal health, both physical and emotional. Expecting
honesty from an active addict could cost you plenty.

Every woman I have ever met who dated or married an addict
has said the same thing: "When he isn't using, he's the best guy in
the whole world." Addicts tend to be pretty charming guys on
their good days. They have to be in order for their partners to remain willing to tolerate the other 80 percent of the time. Nice
guys, good guys, generous guys, big-hearted guys, cuties, sweet-
ies... whatever your euphemism is for them, remember that *most*
of the time they are addicts whose behavior will cause you heartbreak. And chances are good they will always struggle with what
they are currently fighting. That's a guarantee as long as an addict

is still using. The addict's road to recovery is a long and winding one, littered with the lives of women and children who got lost along the way.

Women's Stories

Annie's story illustrates the potentially endless downward spiral a person's life can take if they get seriously involved with an addict.

ANNIE'S STORY

Some of Annie's family members were addicted to alcohol. So Annie felt she was fairly tuned in to the issue of substance abuse. That's why in high school she specifically avoided dating anyone whom she saw at parties drinking too much or using drugs. Instead, she dated Bobby, whom she knew all through high school and had been friends with for years. He was a heavyset guy with a great personality who charmed everyone he met. They both went away for college and reconnected during a visit home. By then, Bobby had slimmed down and had grown up emotionally. The relationship began to build.

Annie had gone to college frat parties. She knew what the scene was about and was not above a little partying herself on occasion. But her alcohol usage, she felt, was truly recreational. She was entering the medical profession and needed to keep her nose clean. So the allure of partying quickly faded as Annie approached graduation and the responsibilities of a career in medicine.

By now, Annie and Bobby had been friends for years and had dated exclusively over the past two years. They decided to marry. She began working a daily hospital shift from 3:00 to 11:00 P.M. while he struggled to maintain consistent work. She wasn't sure what the problem was with his ability to keep steady work. She thought he was trying to "find himself" in his work. He hadn't completed college like she had. In fact, there wasn't much he had completed. But she continued to support his efforts to try to find his niche in the working world.

Cheating girlfriend needs to tell the truth

By Carolyn Hax

Adapted from a recent online discussion.

Dear Carolyn: My girlfriend has told me that she's finally done "sowing her oats." She cheated on me two months into our relationship (she says we weren't exclusive at that point – I argued that we'd slept with each other and were). I just found out that after two years of dating, she slept with two other guys as well. She cried and told me how sorry she was, but I don't know if I can ever trust her. She says she has an extremely high sex drive, but I don't buy that excuse. How can I rebuild trust between us?

racking up lovers while pretending to be someone's girlfriend. She needs to own her behavior one way or the other – either by admitting openly that commitment isn't for her, or by realizing she is ready to change. To make a credible case for the latter, she needs to acknowledge the dark part of her that drove her to cheat and lie, and deplore that side of herself, and articulate the way she wants to be.

I don't see any sign of her owning anything. Without that, expect the status quo: She'll want the security of a relationship, the freedom to do what she wants, and a pass on doing any hard work on herself.

says that with the success of IKEA, "many companies are realizing that designs actually sell. So students know their designs are playing an important market role, and they've been shifting toward more commercial design."

They learn how to listen to company briefings. They observe and analyze lifestyle trends. Ermoli says today's furniture design student studies fashion, art and industrial design. SCAD has a 44,000-square-foot facility with woodworking and metal

See **INTERIORS**, Page **E6**

ral of angels and clouds that graced the dining room of this Fairfield home didn't exactly scream "bachelor pad."

And although the navy-blue walls, burgundy carpet and white light fixtures matched the previous owner's floral furniture, they missed the mark for a single guy and his Great Dane.

To convert this suburban house into a sophisticated, masculine home, interior designer Nancy Bonar of June Surber & Associates introduced fabrics, a

Blanket of snow bring

By Lee Reich
The Associated Press

Y ou might think that snow has nothing to do with garden-

as the soil doesn't get too cold. And a snowy blanket makes it easy to dig carrots, leeks, parsnips stored right where they grew.

Bobby got a job working nights as a waiter. When Annie got home from work after 11:00, he was rarely there. He usually worked until the early hours of the morning. But she wondered whether people really ate out at 3:00 A.M. Soon, money was not as regular as it had been. Bad tips, a slow night, a scheduled night off—he had all sorts of reasons for his dwindling income.

Before long, Annie was totally supporting the two of them. Shortly thereafter, she found out the real reason for his lack of a steady income: He was abusing drugs and alcohol.

Annie was a registered nurse and used her knowledge to persuade Bobby to get into drug treatment. He would emerge from rehab and function well for a few weeks or months, only to relapse eventually. Year after year, the pattern remained the same. Ultimatums were given and broken, and the debt for unpaid rehab bills mounted.

Bobby was arrested and bailed out on such a regular basis that Annie had difficulty concentrating at work. She was constantly distracted with his drug problem, and it was affecting her job performance. So Annie ended the marriage.

Years later she is still getting reports of his constant battle with addiction and homelessness. She feels bad that his life ended up this way, but she does not feel bad that she ended the marriage. That could have been her life too....

Seeing Addictions in Stories from Other Chapters

The following women's stories appear in other chapters. Addictions played a role in the lives of their combo-pack men.

NATASHA

As we saw in the story of Buck and Natasha (Chapter 6, "The Man with the Hidden Life"), sometimes the addiction is to sex and pornography. As is often the case with addiction, mental illness was also a factor. Buck was diagnosed with narcissistic personality disorder. Rarely does an addiction exist outside of other dangerous factors, a reality that makes involvement with an addict that much more problematic.

SIERRA

In the case of Sierra and Chase (Chapter 7, "The Mentally Ill Man"), it was an addiction to thrill seeking, crisis, chaos, and drama that dominated Chase's life, along with dabbling in drugs. Mental illness was also a factor with Chase, as he was diagnosed with bipolar disorder and antisocial personality disorder.

AMY

Amy's story appears in Chapter 9, "The Abusive or Violent Man." There, she paints a picture of her involvement with a prominent professor who was mentally ill, violent, and addicted to alcohol. He also in some ways lived a hidden life. By day he taught at a respected university, and at all other times he drank. Many addicts qualify as men with hidden lives. If he is not public with his addiction, he is living it behind closed doors. Amy's story reminds us that the overlapping qualities of dangerous men can span several categories.

TINA

Tina (Chapter 5, "The Emotionally Unavailable Man") got involved with men who had pseudoproductive (work-related) addictions and thus were emotionally unavailable. Trying to have a relationship with someone who has this type of addiction hurts no less than involvement with someone who has any of the other kinds of addictions. Tina chose men who were always gunning for promotions or were fresh out of college and motivated to succeed (but who never really lived up to their potentials). That kept them working even harder. They never had much time for her, which fit well with (and reinforced) her low self-esteem. Tina says, "The end to that story is I always got what I thought I'd get: nothing. They were so production-oriented that I was barely a second thought to them. Ironically, I would have never dated a drug addict knowing he was messed up. But I *was* dating addicts!"

We must remember that any addiction is life-consuming. It eventually becomes the center of the addict's world. That usually means the addict also qualifies as emotionally unavailable. I haven't met many addicts who were emotionally present for the other people in their lives, because other people get in the way of an addiction.

Red-Alert Behavioral Checklist

The addict

* uses the addictive agent almost daily or in binges or cycles
* devotes a majority of his time, money, or interests to the addictive agent
* suffers mood swings or changes in attitude if he cannot use the agent
* has lost relationships, jobs, or other significant things due to his addiction
* lies about his usage
* lies about his whereabouts so he can use
* doesn't want to discuss the addictive agent
* is rigid about the agent
* has a history of other addictions, or his family has addictions
* places people as secondary to the agent
* causes you discomfort with his attitude about the agent
* is at risk or has been at risk for health problems or deteriorating social relationships because of his addiction

Your Defense Strategy

Addictions, even the pseudoproductive ones, often run in families. But to be able to see an addiction and avoid making the mistake of making it seem normal to you, you first must look into your own family and your own history to see if covert or overt addictions exist or existed there. In my research, the women who did not see an addict headed into their lives either had addicts in their families, and thus were used to being around them, or had not spent any time around addicts, and thus did not know what to look for. In this chapter I have provided clues to look for if you are unfamiliar with the face of addictions.

To begin looking at your own history and that of your family to see if addictions reside there, consider attending meetings of Al-Anon or another twelve-step program. Al-Anon is for family members and friends of alcoholics. Many other twelve-step groups exist for dealing with all sorts of addictions. They are called "twelve-step programs" because they are based on the twelve steps of Alcoholics Anonymous. These groups can help you take what they refer to as a "fearless moral inventory" of yourself and your family to assess if addictions are present. It's important to remember that addicts are often attracted to addicts. A classic combination is for a woman who is addicted to relationships to get involved with a man who is addicted to alcohol and/or drugs.

Once you have looked into your own life and your family's history for the presence of overt and covert addictions, you can begin to examine dangerous men in a new light. In order to recognize an addict, you have to know what addiction looks like—in your family, in yourself, and in him and his family. Your ability to name your family's addictive behaviors will go a long way toward helping you to identify them in a potentially dangerous man.

If you were raised in an addictive family, you are at particular risk for repeating this dynamic by getting involved with an addict. But with the information gained by reading this chapter and by examining and reflecting on your family's patterns, you can develop a strategy of watching even more closely for addicts attempting to come in under your radar. To help you really hone your sense of when an addict is entering your life, consider going to counseling or to Al-Anon and asking friends to help you watch vigilantly.

An addict who is active in his addiction qualifies as a bad dating choice, period, with no exceptions. But what about an addict who is sober or in recovery? In these cases, I say proceed with caution. As I emphasized earlier in the chapter, be aware that just because someone is no longer using his or her drug of choice or no longer engaging in the addictive behavior, that does *not* mean he or she won't relapse. And even if a sober addict never relapses, that doesn't mean he or she has any relationship skills. On the other hand, many addicts successfully stay sober and also go on to grow emotionally and to develop good relationship skills. Chapter 11 lists some signs of a bad dating choice as well as some differences between healthy and unhealthy relationships. Chapter 12 lists some universal red flags. It would be wise for you to familiarize yourself with these lists, as they can be a good way of assessing whether a sober addict is good dating material.

MIRANDA'S STORY

Miranda, who had never been involved with anyone besides her husband, had been married for twenty-five years when her husband divorced her. Soon thereafter she met Roy. He was a sober alcoholic who had been in AA for fifteen years, and he still attended three or four meetings a week. He seemed attentive to her pain and offered her some of the wisdom he had learned at AA. Miranda fell for Roy in a serious way, but he kept avoiding letting the relationship go any deeper. Finally, Miranda asked him about these patterns. He said, "I'm still not good at relationships. They scare me and I really don't want to commit to one." Miranda asked if he would go to couple's counseling with her to find a way of working through his fear of relationships. Roy said, "I'll just go to more AA meetings until I figure it out." Miranda pointed out that he had been going to several meetings a week for fifteen years and was still unable to have a serious relationship. Obviously, she said, he needed more than just meetings. Roy refused counseling, and the relationship ended.

If you want to consider getting involved with a sober or recovering addict, here are some guidelines to follow, in addition to what's recommended in Chapters 11 and 12:

* Understand that years of sobriety do not guarantee lasting sobriety.

* Judge his overall relationship skills instead of his number of years of sobriety.

* Pay attention to how healthy his extended relationships are now—such as those with his friends, his children, his previous wives or girlfriends, his parents, etc.

* Observe what kind of communication skills he has. Can he ask for what he needs without drama, silence, or pouting?

* Observe how he works on himself given the addiction he battles. Does he go to twelve-step meetings? Has he been in counseling or group therapy?

* Observe how much insight he seems to have about his battle with addiction. Is he realistic about its lifelong impact? If not, he is unlikely to continue going to counseling or meetings to promote his recovery.

Women's compassionate side makes them vulnerable to dating addicts, men who are mentally ill, and parental seekers. Women who would love nothing more than to "nurture" a man whose history shows he is in need of love, compassion, and management are prime targets for these dangerous, pathological men. But remember one of the mantras of this book: *You cannot heal what is wrong with this dangerous man.* That is certainly true with any addict. Rescuing someone is not the same as having a relationship with him, by anyone's definition (except maybe that of an addict and his partner). Over time, women come to realize that a life of rescuing and waiting for a man's sobriety leaves them emotionally barren. You have the choice of avoiding that dance of despair by learning to spot an addict before you get involved with him.

To do this, you must recognize signs early enough to allow you a quick exodus before you become fully engaged with him. As we saw in the chapter on red flags, exiting based on a clue is far better than exiting based on hard-core, repeated evidence.

Women's Insights

Annie says:

> Okay, I'm off the hook about the beginning of the relationship because I was clueless. I really didn't know he was using. But I came to know. Everyone deserves a chance to clean up and embrace a lifestyle that can make both people happy. How long you play that out says more about you than it does about the addict. He's just doing what he's craving to do—use and use and use. What concerns me is what it taught me: how to make him look like anyone else so I wouldn't really have to know that he had a big problem. I worry I will overlook it the next time when I am out there dating. I hope not. I've gone to Al-Anon to learn about *me* and why I picked him and why I stayed. Our choices in men are really about us. I wanted it to be about him and his problem, but I stayed even when the reality of the situation was glaringly obvious—so it's about me too.
>
> I am lucky. I didn't lose my job or my career. So many women go down the tubes with the addict by trying to save him. The one thing I'd like to say to women is if you care about the quality of *your* life, don't date an addict. There is no quality of life. And if you *ever* get it, you realize you have paid for it with blood, sweat, and tears, and probably a lot of other things as well. Especially if you have kids—this is a terrible thing to put them through. Recognize addiction in a man early and choose

someone else. We all learn what we are exposed to; we don't need that kind of education, and our kids certainly don't either. It's a lose-lose situation most of the time. In fact, leaving the relationship or not dating an addict at all can be the best thing for his own life and recovery. Women have a hard time under-standing that.

Andrea, whose story you will encounter in the next chapter, dated Rocky, who was pathological, violent, and addicted. Andrea says this:

> I loved that man so much my body ached. It would have been easier for me to throw myself in front of a truck than to leave that man in the middle of his addiction. It just felt all wrong to me. I knew he needed me and my love. I knew it was what would pull him out of his addiction. So I loved harder and deeper. I turned myself inside out for him. Losing my children to Social Services was a big wake-up call. Who else had to be thrown away so this man could heal? Thank God I woke up. We all paid for his addiction, but maybe the kids most of all. They had to go live with complete strangers because Mama was all caught up in lovin' this man sober. Those were my choices— but what crazy choices I made!

Natasha (Chapter 6) has this to say about her marriage to Buck, who was a sex addict in addition to being pathologically disordered and maintaining a hidden life: "Who knows what risk I am at for contracting AIDS? I'm told it's something close to 100 percent. How do I go on with my life and work and maybe date one day with this thing weighing on my mind? It's my whole life that is at stake. Once I knew about all of it, it was certainly a red flag and it was an opportunity to exit. Who in the world would have blamed me? But I didn't. I kept investing in our marriage. Now I'm divorced and maybe safer because of it."

Amy, whose story also appears in the next chapter, says, "How did I miss all the signs? My father was alcoholic and edu-cated and smart; my dangerous man was alcoholic, educated, and smart. For my whole life I used to chant, 'I don't ever want to date someone like my dad.' How in the world did it happen?"

Chapter 9

The Abusive or Violent Man

Here he is: the one we all fear. The one too many women have met, dated, and married. He's the reason we track statistics on domestic violence and homicide. The fact that he continues to succeed at what he does demands that we examine the phenomenon of domestic abuse—not only in terms of his behavior, but also, and perhaps more importantly, in terms of what women are missing in the beginning that causes them to continue getting involved and staying involved with him. Because without victims, violent men wouldn't have much of a career in violence.

Victor the Viper

First, let me emphasize that men who physically assault women aren't the only kind of abusive men to qualify as dangerous. As you will see from Tammy's story, there are many behaviors that are abusive, some less obviously so than others. Many of them are described below, in the section "What Constitutes Abuse?" This chapter is about men who perpetrate all kinds of abuse. One of the most important things to bear in mind about abusive behavior of any sort is that it escalates, almost without exception.

Thousands of women die every year at the hands of violent men with whom they were intimately involved. It is estimated that over 80 percent of homicides against women are perpetrated by boyfriends or husbands. It causes one to wonder how so many homicides could occur in spite of women's red flags. The answer, of course, is that many women who are seriously injured or murdered in episodes of domestic violence are well aware of their partner's tendency toward violence but still do not permanently separate from him. They either tried and their partners pursued them, or they did not try and ended up seriously injured or dead. If there was ever an argument for respecting and responding to your red flags, the possibility of getting involved with a violent man is it.

Very few relationships start with a smack on date number one. If they did, men would rarely get a date number two. Violence in a relationship occurs once a relationship has developed; it begins as a progression of boundary violations that are left unaddressed. If early on a man is allowed to be verbally degrading, emotionally inconsiderate, or physically abusive, and the woman stays with him, she has sent him a message about what she is willing to tolerate. Silence is acceptance to a violent mind. Even if she verbalizes her concerns, her staying equals consent in his eyes. She is training him how to treat her. Many domestic-violence shelters allege that men continue to abuse "because they can." That is, a man gets away with acts of violence because his partner does not report him to the police, she drops the case and does not prosecute, she stays, or she goes back. Although the abuse may begin early in the relationship with verbal and emotional inappropriateness, it eventually grows to dangerous and violent expressions of power and control. Just as addictions are progressive, so is violence.

Violent men have issues with power and control. Why or how these men came to acquire these deadly skills is still widely debated within the mental-health community. But it is at least agreed upon that one of their main issues is the inability to have an equality-based relationship. They have to be top dog. When their power and control are threatened by your individuality or your desires, abuse or violence is a likely outcome. These men were most likely raised in households in which violence was a predominent form of communication. They learned that the solution to what displeased them was violence.

These men have other issues as well. In more than 50 percent of cases, men who are violent also have drug and/or alcohol issues. Violence + addiction = possible death—for you, for him, for anyone else around him. Violence will most likely be compounded when drugs or alcohol are in the picture.

As mentioned above, some of these men are, of course, a by-product of violent childhoods. This means there's a huge possibility of their having emotional problems or mental illness associated with the violence they experienced at the hands of their parents, stepparents, or other caregivers. Some forms of mental illness are intimately connected to the potential for violent behavior. Those diagnosed with borderline personality disorder, bipolar disorder, PTSD, and sometimes schizophrenia can turn violent. Recognizing the connection between mental illness and violence in no way excuses any form of violence. It only helps us look more closely at the potential for danger that mental illness can add to a relationship. These combo-pack men bring with them complicated histories that probably include learned violence, childhood abuse and violence, a dysfunctional upbringing, active addictions, possible trauma-related disorders, and mental-health issues. Trying to find a single source for their violence is like pulling a loose thread on a tapestry. Where it will lead is hard to tell.

Women who date these ticking time bombs may never know the reasons behind their violence. Sticking around to find out why he is so out of control may cost a woman her life. I don't know how badly she thinks she needs to know the "why" of his sad life, but it could turn out to be knowledge that comes at a mighty heavy price.

What Constitutes Abuse?

As I pointed out in Chapter 1 and above, women sometimes miss the signs of abuse if they are only looking for it in the form of a physical assault. Rarely does it begin so abruptly or noticeably. Violence begins with smaller acts of violation and grows into larger patterns of behavior that can span several categories of abuse. The following is a brief description of some of the types of abuse you should be aware of:

Verbal abuse includes calling you names, threatening you, degrading you, swearing at you, and intimidating you with language and volume.

Emotional abuse includes controlling and dominating you by not allowing you to make your own choices; telling you how to dress and behave or whom you can or can't talk to; put-downs that keep you captive and uncertain that you could make it on your own; criticizing you, which ruins your self-esteem so you will lack the confidence to leave; unfounded jealousy; acts of violence toward inanimate objects just to scare you, such as punching a wall or throwing things; publicly humiliating you; isolating you from others so they do not know what is happening to you and so you will not get the help you need in order to leave.

Spiritual abuse includes making fun of or criticizing your spiritual beliefs, trying to dictate or control your relationship with a Higher Power and how that relationship is expressed in your life, or using a distorted interpretation of scripture to justify dominating you because "women are supposed to submit to their husbands."

Financial abuse consists of his controlling all the money as a form of controlling you and so you have no resources with which to leave, concealing assets or shared money so you cannot leave or so you must be dependent on him and go to him for all of your needs, keeping you impoverished so you don't aspire to anything more than what you have with him, and blowing money to demonstrate his power and to leave little or none for you.

Physical abuse includes any act of violence such as hair pulling, choking, hitting, kicking, slapping, pushing, restraining or holding you so you cannot leave, biting, using a weapon, locking you up so you cannot flee, and abduction of you or of your/his children.

Sexual abuse includes any form of physically attacking the sexual areas of your body, forcing unwanted acts of sex on you, rape, sodomy, and forcing you to watch sexual acts or pornography against your will.

System abuse results from his violating and ignoring restraining orders or any other court orders he is mandated to follow, lying about you to the police or to social-service agencies in order to have your children removed or have services discontinued that would help you leave him, violating child-custody arrangements, not paying child support so that you fail financially, and not showing up for court-mandated treatment for batterers.

Who They Seek

It should be obvious that women who will stay are high on the list for abusive or violent men. Having their power cake and eating it too is very appealing to these dangerous men. I don't say this to make light of the very complicated reasons for *why* women stay. I say it to point out from his perspective why a woman's willingness to stay is appealing to him.

A woman who believes an abuser when he says it is her fault, he will change, he will never do it again, he will go to counseling, he will go to church, he only does it because she makes him, or he does it because she needs or deserves it is a top choice for a violent man. Sadly, there are plenty of women who believe men like this and are still waiting through the slaps and kicks to see if he is actually going to act on his pathological promises. Let me save you some time: He isn't.

A woman who is satisfied with good-boy make-up tactics, such as being treated to a new piece of jewelry, a dinner out, or a vacation so she will forget the horrors of last week, is another candidate for an abusive man. When pretty words or pretty things can undo the damage inflicted by acts of violence, this dangerous man has found his comfort zone: Beat and buy.

Women who come from abusive homes are already trained in the ways of violent and pathological people. They know the way it all plays out and are familiar with the rules of the game. Low self-esteem in a woman is an attractive quality for an abusive man, as is a victim stance when it comes to the way she perceives herself. A worldview that says, "I can't get out—this is just the way it is" helps her adjust to her abuser's world.

A woman who already has a history of getting involved with violent men is also a good choice for this type of man. The longer and the more often you've dated abusive men, the better trained you are for him. The new violent man in your life will have very little tweaking to do to get you (and keep you) up to speed.

Some women prefer to think they merely wandered into violent relationships, rather than realizing that their men know what kind of woman they need in order to avoid changing. You are way beyond a coincidence. Your convenience in his life is not a mistake on *his* part.

Why They Are Successful

Abusive and violent men are successful for lots of reasons, most of which have to do with their being good at what they do *and* repeatedly getting away with it. But we women aren't excused from being observant just because certain pathological men are skilled at finding, dating, harming, and sometimes killing women. Nor are we excused from how we *respond* to signs of dangerousness and pathology in a man.

We can minimize the lessons we stand to learn if we simply say, "It's not that I was unobservant; it's that he was *that good.*" Maybe that's one way of looking at it from the grave. But I think there are other ways of looking at it that can help us see in the here and now. The existence of abusive and violent men provides the best reason for learning why dangerous men have been successful in your life and in other women's lives. Just how good are your observation skills? As with other categories of dangerous men, women can miss the signs of abusive or violent men because they don't think they would ever end up in a relationship with one. Women are snookered by these men because they aren't looking for the signs and symptoms of abuse and violence. Whether or not he is good at what he does is no excuse for your being unobservant and then responding positively to him.

An abusive man obviously starts out in the relationship, at least briefly, a little differently from how he ends up. He is charming, attentive, fun, talkative. He is whatever attracts you to him. Compare and contrast this with how he is as the relationship is ending; by then you may not even recognize a flicker of who he once was. But it had to be good in the beginning for you to get involved with him. He is successful when women cling to the image of "how it was" and forget how it currently is. Wanting to get back to that "lovin' feeling" can keep women glued to a dead-end relationship for years. Dating a violent man is never the time to forget about all of the bad times that came after the good times.

He is successful because women violate their own boundaries about what they will tolerate. They fail to live by the one-strike rule. One hit, one fear-inducing gesture, one episode of ugly and degrading language—one anything that causes her to wonder if he *could* get violent—and she should be out of there. Instead, too many women say, "If you hit me one more time" and draw a line in the sand that turns out to be meaningless. It gets erased. Next time, she again says, "I mean it, if you hit me even one more time...." Five years later the line in the sand has been long forgotten—perhaps by both of them.

Domestic-violence shelters have proliferated since the 1970s. There are resources and pathways out of violent relationships for *all* women. There are so many resources and so many forms of assistance that a lack of help is no longer a valid reason for why women stay in violent relationships. Help exists in the form of emergency safe houses, transitional housing, job training, counseling, and more. Everything you need to get out and survive on your own is available now.

These dangerous men are also successful because some women are so embarrassed to have ended up with an abusive man that they would rather try to hide that fact than expose it and get out. Women often linger in these deadly environments out of fear of failure and exposure.

Finally, violent men continue to be violent because even if women leave, they don't always prosecute. This is a huge issue for those involved in prosecuting abusers and in helping victims of domestic violence. It is also a huge issue for the women these men will date in the future. Whether or not you return to the relationship, at least leave a paper trail for your "sister" in the dating world who may date this man in the future. Let there be court documents, police reports, and jail sentences to warn her in case she performs a background check on him. Give her this much information so she can at least make an informed choice!

Women's Stories

Andrea's story illustrates just how much a violent man can cost you. Amy's story proves that men from all socioeconomic brackets and all educational backgrounds can be violent. Tammy's story shows how all abuse—even if it doesn't result in physical assault—is intended to control the victim through fear and intimidation.

ANDREA'S STORY

Andrea was in her late twenties when she got divorced and was faced with raising four young daughters on her own. She had been a stay-at-home mom and had very few career skills. She began working odd jobs to help sustain her new life as sole supporter of her family.

Along came Rocky, a stocky man who built homes for a living. He was radical, wild, and untamed. There was something about that combination Andrea found totally irresistible after her "stick-in-the-mud" husband. Andrea did not investigate his past relationships very thoroughly, and they soon began living together.

It quickly became evident that Rocky had a lot of problems. He drank from early afternoon until he passed out. He smoked pot and crack and drank until he was full of rage and his eyes were wild with fury. But there were times when he did not drink or do drugs and acted "normal" toward Andrea and the kids. Those were the times she clung to and how she chose to remember him as "my Rocky."

Stress was mounting for Rocky. He was losing work so money was tight. His mother was dying. He lost his driver's license because of repeat D.U.I.s, so getting to job sites became a problem. Rocky always chanced it, though, driving without a license because he loved to live on the edge. At least monthly, he was pulled over, ticketed, and taken to jail for driving without a license or insurance. Money allocated for rent was instead spent on getting him out of jail. As the lack of money became an issue, he began dealing drugs for supplemental income. But he was frequently busted for dealing, taken to jail, and bailed out with the rent money.

To make matters worse, their cars broke down, and since there was no money to fix them, Andrea couldn't get to work or drive Rocky to work. Her kids couldn't get to after-school activities. Their world was shrinking to the size of their trailer.

Rocky's temper was clearly mounting. He spanked Andrea's children too hard and too often, punched holes in the wall, kicked car doors, and had barroom brawls with other men. Off to jail again he went, this time for assaults. More rent money was paid to the courts, which meant less money to live on. The cycle of violence and poverty had set in.

Soon, the cops were coming to their home. Rocky beat Andrea on a regular basis, leaving bruises on her arms and chest and cuts on her face. Rocky was referred to a batterer's intervention program, and Andrea was referred to a domestic-violence counseling program. According to Rocky, he didn't have a problem. It wasn't drugs, alcohol, or violence. It was the "damn system that's just out to get me. They need to mind their own damn business."

Weekly and sometimes daily arrests were now common. Rocky was facing an average of seven charges per week in court. All the family's income went to pay for court costs, attorney fees, and jail fines. Andrea went to social services to ask for rent assistance, food stamps, money for transportation, and any other help they could offer. She learned the art of walking softly, keeping the children quiet, trying to anticipate every stressor for Rocky so she could eliminate it and remain safe.

But one night, while Rocky was drinking and drugging, he was triggered by who knows what. He viciously beat Andrea in front of her children. The kids tried to pull him off of their mother, and he flung them to the walls like discarded shoes. He pulled out Andrea's waist-long hair in chunks when he dragged her back into the trailer. He beat her until her face was beyond recognition.

Andrea broke free and fled. Disoriented, she ran through the woods and huddled behind trees. She stayed there until dawn and then went to a friend's house and called relatives, asking them to get her children from the trailer. But by then, social services had been alerted about the beating. The authorities' view of the evening was that she had abandoned her children when she fled for her life, leaving them with a violent and intoxicated man. All four girls were taken from her.

Shaken, Rocky vowed to "kick some ass" until he could "get those kids back for Andrea." Andrea remained hopeful that with batterer's intervention and maybe AA, Rocky could be "my Rocky" again. But in the meantime, it cost her her children. The girls were farmed out to various foster homes. Andrea was allowed one hour a week with them. Crying, hysterical, and depressed, Andrea retreated to her bed after each visitation with her children. But still she remained convinced that Rocky would, somehow, become nonviolent.

Rocky went to the intervention program. He listened and gave his reasons for hitting and drinking, which included lots of references to "the damn system." But not much changed. Then he went to AA for several weeks. Andrea beamed—now they were on the road to a healthy family. But soon Rocky was drinking again. Andrea fled to the women's shelter before he could begin the cycle again. This time, she read the writing on the walls. It had cost her the house, her job, her car, and her four children. The only thing she had left that was her own was the beating of her heart. So she took it and left for good. We can only hope that in the future she will learn to heed her red flags and resist any temptation to get involved with another violent man.

AMY'S STORY

Amy was an only child. Her parents were both educators who prided themselves on achievement and intellect. These were core foundational values in Amy's home. She knew early on that she would go to college and probably to graduate school. It's just what was expected of her.

Even with all of his education and intellect, her father had some defects that wreaked havoc in his private life. He was an alcoholic and would often beat her mother during fits of rage and blackouts. Amy lived in constant fear for her mother. She also feared her father's violence would one day be directed against her. She found her mother sobbing frequently because her dad had other "girlfriends" about whom he was none too subtle. Her father's drinking and irrational behavior started creating problems at work. He was often put on probationary status and would clean up his act, only to relapse again. His job security was always "tentative" at best. The older Amy got, the more her father disgusted her. "Repugnant" and "alcoholic wife beater" are the sorts of terms she used to describe him. Her fantasies included running away to marry someone wonderful and taking her mother with her.

Amy finished her master's degree and went to work for a big college system. She met Edmund, a sophisticated professor and department chair. She was impressed by his credentials and his ability to pontificate on any subject. He, too, was impressed with himself—to the exclusion of wanting to discuss anyone or anything else. In the beginning, Amy enjoyed learning all about the subjects he was interested in, but when she finally began to want to talk about herself, she saw another side to Dr. Jekyll.

He would lapse into deep depressions followed by raging accounts of his own brilliance. Then he would sink into alcoholic hopelessness. He would pull it together and show up for school the next day, but each month that passed brought more hangovers, lower functioning, more lies to cover up. Soon it was obvious to Amy that she had chosen a duplicate of her father as her boyfriend.

Once Amy realized she was dating a version of her dad, she tried to end it with Edmund. That night he beat her. The cycle had come full circle. The next morning, Edmund, in deep horror over his behavior, promised Amy he would marry her and help her get into a Ph.D. program so she could also become a professor. He promised to introduce her to all the important people in academia. He would help her become as well known as he was.

Edmund's promises kept Amy in the relationship for another year, during which time the drinking increased, the beatings continued, and the promises piled up. Then the final dose of reality hit. Edmund was put on probation at work for his "psychological and addictive problems." Amy packed her bag, said good-bye to Edmund, and never looked back.

TAMMY'S STORY

Tammy, a single, thirty-five-year-old writer, knows that replacing one violent man with another isn't very unusual. She says:

> I have dated several men who were controlling, aggressive, and sometimes violent. The first relationship didn't go as far as it could have, nor did he become as violent as I think he wanted to, because I still lived with my parents and he didn't want to answer to them.
>
> But with the latest man I got involved with, I honestly thought I had met the reincarnation of Jack the Ripper. He turned "nutty" on me so quickly. He came on very strong and encouraged me to move into his house as soon as we met. Then he began to control every aspect of my daily life. I was in Europe promoting a book I wrote. Since I was in his country, he decided to jump in and handle my book for me.

Within a few days of my meeting him, he was telling me how bad his childhood was, how much he hated his father, and how glad he was when his father died. He told me how he was bullied in school and had become so neurotic over it that he lost the ability to talk for a year!

He continued to tell me we would get along fine just as long as I did *exactly* what he told me to do. When it was time for me to return to the United States after the book tour, he begged me not to leave him the way all the other women in his life had done. Once I was home, he sent me a box of photos of me that were mutilated, with my eyes gouged out and blood painted on my face.

Tammy's European hottie was obviously a combo man. All of his pathology and mental problems combined to result in abusive, controlling behavior and projected violence that very likely would have turned into real physical violence had she stayed with him.

Red-Alert Behavioral Checklist

The abusive or violent man

* talks down to you, criticizes you, calls you names, or otherwise uses belittling language against you

* refers to his previous partners in negative, demeaning ways

* attempts to control or dominate your life choices, small or large

* tries to dictate your spiritual or religious beliefs

* is frequently irritable

* raises his voice, yells, or screams, even when carrying on a "normal conversation"

* yells and screams and seems "too worked up" when he gets into an argument with you or others

* has a history of assaults against other people

* has harmed animals or treated them cruelly

* has set destructive fires

* becomes violent or out of control when using drugs or alcohol

* punches walls or throws things when angry

* seems to experience anger as his most frequent emotion

* blames you or others for his anger or outbursts

* has trouble in other relationships because of his anger

* has previously been sent to anger-management training

* has previously been sent to substance-abuse treatment

* has been expelled or suspended from school or work for anger or fighting

* hangs around other people known to be violent

* has a short fuse or a hot temper

* gets angry when confronted, questioned, or corrected

* is preoccupied with violent movies, TV, or video games

* idealizes acts of violence and destruction

* uses words such as "killed," "smashed," and "kicked" in his everyday language

Your Defense Strategy

Women end up in long-term violent relationships because they don't leave early. They ignore the warning signs and red flags that pop up early in the relationship, when fleeing is a lot easier and safer. They excuse the behavior, think it is an isolated event, or believe his reasons for it. They ignore clues and wait for confirmed evidence. In the case of abusive or violent men, confirmed evidence is quite painful. It is safer to move on a clue than to wait for its confirmation.

Since violence is progressive, it will increase. Whatever the level of abuse or violence is now, it will get worse. Women have the best chances of escape when they leave early in the relationship, following the *first* episode of violence or inappropriate behavior, and *do not go back.* It is a lot easier to fade out of a dating relationship early in the picture than it is to break up after three years of serious commitment, when a violent man is likely to stalk you. Let me repeat: An early exit can save your psychological well-being—and quite possibly your life.

Abusive and violent men are known for their theatrical displays of remorse and soul searching. They swear on their mother's lives they will never do it again, will go to church, or will go to counseling. They offer lots of seeimgly insightful reasons for why their short fuse went off. There are always reasons why, including, of course, sad childhood stories. However, once you are reunited, the offer to go to counseling isn't followed up with any action. A woman has the most influence over a man's willingness to get help and remain in help when she is out of the home and the relationship. This seems like an oxymoron. But once you are reunited and are dating, living together, or back in the home, his inspiration and motivation for seeking help are eliminated. He has back what he wanted to get back. As he sees it, he really isn't the problem anyway, so there isn't any reason to continue in counseling. Violent men rarely change on their own volition outside of intense counseling, and if they have a pathological disorder, there is almost no chance for change at all.

Staying out of the relationship—and that means not even going on dates with him—and requesting that he go to counseling *for himself* (not couple's counseling) for six months is a sure way of finding out just how interested he is in having a relationship that is based on emotional maturity and health. Women who have followed this simple approach have found the answer they were seeking. I can count on one hand how many men have actually followed through on this. The others were much more inclined to ditch the relationship than they were to work on themselves. This in itself will tell you something about whether the man is healthy and normal. Violent men never want counseling, and if they start it, they don't stay in it. Although this may be painful information to get, it is better that you know his true nature now, rather than later, when his hands are around your throat.

As they do with other pathological men, many women believe they can change abusive men or can provide a stress-free environment in which he "won't have to" get violent. But these things don't change him. The women who are on the local news as victims of domestic violence are the women who failed to believe this. Just ask Andrea.

Be on the alert for other disorders that can go hand in hand with violence, including bipolar disorder or other cyclical mood disorders, addictions, posttraumatic stress disorder, borderline personality disorder, and antisocial personality disorder. (See the Appendix for descriptions of these conditions.) These conditions complicate an already serious problem of violence. Add a pathological or chronic disorder to a pattern of abuse or violence, and you have a situation that will most likely only change for the worse.

Women can take proactive steps to find out about any man they're considering dating. Many services are available to let you know if your new beau has ever crossed the line in ways that could endanger you. Background checks can unearth lots of information from public records about where he has been and with whom. A background check can reveal criminal records, civil proceedings, family-court proceedings, traffic violations, money scams, liens, bankruptcies, protective orders taken out against him, sexual offender status, stalking violations, rapes, assaults, probation or parole violations, and more. Why in the world would you *not* want this information? Some information can be obtained through your local courthouse. Various websites will produce detailed background checks for a small fee. You can check your state's department of corrections website. Private investigators can be hired online. There is virtually no reason not to have a lot of information on a guy whom you are considering dating or marrying. Check the back of this book for some resources you can use now.

Women's Insights

Tammy says:

> I began to sense that he was growing more and more potentially violent. Things he said and *how* he said them were making me uncomfortable. He wouldn't let me out of his sight, and I'd only known him for three days! If I had left early, after those three days, there wouldn't have been much of a relationship for him to come after. He immediately began talking about marriage and plans for our future. I began to sense that I might end up in a situation that I couldn't escape if I didn't get out *right then.* He came on as such a sweet and charming European man. He was every American woman's dream. I was an idiot to ignore what started happening within three days. I was more interested in living a fantasy that I thought I could have with him than I was in staying alive! I could have been killed. That's my gut instinct on all of this.
>
> I even ignored the buttons he pushed in me because he was like my father, who was an Army drill sergeant. I had already resolved (so I thought) that I would never allow myself to be controlled the way my dad controlled me. And yet within three days, this man was running my life—or at least really trying to.
>
> I hate the messages my mother gave me about the abuse of power. She told me I must *give* my power away in a relationship because men demand it and will feel powerless without it. I have fought that message ever since—with my father and now in other relationships. This one, however, was too close to a life-or-death situation. I really could have been killed.

Help for Women in Abusive Relationships

If you recognize that you are in an abusive relationship with a violent man, it is imperative that you take lifesaving steps for yourself and your children, if you have them. As you have read in this chapter, violence is progressive. It will only get worse. You will not remain safe in a relationship with a violent man, nor can you protect your children in the presence of a sick and violent man.

Every community has services available for women trying to break ties and flee from violence and control. The back of this book lists some national resources that can actually help you find resources in your local community. These organizations operate extensive data banks that will help you locate services close to you.

Community resources include the following: safe houses and shelters where you can live while you are getting on your feet and reestablishing your life; court advocates who will accompany you and help you file charges and take out restraining-order papers if you need them; referrals to any social services you may need, such as child-support enforcement or food stamps; counseling referrals for yourself and your children so you have access to healing; local support groups made up of other women healing from violence; law enforcement protection; and legal aid if you are in need of legal resources.

Leaving a violent relationship can present risks to your physical safety, because a woman is most in danger when she is trying to leave and immediately after she has left. It is critically important that you understand this. A woman needs a community of support, legal help, social support, and law-enforcement assistance in order to safely unhinge herself from a dangerous man. *Do not attempt to leave a violent relationship on your own.* You need the advice and support of community agencies. They know how and when it should be done and can instruct you in how to be safe while disconnecting from the relationship. Again, see the Resources, located in the back of this book, and use the agencies listed there to help you get in contact with and seek assistance from organizations in your area.

Chapter 10

The Emotional Predator

Okay, ladies, this is as bad at it gets. The predator has a nose for neediness in the women he pursues. It's his best skill, and he will use it to hunt you down and reel you in.

Howard the Hunter

The emotional predator qualifies as the pinnacle of poisonous and pathological dating choices. He could, in fact, be called the "emotional psychic." That's because it's his ability to intuit and sense a woman's emotional vulnerabilities that places her at risk. *Webster's* defines *predatory* as "having a disposition to injure or exploit others for one's own gain"; it defines *predator* as "one that preys, destroys, or devours." That's a good summation of how this dangerous man operates. Ask yourself if these sound like normal dating behaviors. Who but the most pathological among us would set out to exploit, prey on, destroy, or devour?

In Chapter 1, we learned what pathology can mean. The emotional predator's pathology makes him incredibly successful and absolutely dangerous. These men can actually make the most charming dates, at least initially. However, remember also that if he is pathological, that implies he can't be cured. The more pathologically disordered he is, the more incurable and, ironically, the more convincing he often is. He will home in on your vulnerabilities and read you. If he likes what he reads, he will follow up by inviting you into his scary and dangerous life.

Predators have a natural ability for reading women who are lonely, bored, needy by nature, emotionally wounded, or vulnerable. The predator also has his antennae up for women who put out a subconscious message that they have unfulfilled needs in their lives. He is a master at reading your body and eye language. He puts together the messages you're sending via your body, eye, and verbal language, and from there can pretty much tell whether you've recently been dumped or otherwise hurt. Next, he figures out how he can squeeze into the vacant space in your life and what you need to hear in order to allow this to happen.

Pathological men often reveal that they can scan a room and "sense" which woman will make the best target for them. They don't know why they have this gift or how they acquired it. They just know that since childhood they have been working women over. As a boy, this dangerous man probably exhibited a lot of the same charming traits he has now. Back then, he used his skills on his mother, teachers, and sisters. It's as though the women in his life felt they had no option but to let him get away with whatever he desired. They were no match for this child psychopath. A predator's intuitive sixth sense is untaught (although, as discussed below, it usually results from childhood exposure to an abusive or extremely dysfunctional environment). But as time goes by and he grows more successful at using his charm and insight, he begins to learn what works and what works even better. Early in his career as a budding psychopath, he becomes a master of behavioral psychology. Even an adult's skills can't compete with his abilities to scam, con, and conquer.

All psychopaths (except for those whose condition results from a head injury) begin their careers as pathological children. Recall from Chapter 1 that for a personality disorder to form and to result in psychopathology, the child is usually exposed to abuse and/or emotional deficits early in life—specifically between birth and approximately age seven, when the personality structure is actively developing. Beyond that age, personality disorders are less likely to form. In most cases, this means men with pathological personality disorders endured extremely maladaptive childhoods and have a lot of personal issues as a result. If a man has suffered serious trauma as a very young child, that in itself is a red flag. However, remember, too, that some pathology cannot be traced to a known source—we don't always know why some individuals are pathological.

Remember as well that not all psychopaths are bottom-of-the-barrel criminals. Even Ted Bundy was charming, intelligent, and handsome. Predatory men can hide behind the guises of brilliant businessmen, attorneys, surgeons, or even clergymen. This gives them an even better ability to slip under the radar of women who fail to see their character traits as a sign of problems.

As is probably clear by now, emotional predators also fall into the mentally-ill category, usually under the diagnosis of antisocial personality disorder. Most also have hidden lives. When you couple a predator's natural instincts with a lifetime of skills honed by successfully conning, exploiting, and injuring women, you have a man who is nothing short of extraordinarily smooth and capable of horrific dangerousness.

Predators' motives vary. But you can be sure a predator wants something from you. That is the entire reason for the relationship. He isn't merely interested in a date. A predator, by definition, hunts and uses for his own gain. There is something in you or in your life that he wants. Maybe "all" he wants is your utter adoration or for you to exalt his ego. Maybe he wants to move in with you so he can sponge off of you and not work. Maybe he wants your money, or maybe he wants what you can provide to help establish his image (ever heard of a "trophy wife"?). Or maybe, as in Jenna's story below, he's most interested in the pursuit and conquest of a woman, to the point where he has a hard time accepting it when she tries to break things off with him. If you escape a predator who has these as his only motives, and not death as many of them do, you should count your blessings that things did not go further and learn from the experience.

Other types of predators can cost you much more. If he is a sexual predator, you (or someone else) are a target, whether it be for consensual sex or rape—depending on whichever way it plays out or whatever mood he is in. If he is a pedophile, he may target your children as his prey and you as the vehicle. He needs a close relationship with you in order to earn your trust and gain access to your children. This is especially true for predators who see your children as your vulnerable issue. These men seem helpful because they take on the role of father figure, mentor, minister, church youth leader, role model, scout leader, or athletic coach. Their "in" with you is through your children's needs. Too many stories exist of children who've been abused by a coach, teacher, priest, or camp counselor. Too often, these men's savvy approach has been to date the mom in order to have access to the children. Children have been brutalized at the hands of "helpful" men whom women have met and brought into their lives from Christian singles' ministries, divorce recovery groups, twelve-step programs, dating services, or soccer games.

And, lastly, the most feared predators are those who literally hunt for the kill. At any given time in the United States, it is estimated that there are hundreds of uncaught killers on the loose.

It is hard to imagine that any of these men could make it into your life. But this is what other women have thought—that they would never date a rapist, killer, or child abuser. Because predators don't show up at your door with their offenses tattooed on their forehead, they can slide in under your radar.

By learning to closely heed our red flags, we should only have to shiver at the thought of dating or marrying a predator. For some women who end up getting involved with these dangerous men, like Tori (see below), the outcome may be fairly mild. Her predator was "merely" a deadbeat. Other women, as you will see, end up with predators who are child molesters, rapists, or killers. Again, the predator's motives are as broad as his pathology. The sicker he is, the sicker his actions.

To differentiate a predator from a clinger, who also approaches women with focused and genuine interest, know that a clinger "needs" the relationship. A predator does not. Early on, the clinger focuses more on friendship, whereas the predator is more deliberately romantic. Clingers often establish a connection with women by focusing on the sad histories they share of being "dumped." Predators are shifting chamelons who can be all things to all women. Clingers may be inexperienced in relationships and may come across as a little clumsy. Predators are smooth as silk. Clingers are blabbers who tell you everything about their entire lives, while predators are listeners who give up very little information until they are sure it will align with your history. With clingers women feel more needed, but with predators they feel more intrigued.

Who They Seek

Predators are the most skilled of all the dangerous men at seeking and finding women who will satisfy their current hunger—whatever it is. The type of woman a predator seeks varies depending on the nature of his pathology. His selection is based on his need and your vulnerability. He knows it's a matter of matching need with need. The more he knows about your needs, the better he can meet them.

He has a nose for vulnerability, so women who have unmet needs "smell" especially good to him. He seeks women who need men who can "sense and know" them on almost a spiritual level. Since he is good at this, he will appear to know you well—and quickly.

Women who think an important element in dating is having similar interests, hobbies, and backgrounds will be naturally attracted to this chameleon. He will be whatever you have been. He is your male twin. Women who are impressed by charm and smoothness and whose red-flag system doesn't recognize these qualities will be sought out by predators. The difference between other types of dangerous men and predators is that real predators don't fumble. They are experienced daters who do not blunder, say the wrong things, or come across as inept in relationships.

Because predators know what kind of women respond to their personalized hunting instincts, they seek women with histories. They like women who had absent fathers, mothers who taught them to trust unconditionally, or neglectful or abusive husbands. They also like women who embrace a naïve worldview that says people are basically good and the world is safe. Knowing that many women were trained to believe that people are good at heart, predators present themselves as men of virtue and honor. If you had an absent father, so much the better. The predator will fill that space for you with his own fatherly ways. But because he is a chameleon, he will listen closely to see if you also need a mentor, an advisor on some topic, a spiritual leader, or a male friend for you or your kids.

During counseling sessions I've had with emotional predators, some have verbalized their targets. One said, "I look for naïve women. I like a certain vulnerability to her—that she trusts humanity without asking for proof. Maybe she's been hurt a lot so there is a woundedness to her. Women who are uneducated about the way the real world works are good too. That naïvete and vulnerability makes them believe you, because they *need* to believe you."

Another said, "I like the mentally weak—women who have been pounded down by men and those with childhoods that weren't so good. They are particularly easy."

A third said, "I'm good. I can read the room. Their body language, how they are shy with their eyes, or how they react to a mere compliment sets the stage for my work. Although all the women aren't just shy. Some overcompensate and try to be flashy or cocky. But I know it's the same message underneath. I know what women want and need. It's that easy."

It is important to understand that each predator has developed his own unique style. He has a "type" of woman he prefers because with that type he has mastered the approach, the dating, and the end. He doesn't have to think very hard if he just uses the profile he's had success with. One predator may prefer recently divorced women because he succeeds at playing that angle with them. He talks their jargon. Another might prefer single women or college girls. Other predators seem to get bored and opt to switch the profiles of the women they go after, just for fun.

Why They Are Successful

As mentioned, emotional predators' number-one feature is their unbelievable charm. They have an ability to be a great date and to initiate rapid emotional intimacy. In a day and age when women are sick of men who "don't get it" about what women need, these guys can show a woman they definitely "get it." They show you all the attention that the Neanderthals you've dated until now haven't shown you. They say all the right lines that the men in your past could never verbalize. They are brilliant and insightful about what you need. They seem to know exactly every pain you have suffered.

With more skill than a carnival psychic, the emotional predator can hone in on your every need, sympathize with you in such a way so that you believe you've met your long-lost soul mate, and sweep you off your feet before the foam on your beer melts. He's smoother than forty-year-old brandy and more insightful than a therapist. He "knows" you the way no one else ever has.

This hottie moves fast. He's got to—before you figure out what his true M.O. is. Every woman should be suspect of relationships that seem to be traveling in the fast lane on the superhighway of emotional intimacy. A predator needs to keep you so euphoric with compliments and lover's talk that you aren't listening, watching, or paying attention. He is dripping with sincerity, looking deep into your eyes and clinging to every word you say. "I can't get enough of you" is a masterful line used by the best predators. A predator wants to move in with you or marry you quickly, because time is against him.

To move the relationship along and become indispensable to you, he must act helpful, comforting, and generous. Since he's working against the clock, he must find out what you need and then meet that need. Are your gutters clogged? Any man knows that single women have undone "honey-do" lists. He can become Hank the Handyman immediately. Up on the roof quicker than Rudolph, he unclogs your gutter and notices and fixes some loose shingles while he's at it. Did you just lose a parent? He knows all about the grief process and over a bottle of wine has you crying into his hankie as he pats your hand. Do your kids need attention? He's got them hiking, biking, and fishing all weekend long. Your electric bill is fifteen days late? He'd be happy to help with that—even though you just met him.

While listening to you and observing you, he will glean a lot of information about your hobbies, interests, spiritual beliefs, and value systems. He is the original identity thief. He uncovers and uses for his own purposes everything he can about what makes you you. He will find you amazing, beautiful, bright, and talented—like no one he has *ever* met before. He will align how he portrays himself with your needs and also your interests until you feel like you are looking at your twin.

Finally, another way some predators succeed with women is by preying on their compassion. Most of the examples you will encounter in this chapter are of predators who use a strong, confident, and assertive approach with women. Yet predators will approach a woman in any number of manners, depending on what will work with her. Ted Bundy kept medical props in the trunk of his car. He accomplished one of his final slayings by putting a fake cast on his leg and flagging a woman down on the highway. Other predators fake illnesses, limps, or near-death experiences in order to attract women's compassion. Once a woman is in the grip of a predator, anything can happen.

Women's Stories

Before you think you'd never hook up with someone this wacked out, see what happened to three bright women who didn't bother to consider the possibility that predators had marked them as targets.

TORI'S STORY

You met Tori, a fifty-two-year-old artist, in Chapters 1 and 2. The night Tori met Jay in a restaurant, he had already "spotted" her when she went to the restroom. Eye contact was invitation enough for him. It was his "go" signal. Suavely leaning across the doorway when she exited the restrooms, he politely introduced himself and offered to buy her a drink.

He didn't offer a lot of information about himself. Instead, he asked about her. Tori, an Italian and a talker, told him way too much. Being the good predator he was, he listened well. He noted her language style, things she referenced, her body lingo. He scanned her dress for any hints about her life or tastes.

During their first conversation, Jay presented himself as everything Tori was interested in. Sensing her skill with language, Jay stepped up to the plate with his big words. He quickly tuned in to her love of reading and became a self-proclaimed and frustrated poet, quoting Yeats and Edgar Allan Poe. Sensing they were close in age, he talked about the Vietnam years—something everybody from their generation felt passionately about. Jay said he was a veteran from that conflict. By the end of the evening, he had transformed from a mere soldier to a noble mercenary who was sent on dangerous missions because of his courage.

Noting she was Italian, Jay tapped into food, ethnicity, and religion as topics of mutual interest. Of course, he'd had wild travels to Italy and beyond. He said he was Irish and told stories about the Catholic-Protestant conflict in Ireland. He had been there and had seen that, too. Jay commented on Tori's unusual style of dress, which led to Tori's disclosure of her profession as an artist. Immediately, he was talking about his love of art and about the great cathedrals and museums in Europe. When she said she had a twenty-year-old daughter, he also said he had a twenty-year-old daughter, which led to discussions about their mutual experiences with divorce and as single parents. Tori made a few comments about God, which had Jay bellying up to the altar. His grandfather was a Pentecostal preacher, and his family had a long heritage in the church. In the space of one conversation, everything Tori was, Jay was too. How lucky she was to find a guy her age, an honorable Vietnam vet, a poet at heart, a world traveler with knowledge of literature and art, and a guy whose family was "in the church"!

Notice from Tori's story how a predator utilizes a woman's background to make himself immediately compatible with her. He counts on a woman's overdisclosure about herself. By paying her a little attention, he is sure she will talk on and on about herself. As she does, he mines nuggets from her stories that he can use to help him define himself as her ideal suitor. He banks on the fact that previous men in her life probably didn't want to hear her stories in such detail. He presents himself as interested and having good listening skills. These are traits he knows women find irresistible. He prompts her with open-ended questions like "What do you do?" or "Where are you from?" Such queries promote more disclosure, rather than mere yes or no answers.

Jay waited for Tori to disclose herself and then became something that was compatible with whatever she said. A discussion about her ethnicity was followed by his revealing his ethnicity. Her Christianity was followed by his family's church background. Her interest in the Vietnam War was followed by his war heroism. Whatever she was, he became the same way.

This is not uncommon with predators. Most of them have high IQ's and have enough background information on many topics to talk intelligently about them on a surface level. In fact, Jay, like many predators, read encyclopedias for recreation. He gleaned from them information and tidbits he could use in the future.

Dating Jay was a whirlwind. Within a few months he had moved in with her. Tori's whole life changed. Her normal activities of gardening, hiking, and socializing with friends were aborted for her new life with Jay. His preoccupation with her created the isolation he needed in order to take her life hostage. Soon, without Tori's knowledge, he was screening her mail and phone calls. Friends mysteriously faded away because she didn't get their messages. Not long after he moved in, poor Jay was laid off. Or so she thought. He was out beating the streets for work, or so she thought. But nothing was panning out—or so she thought.

Once Jay was inside her life, Tori began to fund their whole existence due to his "unfortunate unemployment." It cost her all of her life's savings. While Tori mowed the lawn and took out the garbage, he sat in front of the TV, flipping channels to pursue his real intellectual interests: *The Simpsons*. What happened to the guy who'd quoted classic literature?

When Tori had finally had enough, she asked Jay to move out. But, lo and behold, he was diagnosed with prostate cancer. He gave doctors' names, appointment times, and a recitation of his prognosis. He hadn't long to live; wouldn't she just love him into his final days?

Outrageous? Yes! A lie? Of course! He just didn't want to lose his feathered nest. Maybe most of us would have seen this bus barreling toward us, but Tori had learned from her mother to "love the downcast," "play with those less fortunate," and "seek the good in each person." That may be a good philosophy for philanthropic work, but it's not good for intimate relationships.

Tori spent three years with Jay. It took her that long to ponder and weigh his good and bad attributes, wonder whether he could get well in counseling, become sick of his frequent unemployment and abject laziness, and check out her red flags regarding all his preposterous stories. Instead of proactively addressing the problem and asking him to move out, she remained passive and allowed the relationship to die a slow death. When the arrow on Tori's B.S. meter finally pointed to high, she was ready to kick Jay to the curb.

Tori's experience teaches us a lesson. If you don't know how to get out of relationships efficiently, you shouldn't get into them. The skill of ending and leaving relationships in a healthy, safe, and timely way is more important than your ability to get a date.

PAM'S STORY

Pam, a thirty-eight-year-old magazine editor, has just finished her fifth relationship with a dangerous man. For most of her dating life she has been involved in unhealthy relationships. Although she's brilliant at her job of running a mid-sized magazine, her savvy has not thus far translated into an ability to pick healthy men.

Jeff, her most recent boyfriend, pursued her relentlessly. The fervent way he wanted her made her feel sort of "special." Although she had previously dated dangerous men, Pam, like many women, never spent time examining her patterns and her selections so she could learn from past mistakes. Jeff came screaming in under her radar.

Jeff showed a huge interest in Pam's "intriguing past," so she talked on and on about her family upbringing, her failed relationships, her daughter, and her hobbies and interests. She loved the beach; so did he. That meant they could travel together, he said. She was from a big family; so was he. He asked if he could meet her family (but didn't invite her to meet his). She loved to dance; he was a great dancer, according to him. She was lonely; so was he. Her work was demanding; so was his.

Pam's head was kept in a whirlwind from all the wining, dining, flowers, calls, work visits, dancing till dawn, and vacations. She was breathless from the pace of the relationship. Jeff told Pam her beauty, coolness, and brilliance had him "spellbound." Although he seemed intensely interested in her past and her life, he never talked about himself. Pam mistook his avoidance of her questions about himself for humility.

Jeff was an advertising account executive for a computer company. His life was interesting and fast paced, and he was always "psyched" for the next sale and pursuit. Pam enjoyed his high energy level and the way he lived his life. She had no idea she was his next "pursuit." It took months before she realized her appeal to Jeff was based on his wanting something from her besides her charming company: He was trying to get a reduced rate for advertising in her magazine. Sleeping his way into a bargain did not rattle his ethics in the least. He would win a ten-thousand-dollar bonus if he scored the most advertising bang for the buck, and wooing her was just what he did to win. His next promotion—complete with company car and an expense account—would be guaranteed. Besides, it wasn't like he hadn't worked women in the past to get what he wanted.

Unimaginably worse, however, was how he exploited Pam's trust in him to prey upon her eleven-year-old daughter. He became particularly involved with the child. Eventually they took her with them on some of their beach vacations. While Pam showered, Jeff molested the girl and threatened her if she told. On the nights when Pam worked late, Jeff would pick up her daughter from school, take her to dinner, and then take her home and "help her with her homework." He said he was doing it because he knew Pam's job was "very demanding." In reality, during those times he was showing Pam's daughter pornography, giving her wine, and fondling her. He had free access to Pam's home when she wasn't there, and he installed some Web cams to film her daughter's bathroom and bedroom.

During a romantic vacation at the beach, Jeff got his wish. He got Pam to sign a multiyear advertising deal at an unbelievable price. Before the ink was dry, Jeff's promotion was in place and he shipped out to his new job on the other side of the country. When Pam didn't hear from him for a few days, she worried. He didn't answer his cell phone, and soon it was disconnected. She went by the address where he'd said he lived, only to discover he had never lived there. She went by his office and learned he had been promoted and transferred from the Southeast to the Pacific Northwest.

He never called to say good-bye. But the greater shock and devastation, of course, came when Pam's daughter told Pam how Jeff had violated her.

JENNA'S STORY

Jenna comes from what she refers to as a "normal, middle-class family." She had a stay-at-home mother who was attentive and a

working father who gave her healthy attention. She had good relationships with her siblings. She thought her family communi-
cated well, and she grew up believing that all people did. Her
family supported her interests and told her to trust her instincts.
She enjoyed her female friendships and didn't date much in high
school. Jenna's upbringing gave her a sense that she had her "head
screwed on right."

Jenna began to date when she left home to go to college. She
didn't strike up anything serious, which was fine with her. She
just wanted to enjoy college and get through the piles of work it
seemed to demand. She chose journalism as her major. Soon she
met and began to date Cory. Her grounding in her family's con-
structive patterns of communication tipped her off that something was astray with Cory. She had a sense of what "healthy"
was, and she felt this guy "didn't feel quite right." She couldn't
put her finger on it, but something about their interactions didn't
sit well with her. Still, she kept dating him, thinking she was
probably being too nervous.

Jenna tried to check out her gut instincts with people who
knew Cory. On the surface, after all, he looked pretty good. He
had a good-paying job, was friendly and outgoing, and had several
friendships. So why did she still have that nagging feeling? He
was charming, but too charming. He seemed to agree with everything she said and every opinion she held. But conversations with
him were superficial and trite. As Jenna said, "He was as deep as
Formica." So Jenna made it a point to dig deeper for answers, to
listen closer to his friends, and to ask more pointed questions of
his family. Cory had a history of failed relationships. Nothing ever
panned out, even though he was handsome and a great conversa-
tionalist. Women must have seen something they didn't like. He
was bright and did well in his job—but that "something" kept
Jenna's gut tied in knots.

It seemed to Jenna that Cory "tried too hard" in the relationship, so she thought she would see what his real opinions were.
She began to change her views whenever she talked with him,
just to see how he would handle it. Cool Cory bought right in to

any new opinion she expressed. He'd say he felt exactly the same way. It was then that Jenna saw there were real problems with him. She broke it off, but within weeks Cory was coming around with a new batch of lines. He would call or stop by, saying he was "concerned about her" because she "obviously had problems." He said his checking on her was just an act of "kindness from a friend" because of the relationship they once had.

Jenna saw his story for the crock it was. Once she'd busted him for faking opinions with her, he tried to turn the table and make it seem it was Jenna who had emotional problems. Equally troublesome was his persistent pursuit of her when she'd made it clear she was no longer interested in him. He seemed excited by the idea of conquering Jenna and winning her devotion. Jenna finally broke it off with him for good, and thanked her lucky stars she eventually paid attention to her red flags.

Any Woman's Story

What happens when the predator is a professional? How much more convincing is he when he is also your doctor, dentist, therapist, attorney, or accountant? This situation is far from unusual. Since predators are usually bright and persuasive, it's possible for a woman to invite a predator into her life by requiring his professional services.

That is what occurred in a small North Carolina town. It was eventually noticed that a particular doctor had "different practices" for single women than he did for those who were married or who brought family members to their appointments. He overmedicated many of his women patients until they developed drug dependencies that kept them reliant on him. He collected emotionally dependent and drug-dependent women as trophies. He saw these patients more frequently than he did other patients and prescribed more drugs for them than he did for other patients with the same diagnoses. He raged at any of his staff who questioned his practices. It is not uncommon for patients to think doctors are above reproach and to avoid questioning the medical care they receive. Such a mindset gives professional predators all the bait they need to reel in their prey.

The doctor camouflaged his abuse of patients by focusing the other half of his practice on "holistic approaches to health." By referring patients for acupuncture, using guided imagery, and suggesting vitamins, herbs, and other alternative medicines, he appeared to be a progressive health practitioner instead of the predator he really was. When accusations arose that he was overmedicating some of his patients, he would point to his holistic practices and claim, "That's not what I am all about. This is what I believe in." Meanwhile, the unfortunate women who fell prey to him had succumbed to the attention he paid to their every need and to the narcotics he prescribed that helped them escape their lonely lives. Most of them became addicted—both to the meds he prescribed them and to the attention he paid them.

One of the women who came under the doctor's spell was Jo, a single sixty-two-year-old who had lots of emotional problems. She also had a blood disorder that kept her confined to her home, mostly by her choice. Her only daughter lived in another state, and she had few friends and no other relatives. Her only link to the outside world was the doctor.

He made house calls to see Jo after hours. She would meet him at the door with a bottle of wine and a plate of cheese, wearing her best frilly lingerie. They chatted and drank wine and acted as if it were a social visit. Jo would flirt with him and report on her mounting pain and anxiety. The evening would end with a new stack of prescriptions for Jo and a promise from the good doctor to visit again soon for their "special time together."

Jo's daughter arrived for a visit and was shocked to find nearly twenty bottles of similar medications, all of which her mother was taking at one time. When the daughter asked to meet with the doctor to discuss the medications, he refused. Once an investigation was opened into his practice, there turned out to be dozens of other single women with no families who were sharing bottles of wine with and receiving stacks of prescriptions from this dangerous doctor.

Jo died an early death one night in her sleep. The cause of death was attributed to her blood disorder. But those who knew her and who knew the doctor know that the underlying reason for her death was the misguided trust she placed in a predator.

Red-Alert Behavioral Checklist

The emotional predator

* has a natural instinct for sensing vulnerable or "sensitive" women

* senses women with low self-esteem

* senses women with weak emotional and sexual boundaries

* senses women who want or require relationships in order to feel needed or fulfilled

* senses women who are bored, lonely, or needy

* senses women who are on the rebound from having been recently dumped, divorced, emotionally ignored, or wounded

* senses women's body and eye language

* listens closely to what a woman says in order to pick up clues he can use in later conversations

* senses unfulfilled physical-intimacy needs and sexual needs

* creates a sense of fun and mystique to draw you in

* is smooth and seems to have all the right lines and insights into you

* comes on fast and strong and sweeps you off your feet

* is overly interested in every detail of your life

* wants to move in together or get married quickly

* implies that he "knows" you well before he has spent enough time to really get to know you

* pushes you to quickly disclose a lot about yourself to him

* tries to fulfill your physical, financial, or emotional needs

* seeks to fill roles in your life, such as advisor, father figure, spiritual leader, mentor

* is overly helpful, comforting, and understanding

* has the exact same interests, values, hobbies, etc., that you do

* is a chameleon who can be all things to all people

Your Defense Strategy

A common problem in many women's dating behavior is disclosing too much too soon to men they do not know. I (not so affectionately) refer to this habit as "verbal bulimia." It's a catch-22, because one of the ways you get to know someone is by talking. But in this dangerous age, I encourage women to listen twice as much as they speak. In fact, turn the tables and ask open-ended questions yourself. Don't immediately tell a new man about your interests, your past relationship failures, your family history, or your career. Instead, listen to him and remember what he says. The next time you talk with him, see if his story lines up with what he said before. Use his disclosures to find out if you have anything in common. You decide! Don't give him enough information for him to become everything you ever wanted.

Monitor how he acts when you don't give him the information he is trying to get from you. Does he simply "work harder" to try to get you to talk about yourself? If he doesn't have information about you, does he answer questions about himself in vague ways, trying to avoid committing to any particular description of himself? Too many women, when they are given a little attention, begin telling about herself at warp speed. That's not a safe approach when you're in the presence of a man who might have predatory instincts.

Remember also that being "swept off your feet" simply means you are no longer grounded. That is, you no longer have your feet firmly planted on the ground so you can face reality eyeball to eyeball. If your new relationship is a whirlwind, that's a clue. If he insists on spending day and night and day and night with you right away, you'd better put on the brakes, open the car door, and bail!

Most of us know that men really aren't *that* interested in the minute details about our feelings, thoughts, and routines. If he hasn't blinked or breathed since you started talking, that's a heads-up. If he seems too familiar with women's feelings, ask yourself how he got that familiar.

These smoothies come on so convincingly that they make you forget your own value system. If you are doing things you never thought you'd do and it concerns you—*stop!*

Women's Insights

Pam wonders if she is repeating familial patterns that were similar to her relationship with her father. She says:

> I was intoxicated by his attentions. He got way too serious way too fast. These guys are charming and intelligent. They are mysterious, exciting, and elusive. I don't know why that didn't clue me in. I was just so excited that someone found me that "cool." I think my low self-esteem was a marker for him in selecting me. And it's also probably the reason they don't stay around, either.
>
> This was my fifth dangerous relationship! You'd think I'd see it coming by now. On some level, I must think these guys are a personal challenge. Of course, it's a challenge no woman *ever* wins. But since when is dating about liking a challenge? If you want a challenge, get a good career. Don't date men to challenge yourself. That's ridiculous! How did I ever come up with that?
>
> I kept picking predators—people who are fake and would never get close to me because they don't get close to anyone.

Predators are in and out before you know it—if you're lucky. At least mine weren't deadly.

I don't think I knew on a conscious level that he was a predator. But something in me kept getting involved with these types of men in order to avoid having a real relationship. It cost my daughter this time. And that was the big wake-up call for me. My own *sick* choices harmed my child. I'll be in therapy for a long time over this one.

Jenna remembers how her red flags flared up when she met Cory:

There was something wrong from the beginning with this guy. He mirrored back opinions that I held. It was like he was parroting words back to me and was working hard to make it sound like we shared similar beliefs and interests. But there was a recognizable fake quality to it—an insincerity and a lack of depth to his comments.

He had a good job with a good salary and had friends who thought the world of him, so I kept discounting my red flags. But in the end, he couldn't emulate being a real person. He just didn't quite have the real heart and soul and emotional depth to pull it off convincingly. When I tried to end it, he pulled out the verbal tricks and told me he was concerned about me and felt that I obviously "had problems." It was so clearly manipulative that I just ended all contact after that.

I realize now that I was one of the lucky ones to make it out fairly fast. I learned that I shouldn't allow myself to be too attracted to really glib conversationalists who have a lot of superficial charm. Often, such a person is not just avoiding emotional depth out of nervousness; they really don't possess the ability to be any deeper. In fact, "charm" in general is something I really pay attention to now.

Jamie, from Chapter 5, ended up as predatory bait in another relationship. She says the following about her comfort level with men:

There is a certain mystique surrounding predatory-type men that speaks to most women—a sense of power within the struggle for their affection that is elemental and basic. My life is full of them because I find myself more comfortable with men than with women, so I end up in relationships with them that I had no intention of getting into. I think I am getting a male friend, but I am really getting yet another predator.

They can smell me, I think. I ran a personal ad in a paper, and several men wrote me and said they could tell from those few sentences that I was submissive and available to them. It scares me to think I have the word *target* stamped on my forehead.

Jacey lacked much dating experience. Through a friend, she struck up a correspondence with a prison inmate and began seeing him after he was released, even though lots of people told her not to. The result was disastrous and devastating. She views early conditioning and messages from her family as the cause behind her willingness to get involved with a convicted felon:

I am a naïve person. It doesn't take long to figure that out when you talk to me. I am also shy and have low self-esteem. My mother was the same way. We were raised to believe that people are good. You just don't question that, and you give everyone chances to change.

That's why writing to a man in prison didn't seem risky. I thought I was doing something good and kind by writing to him. I thought he could change and probably did change while he was in there. It took being raped several times by him before I realized I shouldn't always believe that people are who they say they are. I now know that some people will pretend to be something they are not in order to get what they want.

I am just not people-oriented enough to get the clues up front. Anyone else would have realized that if this guy was in prison, obviously something was wrong with his character. However, I don't tend to think that way, nor was I raised to think that way. So I know I live "at risk."

Chapter 11

Signs of a Bad Dating Choice

The preceding several chapters have tried to illustrate what the different types of bad dating choices look like. I have included a lot of detail about each category of dangerous man because you cannot acknowledge and change what you do not label and describe.

This chapter offers one more way of labeling and describing the signs of bad dating choices. These signs represent boundary issues that can inform you about the suitability of a potential date. The last section in the chapter contains an exercise that walks you through the challenge of finding out if you are at risk for repeating the behavior of dating dangerous men. Having that information will help you decide what sort of intervention you need in order to avoid destructive choices in your dating future.

Boundaries and Their Role in Healthy Relationships

Boundaries are indicators of where we start and end, and where other people start and end. We set limits—or boundaries—in relationships to protect our bodily selves and our dignity. Good boundaries demonstrate that we have an awareness of what we stand for; they are statements about what we will tolerate. A healthy relationship involves two people with clearly defined senses of their own identities. Neither is trapped in fear of the other person being different from oneself; neither sees differences as threatening.

Healthy boundaries allow us to separate our own thoughts, feelings, and needs from those of the people around us. The lack of an ability to separate these aspects of ourselves from those of others is called *enmeshment*. Enmeshment occurs when a person begins to take on the thoughts, feelings, and needs of someone else, even when those thoughts, feelings, and needs do not reflect his or her own best interests. It occurs when one person begins to draw his or her identity from another person. Drawing your identity from a dangerous man, as the stories in this book so dramatically illustrate, can have disastrous outcomes. Giving yourself up for a relationship is a huge sign that you have unhealthy boundaries.

Women without boundaries or with weak boundaries often attract all types of dangerous men. Emotional predators are bloodhounds for weak-boundaried women. It is the hallmark of their snout to find you. Emotionally unavailable men count on your inability to send them home to their wives or to send them packing when they prove "too busy" to truly commit to a relationship with you. Parental seekers and permanent clingers know you lack the internal fortitude to kick them to the curb as they whine and cling. Addicts gamble on your codependency as a way of keeping their foot in your door. A mentally ill man recognizes that you will probably confuse sympathy with love. An abusive or violent man knows darn well that you are probably too afraid of him to say what you mean and mean what you say.

In these cases, silence equals consent, and staying equals compliance. Women with weak boundaries fail to verbalize and take action on what they need. They stay quiet and hope "somehow" it will all work out. Women with poor boundaries commonly nurse fantasies of healthy relationships that magically don't require any work. But the message your silence sends to a dangerous man is that you consent to his inappropriate behavior. That's why developing good boundaries is so crucial for women who want to avoid dangerous men. An ability to confront unhealthy boundaries and behavior in the beginning of a relationship can help you determine early on whether a new man is a viable candidate for a healthy relationship with you.

Some women with poor boundaries are not passive, weak, or silent. By contrast, they can be aggressive and assertive. Such a woman violates her man's boundaries by trying to change his dangerous and annoying behaviors. She becomes focused on redirecting his "misguided ways." She might resort to nagging, suggesting, scolding, moralizing, raging, or threatening—all with the hoped-for outcome that such tactics will result in positive behavioral change. But of course, that doesn't happen. The behavior of the "steamroller" woman described here is as ineffective as that of the "doormat" woman described above. This kind of unhealthy, boundary-violating behavior doesn't change anyone or anything.

Boundaries are also important because they are a way for partners to respect each other's private lives and each other's ability to run his or her own life by himself or herself. Women who get involved with dangerous men are at risk for letting men have excessive influence over their lives. Boundary violations are great indicators of future relationship problems and should be viewed as pertinent information that is not to be ignored.

Our boundaries reflect our very selves—our life choices, friends, career choices, preferences, and dislikes. In healthy relationships, neither party impinges upon these areas of the other's life without an invitation. Boundaries are like gates through which we invite others into certain areas of our lives. If someone crashes your gates without an invitation, you can be sure that person will try to live inside your gates and invade your personal business without invitation. Men who are boundary violators, by definition, feel entitled to run your life.

On the surface, a boundary violator may appear to be merely opinionated or overinvolved. But men with chronic patterns of boundary violations are much more than just opinionated blowhards. Some of the types of dangerous men described in this book are defined by their habits of violating the boundaries of the women they get involved with. Women could avoid a lot of the dangerous situations they place themselves in if they could only recognize boundary violations by either party as the serious impingements to healthy relationships that they truly are. If a woman would recognize that each boundary violation pushes her closer to the edge of tolerating or doing all those things she said she would never tolerate or do—things that in the end rob her of her dignity—she might respond to the violations as soon as they begin.

As has been shown repeatedly in the stories of women who've gotten involved with dangerous men, women can quickly develop an increased tolerance to boundary violations. This can result in "hypertolerance"—a frame of mind in which abnormal behavior becomes normalized. Each time a boundary is ignored, the line in the sand is erased and is redrawn closer to you. Eventually, you have no line to show what you will and will not tolerate. Your "no tolerance zone" has been reduced to nothing, with your consent.

Let us not forget what the discussion of pathology in Chapter 1 taught us: Boundary violations committed by those who are pathologically disordered can be exceptionally dangerous. The greater the boundary violation, the more it points to chronic and unrelenting pathology in the perpetrator. Dangerously advanced forms of boundary violation include the following (these are risk factors that should be considered when assessing for psychopathology):

* Threatening to kill anyone or anything

* Assault on a pregnant woman

* Assault in front of other people

* Forced sex in any capacity, even with a known partner

* Violation of court orders

* Stalking anyone for any reason

* Repeat offenses of any of the behaviors on this list

Healthy Versus Unhealthy Relationships

So how can women compare and contrast what is healthy and what is unhealthy in terms of boundaries? What kinds of things are unhealthy in a relationship? The following table provides a few answers to these questions:

WHAT IS HEALTHY?	WHAT IS UNHEALTHY?
Open and honest communication	Game-playing and manipulative communication
Having friends outside of the relationship	Few friendships other than with one's romantic partner
Taking responsibility for the outcome of one's own life and happiness	Making others responsible for one's happiness
Having one's own identity	Feeling complete only when involved with someone else
A balance of time together and time apart	Too much time together or too much time alone
Emotional intimacy that is built without drugs or alcohol	Use of alcohol or drugs to achieve false connection
Appropriate level of commitment in the relationship	Over- or undercommitment (based on the length of the relationship so far)
Flexibility in the relationship	Rigidity in the relationship
Knowing what one needs	Being clueless as to what one needs
Asking for what one needs	Afraid to express what one needs

(Adapted from the website http://groups.msn.com/ PSYCHOPATH/home.htm, with permission.)

Boundary violations in these areas and others may be early warning signs of more serious violations that could follow.

Specific Signs of a Bad Dating Choice

In addition to developing good boundaries and getting in the habit of safeguarding them, learning the signs of a bad dating choice that are listed below will assist you in gaining a new level of awareness for spotting dangerous men before you get involved. But these are just general guidelines. The most reliable list of "danger signs" would be the one you make based on your own specific relationship history. The workbook that accompanies this book contains exercises to help you do just that.

A man might be a poor dating choice if he

* doesn't respect your need for time alone

* pushes to see you all the time

* discourages your outside interests, family, and friends

* asks you to do things you are uncomfortable doing (e.g., lying, lending him money, sex, etc.)

* uses drugs (any kind of drug use should be a red flag)

* uses alcohol too frequently and/or abundantly

* is frequently unemployed (except while in school)

* changes jobs frequently or is frequently fired or dismissed but always explains it away

* wants to control your hair, dress, behavior, friends, jobs, or how you express your spirituality

* wants you to quit or change jobs or friends for him

* has had multiple unsuccessful relationships

* has had any sexually transmitted disease, currently or in the past

* has a reputation for lying

* conceals important information about himself that you only discover later

* is physically, emotionally, verbally, or sexually "rough" or "weird"

* is too charming, has all the right lines, comes across as excessively smooth

* has a history or previous diagnosis of mental illness, especially
  - untreated depression
  - anxiety (appears "keyed up")
  - bipolar disorder (manic depression), especially if untreated or sporadically treated
  - conduct disorder or antisocial personality disorder
  - schizophrenia or any other psychotic disorder
  - narcissistic personality disorder
  - substance abuse (unsuccessfully treated) or other addictions
  - borderline personality disorder
  - posttraumatic stress disorder (PTSD)

* has a criminal record, especially:
  - repeat speeding violations
  - D.U.I.s
  - assault on a female
  - battery of any kind
  - other assaults
  - any sexual offense
  - forgery/bad checks

* has "deadbeat dad" issues

* is inflexible—cannot change to meet a spontaneous request

* believes the rules are for everyone else except him

* feels or acts like he's "special and unique."

For Women Involved with a Dangerous Man: Deciding Whether to Leave or Stay

By now, I think the argument has been sufficiently made about why dangerous men should never be a relationship choice for any woman. The hopeless outcomes of getting involved with dangerous men have been documented throughout this book by women who want you to know why doing so is futile and harmful; the research has demonstrated that you and your man are not going to be exceptions to the rule; and the case for responding to your red flags and exiting dead-end, destructive, and potentially deadly relationships has been made. Now that it's time to put action behind knowledge, the ball is in your court.

As I stated in Chapter 8, making the decision to leave is yours alone. But be aware that acquiring resources and reinforcement to leave often requires getting other people involved to support you in this process. This is definitely true if you're leaving a violent or potentially violent relationship.

If you are ready to leave the relationship, contact resources in your community for help, support, and advice on how to do so safely. In addition, find resources for obtaining counseling or group therapy so you can understand how and why this occurred in your life and what your choices can teach you. Create a healing community of supporters to ensure that both your exit and your future are safe.

Women need to understand and heed the universal signs of dangerous behaviors. This chapter has provided an overview of signs and symptoms that should be of concern to any woman if she sees them in a man she's considering dating. But I encourage you not to stop here. Take the next step: Re-engage your internal red-alert system so that you can experience your red flags and compare what they tell you to the lists contained in this chapter. Regaining awareness of your emotional, physical, and spiritual red flags is critical; the next chapter addresses this issue. An additional step would be to utilize the workbook that accompanies this book to create your own list of do-not-date characteristics.

Completing this workbook exercise will help you personalize the material you've learned so you can determine which kinds of men you should avoid in the future. Memorize the signs of a bad dating choice listed above, listen internally, and create your list.

Questionnaire: Am I in Danger of Dating More Dangerous Men?

Determining whether you're at risk for dating more dangerous men can be an incentive to take the next steps in the process of creating a new future for yourself—a future free of dangerous men and full of the promise of new, healthy relationship possibilities.

Give yourself two points for each "yes" answer, and zero points for each "no" answer:

_____   I have dated more than one dangerous man.

** _____   I have dated more than three dangerous men.

** _____   I have dated five or more dangerous men.

_____   I have broken up with and then gone back to a dangerous man.

** _____   A dangerous man I've dated would qualify as violent.

_____   A dangerous man I've dated would qualify as an addict.

_____   A dangerous man I've dated would qualify as mentally ill.

** _____   A dangerous man I've dated would qualify for any combination of violent, addicted, and mentally ill.

_____   I have a pattern of ignoring my red flags.

** _____   Ignoring my red flags has put me at risk with dangerous men.

_____   I don't even know what my red flags are.

_____ Friends and family are upset over the types of men I pick.

_____ I have dated emotionally unavailable men more than once.

_____ I don't know what healthy relationship patterns are.

_____ I fluctuate between men who are emotionally un-available, have hidden lives, or are violent, and men who are permanent clingers or parental seekers.

_____ I don't fluctuate in the type of man I date; I keep picking the same type of dangerous man, even though it hasn't worked in the past.

_____ I grew up being taught to trust people unconditionally and to ignore my own feelings and intuition.

_____ TOTAL POINTS

THE DANGEROUS-MAN RISK SCALE

(Note: This is not a clinically verified scale.) When considering your risk for dating dangerous men, in addition to adding up your points you must also consider _which_ questions you answered yes to. Those marked with ** indicate higher risk; if you answered yes to _any_ of these starred statements, that should raise additional concern.

0–8 points   Lower risk (unless you answered yes to any questions marked with **)

10–18 points   Moderate risk (unless you answered yes to any questions marked with **)

20–34 points   High risk (exceptionally high if you also answered yes to any questions marked with **)

Women who score in the moderate- and high-risk categories need to seek intervention on their own behalf. A first step toward doing so would be to work through the exercises in the workbook designed as a companion to this volume (see Resources), which can help you dig deeper in order to uncover, learn from, and change your self-sabotaging patterns. Beyond working through the Dangerous Man curriculum, you might also consider getting professional counseling to help you dismantle your destructive life patterns.

Chapter 12

To Thine Own Self Be True: Learning to Heed Your Red Flags

The previous chapter was about what "he" does that might indicate he's a bad dating choice for you. This chapter once again returns the focus to you. It is about what *you* do that should be a red flag for you. Focusing on men's behaviors removes only 50 percent of the equation. The other 50 percent lies in your own experiences and behavior patterns. Examining them provides an opportunity to learn from them and to change them.

How Women Fail to Honor Their Red Flags

In general, there tend to be three ways in which women fail to live in accordance with their internal red-alert system: They don't notice their red flags, they focus too much energy on blaming "him," and they don't question the training and conditioning they've received from their family of origin. Let's take a look at each of these three patterns.

NOT NOTICING

Defining a man's dangerous behavior is an important step toward making better choices about dangerous men. Equally important is noticing your own reactions (or lack of a reaction) to dysfunctional behavior, *and then paying attention to—not ignoring—your reactions*. These are your natural red flags, and reconnecting with your red-alert system is paramount when changing how you respond to dangerous men. In Chapter 2 you learned that your body, mind, and spirit will communicate with you about how they read any man—if you will listen. Throughout the book we have shown that what often occurs is that a woman grows unaware of the signals her red-alert system sends her. This happens over time when you consistently ignore your red flags, and it is a destructive pattern. It's also why we say there are no victims, only volunteers. Being true to yourself and changing your selection patterns means tuning in to how you feel about a particular man emotionally, mentally, physically, spiritually, and sexually. Not noticing these inner promptings is a self-sabotaging defense mechanism. Instead, listening and acting on them is your choice. It's also your opportunity for change.

BLAMING

In order to successfully change your patterns, you must move from a position of blaming all the men in your past (and present) for what happened in your relationships. Instead, you must see yourself as jointly involved with them in the selection and dating process. I am not talking here about rapes or other instances of violence from strangers. I am talking about mutual relationships between consenting adults. The concept of mutuality in partner selection can be unpopular with some feminists. But I take exception to a line of thought that implies women merely wander repeatedly into dangerous relationships and that all of the resulting damage is caused by men.

This notion oversimplifies the complex issues surrounding the interactive and personal psychologies of both the man and the woman. It also relieves the woman of any responsibility for her own lack of awareness, recurring choices, mental health, self-sabotaging behaviors, and growth. It labels her as a victim, implying she's powerless and impotent. On the other hand, if a woman's choices are her own and she continues to have problems resulting from those choices, her opportunities for growth, insight, and change are all in her ballpark. She is the master of her ship and of where she steers it. Playing the blame game can curtail a woman's taking responsibility for her part in things, a mindset that doesn't help her to be any safer. It offers her a dangerous loophole for her thought and behavior patterns. If it's all his fault, there is nothing she can do or change. How can believing this possibly keep her safe?

ACCEPTING FAULTY FAMILY TRAINING

Your family upbringing and training may have left you predisposed to accept dangerous men as dating partners. Part of developing a defense strategy involves becoming keenly aware of how your mind sets you up to overlook the behavior of dangerous men. Some of these mental gymnastics date back to childhood, when family members or family dynamics may have conditioned you in the following ways:

* To normalize abnormal behavior
* To downplay danger
* To override your feelings of fear, concern, or discomfort
* To accept abusive behavior
* To expect addictions in men
* Not to expect people to earn your trust, but instead to trust them immediately
* To violate your own values and morals and accept married men as dating partners
* To allow people to violate your boundaries without consequences
* To avoid speaking up when you feel you should
* To accept any kind of male attention and be glad to have it

* To rescue unstable men from their own lives

* To never give up on failing relationships and to remain forever optimistic that *all* men can, and will, change and grow

* To rename problem behavior as something less threatening

* To never say no

* To not refuse dates

* To resist labeling a man "alcoholic," "mentally ill," "problematic," or anything else that may make you not want to date him

Continuing to live following unsafe family messages such as these is another destructive way in which your behaviors and beliefs can align you with dangerous men.

Universal Red Flags

Some red flags indicate undeniable truths. Women everywhere respond to these universal red flags when they're in the presence of a dangerous man. The wise woman will memorize, pay attention to, and *utilize* these signs as opportunities to reexamine the relationship—or to exit, if necessary. Here are some of them:

* You feel uncomfortable about something he has said or done, and the feeling remains.

* You feel mad or scared, or he reminds you of someone else you know with a serious problem.

* You wish he would go away, you want to cry, or you want to run.

* You dread his phone call.

* You are often bored with him.

* You think no one else in his life understands him.

* You think no one else in his life has ever really loved him or helped him.

* You think you are the only one who can help/love/understand him.

* You want to "love him into emotional wellness."

* You think you can help him "change" or "fix" his life.

* You let him borrow money from you or your friends.

* You feel bad about yourself when you are around him.

* You feel he wants too much from you.

* You are emotionally tired from dealing with him and feel he "sucks the life out of you."

* Your value system and his are very different; you frequently are not on the same page about your beliefs, and it is problematic.

* Your past and his are very different, and the two of you have conflicts over it.

* You tell friends you are "unsure about the relationship."

* You feel isolated from other relationships with friends and family.

* You think he's too charming or a little "too good to be true."

* You feel in the wrong because he is always right and goes to great lengths to show you he is right.

* You are uncomfortable because he continually says he knows what is best for you.

* You notice he needs you too frequently, too much, or too intensely.

* You wonder if he really understands you or instead just claims to.

* You are uncomfortable because he has touched you inappropriately or too soon.

* You notice he quickly discloses information about his past or his emotional pain.

* You sense he is pushing too quickly for emotional connection.

* Although you don't believe it, he claims to feel an immediate connection with you (a sign of false intimacy).

* You see him pushing too quickly to get sexually involved with you, and you find yourself willing to abandon your sexual boundaries with him.

* You see him as a chameleon; you notice he can change to please whoever is in his presence.

* You notice how soon he tells you about his earlier failed relationships and about his previous partners and their flaws.

* You notice he mostly talks about himself, his plans, and his future.

* You notice he spends a lot of time watching violent movies or TV or playing violent video games; he can be preoccupied with violence, death, or destruction.

* You have heard him confess to a current or previous drug addiction.

* You have information about major relationship problems that he handled poorly.

* He confesses he has been violent in the past or uses drugs or alcohol when stressed.

* You know he has multiple children by multiple partners, is inconsistent in paying child support, and rarely sees his children; you find yourself blaming the mother of his children for these behaviors.

* You find yourself accepting him "for now," even though you have plenty of red flags that would help you terminate the relationship if you paid attention to them.

* You make excuses about why you are dating him.

* You make excuses for his character and minimize his behavior.

Mythical Assumptions

I wish I could say that all the women who appear in this book learned from their experiences with dangerous men. After all, they took the time to share their stories with you, which means they obviously care about the quality of their lives. But sadly, some of them have gone on to make more dangerous choices.

The mistakes made by women who get involved with dangerous men are based on myths. These women grew up believing false information taught to them and lived by their families. Or they developed their own mythical beliefs about relationships by repeatedly dating dangerous men. Each go-round with a dangerous man teaches women falsehoods that they adopt as a part of their internal way of thinking about men and relationships. We have looked at this issue in different ways throughout the book. We looked at it from the perspectives of dysfunctional family training, unspoken societal truths, gender roles, and cultural backgrounds. Based on my conversations with women, the following represent the most commonly held faulty beliefs women have about dangerous men:

Mythical Assumption #1: Dangerous men must have dangerous professions—like drug dealer. Dangerous men couldn't possibly be firemen, social workers, teachers, or ministers. WRONG!

Mythical Assumption #2: Dangerous men must come from dangerous families. Dangerous men couldn't possibly be the only dangerous person in their family. WRONG!

Mythical Assumption #3: Dangerous men look dangerous. Dangerous men couldn't possibly be clean-cut, handsome, conservative, or classy. WRONG!

Mythical Assumption #4: A dangerous man will only come into my life once. If I've already dated one, I probably won't date another one. Surely I've learned. WRONG!

Mythical Assumption #5: Dangerous men aren't likely to spend a lot of time getting to know me. I've talked to this man on the phone for weeks now without going on a date with him. He couldn't possibly be a dangerous man. WRONG!

Mythical Assumption #6: Dangerous men don't go to church, volunteer, or give to charities. The man I'm interested in is an elder in his church, helps his elderly mother, and is a volunteer at the hospital. He couldn't be a dangerous man since he participates in these types of activities. WRONG!

Mythical Assumption #7: Dangerous men don't disclose information about themselves. The man I am interested in has told me all about himself, so he couldn't be a dangerous man. WRONG!

The Many Stories of Katie

Katie's story shows how mythical assumptions can get played out in revolving relationships with dangerous men. Her tale is sadly familiar because many women don't stop dating long enough to challenge their own myths. They keep believing them even after the myths have proven to be exactly that: only myths.

Katie is a bright, attractive bank executive who has dated just about every type of dangerous man described in this book. This happened primarily because she failed to glean information from her past dating choices, failed to examine what was going on with *her* that caused her to continue her dangerous patterns, and failed to challenge her own mythical belief system about men and their characters. She says:

My first marriage was to Tom, a man I didn't even like. He was the first man to show any signs of interest in me. He was twenty-one and I was eighteen when we married. I hardly even knew him. I knew I probably shouldn't be with someone I hardly knew and didn't even like, but I didn't listen, even to myself. He had cystic fibrosis, which was terminal. I felt I could take care of him during the years he had left. He seemed to want someone who would care for him in his disease. Within a few months of marrying him, I knew I'd made a terrible mistake. One night I came home and he was passed out on the floor. When I tripped over him, he woke up in a fit of rage, hitting me, cursing, and throwing furniture at me. I moved to my parents' house and filed for divorce. I didn't pursue counseling for this disastrous choice—I simply moved on.

My second relationship, with Robert, happened quickly after my divorce from Tom. We dated for about a year; then he said he was moving to Miami and wanted me to move with him. So I gladly went. He didn't ask if this was what I wanted—it was just the way it was going to be if I "wanted to be with him."

He wanted me to watch pornography, which I was hesitant to do, having been raised Catholic. He said there wasn't anything wrong with it. He had a way of convincing me to do things even when I didn't think I should do them—like he had some power over me, or something. So we began to dabble with porn despite my discomfort about it.

His job was ready to take him elsewhere, so I told him either we married or I wasn't going. He agreed, and we married. But it felt like he never really connected to the marriage or to our relationship. Sure enough, within two years he was moving out and wanted a divorce because there was another woman. How could I never have suspected anything? I resented that I had fallen into watching pornography for a man who would turn around and leave me.

I was devastated but *determined* not to be alone for long. I began dating James the same year. I wasn't quite divorced, but he came along when I needed him most. He was divorced with two kids and he paid child support, so he never had money or groceries or even a car. I began buying him groceries. I gave him my car and bought a new one for myself. He was a recovering alcoholic with lots of body pain that required pain medication. I thought, No problem, I can take care of him. During our thirteen years of marriage he went from one pain medication to the next. He was also insecure, so I never had friends outside of the relationship. I stayed away from many family gatherings as well. He told me how he never had a close relationship with his mom and how he had gone from foster home to foster home. On many nights he wanted me to stroke his head and tell him everything would be okay. He had such a childlike, frightened look in his eyes.

He didn't function well, so I did all the cooking, cleaning, shopping, and bill-paying. I was feeling overwhelmed with caring for myself and him, and when I told him this, he said, "You aren't the woman I married." So we called it quits when all I wanted was for him to learn to take care of himself. I did enter counseling at that point to try to look at my unsuccessful relationships.

Within a year I met Daniel, who was "going to get divorced any day" but hadn't quite filed the papers yet. He had a young son, and he seemed to want to recruit me to be the boy's "mother." Through months of dating he repeatedly promised to file the paperwork for his divorce, but it never quite happened. He asked to borrow money from me for the attorney, but I refused. Since he had a young son, he spent frequent time away from me to be with him—or so I thought. But I think there were other women, as I caught herpes from him. When I confronted him, he was out of there. I started going to twelve-step meetings to look at the patterns in myself that I now recognized. After getting herpes, I was sure I "got it" about these men.

I took a few months off from dating to get a grip on having contracted an STD and to work the twelve steps, and then I met Gary, a neighbor. I liked his smile and how outgoing he was. He made me laugh. I knew he was involved with another woman who lived on my street. When I asked about her, he said he was breaking up with her but had some problems to work out first. Still, I gave him my phone number. The moment I did it, I knew I shouldn't have. I had my first red flag, but instead of telling him not to call or changing my number, I ignored what I knew.

He called that evening and asked me to meet him at the beach. Immediately he was grabbing my breasts and crotch. Although I was taken aback by it, he complimented me on how sensual and uninhibited I was. That felt good to a Catholic girl. He said all the right things. Just when I was getting uncomfortable, he would say something that would ease me into his way of thinking. He had a big Harley, and I felt wild and free with him.

He said he had to date incognito for a while until he was fully broken up with his girlfriend. My gut began to tell me some things, and when I asked questions, I was right. The girlfriend had a drug and alcohol problem and was a stripper. Still, it didn't occur to me to wonder what *he* might possibly be! He would drive his girlfriend to work and then meet me for sex. Then he started asking for weird and bizarre sexual behaviors. I was unfamiliar with what he asked for and uncomfortable with the idea. I had major red flags that maybe he was a sex addict or something. And, of course, I was right—he began sending me porn through e-mail. I asked him to stop, but he continued. It felt like he was stalking me through the Internet.

When I said I wanted to end it, he was angry and I was afraid of him. I always had the sense that at the edge of his wildness was a lot of out-of-control anger—like he could become crazy easily. Two weeks later he called and asked me to meet him so we could talk. He really just wanted to have sex; he was still with his girlfriend. But still I responded. Now I don't even hear from him.

I question why I would *even* have allowed myself to be sucked into such an unhealthy relationship. But when I look at my past and at my marriages, it's just one bad relationship after another. I am a bank executive! I am a professional! Why do I pick men like these and why don't I see it when I'm in one of these relationships? Why do I ignore what I feel and sense? For God's sake, I'm forty-five years old. This shouldn't be happening to me.

Katie began attending a twelve-step group for sex and love addicts. She recognized that her relationship issues were not merely "problems," but life-threatening addictions that could permanently harm her. She had already contracted an STD and had dated emotionally unavailable men, clingers, seekers, a predator, a man with a hidden life, addicts, a man who was violent, and some who came close. Her life was clearly out of control.

Katie felt committed to the twelve steps. She attended several meetings weekly and spent a few months "relationship free." She thought she was well on her way to relationship recovery—enough so to violate her recovery plan and begin dating Bill.

This one was different for lots of reasons, according to Katie. She had been through some counseling and now had some twelve-step experience behind her. She thought her "eyes were open." The amount of pain she had racked up over the years surely was a good teacher. She thought the fact that she had been so badly hurt was the best predictor that her choices from here on in would be better. And not only was she different, but he was different, too. Their first date involved a trip to church and breakfast! What a change—from Gary and pornography to Bill and church. She was tickled that things could be this different.

Within no time, Katie was no longer attending twelve-step meetings. Bill was the center of her world. Her old patterns began setting back in. Red flags waved, and Katie chose to ignore them as she had in the past. Her support group was just a memory.

When Bill's stories didn't add up and Katie finally allowed herself to respond to the red flags that besieged her, she tried to end it with Bill. But he kept calling and pleading for a second chance. He would drive to her house despite her repeatedly sending him away. He called her neighbors and asked about her, showed up at places where he'd heard she'd be, e-mailed her when she asked him not to, and sent her letters. Katie was being stalked. She got a restraining order against him. Obtaining police protection is what it took to end her relationship with this *sixth* dangerous man. Katie is back in twelve-step recovery once again.

Mythical Conclusions

Katie is an example of a woman who ignored her red flags and all that her previous relationships could have taught her, starting as young as age eighteen. Ignoring her red flags landed her in relationships that became increasingly dangerous with each new man. Katie needs counseling that will help her look at her patterns, her selections, her mythical assumptions, and her "will do anything for love" approach to men.

Katie's story shows that she bought into *every one* of the mythical assumptions listed on pages 217 and 218:

> She was naïve in thinking that in order to be dangerous, a man had to have a dangerous profession, come from an obviously dangerous family, or look dangerous (assumptions 1, 2, and 3).

> She stopped looking for dangerousness after she recognized it in the first few men, believing she would not encounter it again since she had already been involved in dangerous relationships (assumption 4).

> At least one dangerous man slid under her radar by taking her to church on their first date (assumption 6).

> Others were highly verbal and disclosed a lot of information about themselves, which made her believe they were being truthful about their history (assumptions 5 and 7).

Additionally, as is true with many women, Katie's behaviors up to now seem to imply that she believes it is better to be with someone who is sick than it is to be alone but emotionally healthy. She needs help looking at why she ignores her screaming subconscious while trying to make things work *this* time, in *this* relationship, with *this* dangerous man. She hasn't yet done the work of closely examining the types of men she has been with or their behaviors. Staying out of dangerous relationships and learning how to choose differently will require that she list, define, and categorize her relationships, and then develop her own do-not-date list.

Katie hasn't noticed that she allows her entire life to change each time she gets involved in a new relationship. The healthier parts of her life are put aside. Friends are gone, twelve-step meetings are discontinued, church gets ditched, and any other healthy way she took care of herself and balanced her life is put on hold when a new dangerous man enters her life. She cuts off any opportunity for healthy input that could influence her thinking. This in itself should be a red flag to Katie. Once another relationship crashes and burns, she begins to look for answers that she thinks can be found in a two-month period of celibacy and by attending twelve-step meetings while white-knuckling it to stay away from men. Twelve-step programs are a wonderful part of a recovery plan, as long as you are also telling yourself the truth about your behaviors and patterns. However, assuming that two months of attending meetings can change your life is not telling yourself the truth.

So far, Katie's brief stint in twelve-step groups hasn't worked. But this isn't an uncommon approach for women. Many go to counseling, group therapy, or twelve-step meetings while they are *between* relationships but stop going once they begin dating someone new. Maybe they are afraid that if they continue participating in healthy interventions for themselves, they might "see" aspects of the relationship early on that they don't want to see. If they aren't in counseling or going to meetings, it's easy to say they relapsed because they "stopped going to meetings." In twelve-step parlance this is called "setting yourself up." You set yourself up when you discontinue support and then attribute bad choices to "relapse," when on some level you *made a decision* to stray off your recovery path and into a dangerous relationship.

Katie's twenty-seven-year dating history has taught her far more than a mere two months of meetings can undo. She hasn't yet developed a true respect for the depth of her dating training and for how much it will take to undo it. If Katie chooses to persistently stay in counseling and go to meetings, her life can be different and healthier.

Katie's relationships will change when she sees that it's *she* who needs to change. The outside circumstances of our lives change when our internal relationship to those circumstances changes. When we gather wisdom and insight that motivate our character to grow, our outer world changes in relationship to our new inner condition. When we gather courage to challenge the parts of our lives that do not work, we can create new realities for ourselves. Thoreau said, "Things do not change, we change." Reflecting on that bit of wisdom can help us to see that our failed relationships and dangerous choices are mirrors that reflect our character deficits. As such, they can point the way and light the path to the solution.

Denial, minimizing, rationalizing, choosing not to see, or anything else we use to blame others and avoid growth never helps us to stay safe or to learn. Self-honesty, critical evaluation, accountability, and responding to previous negative patterns are our only hopes for changing our lives.

Chapter # 13

New Life, New Choices

Let us return to the stories of two women you met earlier in the book.

Sierra's Success Story

Sierra, from Chapter 7, says her life is different today. Although Chase served time in prison and is now out and living in the same town as she, Sierra feels her life is immensely saner.

> I've seen him around town, and I was very clear in setting my boundaries and refusing to open that door by having conversations with him that he could construe as an invitation. Especially given how his mind works! I changed my phone numbers when I heard he was out. I trained my children about what to say if he ever approached them. We developed a family safety plan about what to do if he ever called, came by, or ran into us.
>
> But more importantly, I have done an inventory of my life and choices. I am not in a place to date. I have told that to my closest friends so they can help me live by that decision right now. They are my accountability partners until I have worked through how and why this happened in my life. I don't think this is a matter of a six-month emotional review and dating hiatus. I have been in two dangerous relationships. I surely think I can invest in more than a few months without a man in order to change my life and my future!

I am finding ways of making my life complete without a man. If I need a man to complete me, I am setting myself up to let just anyone fill that need. I have to have a life that I am happy with, even if no special male comes into it. I have increased my outside friendships and activities. I spend a lot of time with my kids, too. God knows that with what they lived through, they need it!

Most of all, I am aware of my red flags now when I talk to people—anyone. I am just practicing using them and paying attention to what I sense and feel again. I also sort of "eavesdrop" on my thinking when I am talking to a man. I want to see how I'm doing. Sometimes I catch myself glossing over important clues about him. When I am glossing things over, I am minimizing or choosing to ignore something so I can later say, "I didn't know that. Oh well, we're already dating now." This is why I am still not dating. I can see I still gloss over some things, and that isn't going to keep me safe.

I need to consistently call a spade a spade and not just call a mental illness an imperfection. Calling a disorder an "imperfection" suggests that since we're all not perfect, I should just accept that problem in the person, like they should accept whatever is imperfect in me. I can accept problems in people I don't have an intimate relationship with, but in my dating life I need to shoot higher than a man riddled with mental illnesses. Mental illness is sad, but a man with it isn't right for my life or my children's lives. I know now that accepting mental illness is accepting the death of a relationship; how can it be anything else? Certainly Chase taught me that.

For me, my sanity right now involves not putting myself back out there and also not feeling pressured to date. I don't feel like I am avoiding. I feel like I am healing.

Sierra is in a great space. She has allowed herself some healing time without succumbing to society-induced pressures to date or hook up. She has put herself first and is focusing on her recovery, on the changes she needs to see in her thinking, on making sure she consistently responds to her red flags, and on examining how previous relationship problems occurred in her life.

Women everywhere could benefit from taking a "time out" from dating. Unfortunately, few women give themselves time off from dating because of a fear of being alone. It should be a red flag to women if they feel this way. Women consistently ask me "how long" they should take off from dating before they can "begin again." It's as if they are white-knuckling it and chomping at the bit. They want to know how to "speed the process along." Can they read more books, go to meetings or counseling—do anything to make them ready to get back out there? The answers to these questions are different for every woman. Suffice it to say that in my experience, most women allow themselves ridiculously short periods of time for a hiatus from dating, especially in contrast to how many years they've dated dangerously. Twenty-seven years of bad relationships, like Katie had, can't be undone and new lessons learned in six months of celibacy. Insight is never achieved through speed-recovery tactics.

Jenna's Success Story

Jenna, from Chapter 10, has also learned a few things.

> When I met Cory, I was young. I was just barely in college, and I really didn't have many relationship skills. I pat myself on the back for getting out as soon as I did, considering how young and naïve I was.
>
> I spent the next couple of years just barely dating. I knew I should let my experience with Cory sink in if I wanted to ever have a successful relationship. (I don't know how I got that smart so young.) So I just dated in groups. I told guys on the first date that I wasn't going to get serious. And I held to it. Then I watched myself interact with men. I listened just as if I were listening to someone sitting at the table next to me. I critiqued myself and noticed what I was and was not doing.
>
> I especially paid attention to the kinds of things I had learned from the predator—superficial charm, glib conversational skills, a knack at becoming whoever I was. I got pretty good at recognizing those kinds of guys, but I knew they

weren't the only kind out there. I don't know how to explain how I turned all this around. Awareness, I guess. And giving my male and female friends permission to kick my butt if they saw me making bad choices or allowing bad behavior from men.

Today, I am ten years older and in a great relationship. I am a columnist writer, and we have a nice, healthy life together. He is gentle, open, and kind... but he had to wait it out with me. I wasn't going to rush into anything for anyone again. And I figured if he didn't like all that waiting—well, that just said something up front that I needed to know, and he probably wasn't for me.

Now women come to me about their dangerous choices in men. I always tell them the story of the predator and how I chose early on to learn from that experience. If I had merely blamed him for being sick and being in my life, I would have missed the whole lesson for *me* that finally got me to a point where I could choose a healthy man. It wasn't only his fault. We mutually dated. I decided I was going to take every bit of learning I could from that experience because I didn't want to spend my whole life doing the same thing over and over again. It worked for me!

Jenna's success is a breath of fresh air. She didn't rush out and try to medicate her wounds from her involvement with a dangerous man by finding another one. She took a long breather. She didn't blame him. She looked to the experience for what it could teach her so she could extract the wisdom and choose more wisely the next time. When she finally dated, she went slowly and decided that if a guy didn't like it, that was information about the relationship she should pay attention to. Everything taught her something. She remained open and nondefensive about her choices. She put herself in a position to learn from everyone and everything.

Today, Jenna is a dynamic and well-balanced young woman with an amazing career. And, as she said, she's a very happy person, too.

Your Success Story

What will you write in the book of your life? Will you tell of a cyclic pattern of choosing dangerous men and wasting years in potentially harmful and pathological relationships? Or will you choose to let your experiences teach you the lessons that will grant you insight, wisdom, and serenity—qualities that, down the road, might lead to a healthy relationship that could last a lifetime?

Only you can clear out space in your life to make room for healing. Only you can give yourself the time and patience that will let you learn from and change destructive patterns in how you select and respond to men. You are worth every bit of positive energy that you put into a healthy way of being. Today is the first day of new choices for your life. What will your story say?

In Closing

There are never guarantees of happiness in any relationship. Still, it is everyone's hope that their intimate relationship will provide a measure of satisfaction and happiness. Why else would anyone seek a relationship?

Dating or marrying dangerous or pathological men is an assurance of misery. It's banking on a future that will pay dividends of dysfunction, unhappiness, and pain. It is a guarantee of the worst kind.

How to Spot a Dangerous Man Before You Get Involved is your "get out of jail" card. Use it to help you find the way out of the prison of your past patterns and into a healthier way of relating. As I've stated, I am convinced from fifteen years of practice in the mental-health field that the reason why women date dangerous and pathological men is because they lack the information to know how to avoid doing so. Now you have this information.

Women I have successfully treated learned to spot dangerous men; in effect, that means they learned how to stay out of dangerous relationships. You can, too. You are already on the road to making more informed choices and having new respect for your internal red-alert system. You understand the symptoms of harmful and pathological behavior; you've begun to take a look at your own self-sabotaging behaviors. You are armed with a list of the signs of a bad dating choice. Completing the workbook will give you further insight into your relationship patterns and help you create a personalized do-not-date list. From there, you will instinctively know whether you should get more professional help, either in the form of counseling to help you look at your patterns or in the form of advocacy or other support if you are exiting a dangerous relationship.

You now have knowledge you lacked when you began reading this book. You can steer your future into the happy and healthy one you've always dreamed of. Good luck.

Appendix

Descriptions of Mental and Emotional Disorders

Below are brief descriptions of some of the mental and emotional disorders discussed in this book, especially in Chapters 1 and 7. Note that these do not represent every category of mental illness that could prove to be dangerous in a relationship. See a mental-health professional if you are concerned about characteristics in another person or in yourself.

(For more information about the diagnoses described here, see *Diagnostic and Statistical Manual of Mental Disorders,* 4th edition, Washington, D.C.: American Psychiatric Association, 1994.)

Childhood Disorders

CONDUCT DISORDER

Characterized by behaviors that ignore or disrepect the rights of others and that society would recognize as "wrong," including displaying hostility by threatening others verbally or physically; committing property damage; dishonesty; stealing of insignificant, unnecessary items; repeatedly breaking rules like curfews and school attendance.

Individuals who are diagnosed with conduct disorder as children are often later diagnosed with antisocial personality disorder, which represents the most serious diagnosis on the pathology continuum.

Mood Disorders

MAJOR DEPRESSIVE DISORDER, RECURRENT

A person is considered clinically depressed if he or she is notably depressed and disinterested in most of his or her normal daily routines and outside interests for at least two consecutive weeks. The condition is considered "recurrent" if there is a two-month break in symptoms and then they resume.

Other qualifying symptoms include problems sleeping; weight gain or loss, agitation, decreased energy, unnecessary guilt, feelings of unworthiness, trouble making decisions and concentrating, and/or suicidal thoughts or fantasies.

BIPOLAR DISORDER

Involves "manic" cycles or "mixed" cycles. During a "manic" episode the individual seems either unusually high, happy, giddy, or unusually irritable. He or she may sleep less than usual and talk more than usual; may be abnormally boastful; may "flit" quickly from one thought to the next; may stay extraordinarily busy; may make bad choices like drinking and driving, having affairs, spending too much money, or abandoning jobs or responsibilities. During a "mixed" episode, the patient cycles rapidly between manic behavior and depressive behavior (described above).

Anxiety Disorders

OBSESSIVE-COMPULSIVE DISORDER (OCD)

The person with OCD struggles with recurring thoughts (obsessions) and/or repetitive actions (compulsions). These thoughts and actions tend to take up a great part of the person's day, which renders him or her fairly ineffective in daily life.

The obsessive thoughts of a person with OCD do not make sense, based on what the person is experiencing. He or she usually knows the thoughts are nonsensical but lacks any control over them. The person may try to ignore the thoughts, hoping to stop them, but this is never effective.

Repetitive actions can include things like hand washing or checking to see if he or she has turned off the stove or has run over someone with his or her car. Compulsive actions, like obsessive thoughts, are nonsensical; the person tries to suppress the desire to do the action, but trying to suppress it only increases his or her anxiety.

POSTTRAUMATIC STRESS DISORDER (PTSD)

PTSD occurs following a dramatically stressful event (often called a "trauma"). Well-known after being diagnosed in many Vietnam veterans, the condition is now recognized as occurring after all types of emotionally traumatic events, such as rape, seeing someone killed, or being in a disaster like the World Trade Center bombing. Symptoms include flashbacks to the traumatic event, the inability to distinguish between a flashback and the actual event, and fear and anxiety triggered by something that reminds the person of the event. The PTSD sufferer responds to symptoms by trying to avoid places, thoughts, and feelings associated with the event. Often the individual's memory of the event is incomplete and his or her sleep is disrupted. His or her emotional state seems flat and depressed, detached and unresponsive, or agitated, jumpy, and anxious. The sufferer often believes he or she will die prematurely.

Personality Disorders (Pathological Disturbances)

PARANOID PERSONALITY DISORDER

Persons with this disorder harbor a deep distrust for others. They distrust others' basic motivation toward them and believe that others wish to harm them in some way, even though there is often no evidence to support the belief.

Individuals with paranoid personality disorder justify their distrust by reading more into people's casual statements than was meant. They resist disclosing much about themselves for fear that others will harm them with their own words. They experience difficulty in close relationships because they persistently accuse their partners of unfaithfulness, often without evidence.

ANTISOCIAL PERSONALITY DISORDER

The main symptom of this disorder is a chronic disrespect for the rights of others or the rules of society. The pattern usually begins in childhood or early adolescence as symptoms of conduct disorder (see page 232). In adulthood, antisocials have ongoing behavioral problems arising from their disrepect for the rules and laws of society. Antisocials are pathological liars and con artists. They will lie to and manipulate even their closest family members. They are impetuous and will react in a knee-jerk fashion without much thought or planning. Their behavior results in inconsistency in most areas of their lives, including child rearing, working, and paying bills on time. Their only skill for resolving conflict tends to be aggression, a pattern that often results in repeated assault charges. They enjoy pushing the limits of safety and so will often engage in impulsive or daredevil behaviors like speeding or reckless driving. Antisocials have very little ability to show conscience and remorse for things they have done.

BORDERLINE PERSONALITY DISORDER

Borderlines are well known for their unending relationship problems, their inability to regulate their impulses, and their rapidly shifting perception of themselves.

Borderlines fear being alone and can conjure up ideas of people leaving them even before a separation has occurred. Their relationships are up and down. A person in a relationship with a borderline hardly knows what has occurred to make the person so upset or angry.

Borderlines have rapidly cycling emotions and can put on great displays of rage and fear. They engage in a range of self-defeating behaviors that can include abuse of drugs and/or alcohol, overeating, mutilating various body parts, indiscriminate sexual behavior, and feeling constantly suicidal.

NARCISSISTIC PERSONALITY DISORDER

The notable features of a narcissist include the individual's sense that he or she is very important, a showiness about his or her talents or abilities, and a large egotism that far exceeds his or her real abilities. Consequently, narcissists are rarely in tune with others' needs or feelings, focusing only on their own. They are only satisfied when they are the center of attention and are receiving adoration from others. They often embellish their real talents and achievements in an attempt to gain even more adoration from others. Most of the narcissist's thoughts are focused on achieving even more; most think that fame is within their grasp. Narcissists tend to feel the rules are for other "little people" and that a different set of rules exists for people like themselves. They have very little ability to anticipate how others might feel, and they lack the ability to feel sympathy for others.

AVOIDANT PERSONALITY DISORDER

Individuals with avoidant personality disorder feel "less than" others; consequently, they don't enjoy being around other people, and when they are, they feel as if everyone is talking about them in a negative way. Small complaints about their behavior feel large and signficant to them, which makes them want to avoid others even more. Most avoidants like to work alone; they avoid situations that require them to work closely with others. They also avoid social situations for fear that others will reject them. In intimate relationships their fear of rejection causes significant problems that eventually adversely affect the relationship.

DEPENDENT PERSONALITY DISORDER

This disorder is noted by the persistent need or desire to be taken care of. Dependents feel as though they are unable to take care of themselves; thus, they consistently look for others to do so for them. They hate the idea of being alone or of trying to make decisions for themselves on a day-to-day basis. In order to keep others in their lives, they become passive and needy. They rarely verbalize their real needs. As soon as a relationship ends, they frantically attempt to replace it with another, and the cycle repeats itself.

Psychotic or Delusional Disorders

SCHIZOPHRENIA

Schizophrenia is characterized by hallucinations, delusions, and odd behavior and language. Schizophrenics' emotions are often blunted or inappropriate. They hear and see things that do not exist and "sense" things that are not occuring. Schizophrenia is often debilitating in nature.

Substance-Related Disorders

SUBSTANCE ABUSE

Substance abuse results in increased usage that begins to negatively impact the person's life. The addict tries to fulfill his or her obligations, such as work, child rearing, etc., but over time becomes less and less able to do so. Relationships are affected. Usage can result in criminal behavior. Attempts at stopping use, even with assistance, are frequently unsuccessful.

Resources

Workbook

How to Spot a Dangerous Man Workbook. Sandra L. Brown, M.A. Alameda, CA: Hunter House, 2005. A companion to this book, the workbook walks the reader through an intensive process of scrutinizing all of her previous relationships with dangerous men so she can identify patterns in her dating choices. From there, the reader develops a personalized do-not-date list.

Author Contact / Website / Workshops

Sandra L. Brown, M.A.
P.O. Box 15
Penrose NC 28766
Telephone: (828) 226-7946
E-mail: sandrabrownma@yahoo.com
Website: www.saferelationships.com

Workshops, lectures, and retreats are offered on the subject of this book as well as on others related to self-help, mental health, and relationships. The website, **www.saferelationships.com,** offers information on dangerous men, relationships, and safe dating practices. Contact the author for workshops on dangerous men or to develop a workshop for your group.

Resources for Women in Abusive Relationships

www.ncadv.org — National Coalition Against Domestic Violence. Call toll free (800) 799-SAFE (7233). This organization maintains a data bank of domestic-violence shelters in communities all across the country. It can refer you to one located close to where you live.

www.nsvrc.org — National Sexual Violence Research Center. This website lists locations and phone numbers of state and territory coalitions.

www.ncvc.org — National Center for Victims of Crime. A website full of information on various victimizations that also includes national resources and contacts.

www. ndvh.org — National Domestic Violence Hotline. A national data bank for referrals to local resources.

www. womenslawproject.org — The Women's Law Project. A national organization devoted to legal issues relating to women.

Any sheriff, police dept, social services office, victim advocate, or shelter can help you find the necessary local resources to get the support and assistance you need in order to get out of a dangerous relationship, but you must reach out. Call one of these professionals today.

BOOKS

On Domestic Violence and Abuse

Ditch That Jerk! Dealing with Men Who Control and Hurt Women. Pamela Jayne, M.A. Alameda, CA: Hunter House, 2000.

Free Yourself from an Abusive Relationship: Seven Steps to Taking Back Your Life. Andrea Lissette, M.A., and Richard Kraus, Ph.D. Alameda, CA: Hunter House, 2000.

When Violence Begins at Home: A Comprehensive Guide to Understanding and Ending Domestic Abuse. K. J. Wilson., Ed. D. Alameda, CA: Hunter House, 1997.

On Relationships

What Men Won't Tell You but Women Need to Know. Bob Berkowitz and Roger Gittines. New York: Avon Books, 1990.

Loving Your Partner Without Losing Your Self. Martha Baldwin Beveridge. Alameda, CA: Hunter House, 2002.

Women Who Love Too Much: When You Keep Wishing and Hoping He'll Change. Robin Norwood. New York: Pocket Books, 1990.

Loving in Flow: How the Happiest Couples Get and Stay That Way. Susan K. Perry, Ph.D. Naperville, IL: Sourcebooks, 2003.

On Pathology

The Destructive Narcissistic Pattern. Nina W. Brown. Westport, CT: Praeger Publishers, 1998. (On narcissistic personality disorder.)

Without Conscience: The Disturbing World of the Psychopaths Among Us. Robert D. Hare, Ph.D. New York: Guilford Press, 1999. (On antisocial personality disorder and psychopathology.)

The Two-Edged Sword: A Study of the Paranoid Personality in Action. William H. Hampton, James C. Smith, and Virginia S. Burnham. Santa Fe, NM: Sunstone Press, 2003. (On paranoid personality disorder.)

I Hate You Don't Leave Me. Jay Kreisman, M.D., and Hal Straus. Naperville, IL: Price, Stern, Sloan, 1989. (On borderline personality disorder.)

On Chronic Mental Illness

I Can't Get over It: A Handbook for Trauma Survivors, 2nd ed. Aphrodite Matsakis. Oakland, CA: New Harbinger Publishers, 1996. (On posttraumatic stress disorder.)

Bipolar Disorder: A Guide for Patients and Families. Francis Mark Mondimore. Baltimore, MD: The Johns Hopkins University Press, 1999. (On bipolar and other cycling mood disorders.)

Tormenting Thoughts and Secret Rituals: The Hidden Epidemic of Obsessive-Compulsive Disorder. Ian Osborn, M.D. New York: Dell Publishing, 1998. (On obsessive-compulsive disorder.)

Surviving Schizophrenia: A Manual for Families, Consumers, and Providers, 4th ed. E. Fuller Torrey. New York: HarperCollins Publishers, 2001. (On schizophrenia.)

On Addictions

Twelve Steps and Twelve Traditions. Alcoholics Anonymous World Services. Minneapolis, MN: Hazelden Information Education, 1996.

Don't Call It Love. Patrick Carnes, Ph.D. New York: Bantam Books, 1991. (On sexual addictions.)

Twelve Steps for Adult Children. Friends in Recovery. Recovery Pub, 1996.

The Addictive Personality: Understanding the Addictive Process and Compulsive Behavior, 2nd ed. Craig Nakker. Minneapolis, MN: Hazelden Information Education, 1996.

WEBSITES

Information

www.Mentalhealth.com — An encyclopedia describing mental illnesses, treatments, and medications.

www.Hare.org — Lists books on psychopathy and features the Hare checklist of psychopathy symptoms.

www.Crisiscounseling.com — Click on "Problems and Disorders," where you will find a variety of explanations regarding various mental-health issues, including signs of psychopathy.

www.Oregoncounseling.org — Various useful articles on cyber-addiction, stalking, and psychopaths.

www.Geometry.net — Research bank offering descriptions of many psychological disorders, including personality disorders.

www.QuestionsBeforeMarriage.net — Good dating information. Click on "Dangerous Mates" to see a list of red-flag behaviors.

www.CrimeLibrary.com — Interesting, true stories about some of society's most infamous psychopaths.

www.ama-assn.org — Information from the American Medical Association on violence prevention.

www.end-harassment.com — Harassment hotline: Information and resources for victims of stalking and sexual harassment.

www.rosefund.org — ROSE stands for "regaining one's self-esteem." Assistance with rebuilding your life after violence.

www.vaw.umn.edu — Violence Against Women online resources. Law, advocacy, and social services.

www.nicp.net — U.S. National Crime Prevention website.

www.justicewomen.com — Website for Women's Justice Center, which is part of the U.S. Department of Justice.

www.groups.msn.com/narcissisticpersonalitydisorder/home1.msn — Website on narcissism as a mental-health problem.

www.groups.msn.com/psychopath/home.htm — Website on psychopathy.

Services

www.serenityfound.org — Twelve-step organization.

www.TrustMeID.com — Self-identification background checks. You can run a background check about yourself, then allow others to see it as verification of what you are claiming about yourself and your history.

www.Verifiedperson.com — Background searches that include nationwide criminal history, sex offender status, age, identity, city of residence, living status, marital status, children in the household, work history, educational history, professional licenses, professional references, and U.S. employment eligibility.

www.Peopledata.com — Background searches and satellite photo services.

www.Rapsheets.com — Criminal background checks.

www.Datesmart.com — Private investigation services into any area of a person's background.

www.Entersect.net — Identity online validation systems that search court records, civil histories (i.e, marriages and divorces), addresses, etc.

Index

autonomic nervous system, 33
avoidant personality disorder:
    described, 236; and the perma-
    nent clinger, 60, 61; similarity
    to other dangerous men, 130

B

background checks, availability of,
    176
behavior, changes in women's,
    35–36
behavior, dangerous, seen as
    normal, 11
biological impairment, 21
bipolar disorder, 134; and addic-
    tion, 148; as chronic disorder,
    25; described, 233; mixed
    cycles, 233; personal story of,
    143; similarity to other danger-
    ous men, 130; unmedicated,
    132; and violent men, 129, 131,
    132, 163, 176
bisexuality, 93
black-and-white thinking, 42
blame, 31–32, 212–213, 225
borderline personality disorder,
    137; and addiction, 148;
    described, 235–236; personal
    story of, 144; similarity to
    other dangerous men, 130; and
    violent men, 129, 163, 176
boredom, and choosing dangerous
    men, 50, 54, 100
boundaries, personal, 54–55,
    200–203; hypertolerance to
    boundary violations, 203; viola-
    tions of, 162, 167, 203
brain chemistry, and the mentally
    ill man, 128
Brown, Bobby, 12
Bundy, Ted, 19–20, 21, 23, 181,
    186

C

career, devotion to (emotionally
    unavailable man), 90–91

caregiving fields, women in: and
    involvement with mentally ill
    men, 130; and involvement
    with parental seekers, 77–78,
    80
charm: of emotional predator, 179,
    185, 198; of permanent clinger,
    70; as a red flag, 58
chemical impairment, 21, 128
childhood abuse: and development
    of emotional predator, 180–181,
    182; and development of
    emotionally unavailable man,
    93; and development of
    parental seeker, 74; and devel-
    opment of violent men, 163;
    women as victims, 44, 77, 150,
    165–166
childhood disorders, 232–233
childishness of parental seeker, 73,
    74, 84
chronic illness, childhood, 86
chronic mental disorders, 24–25
chronically busy men. *See*
    emotionally unavailable man
codependency, 87
combinations of dangerous cate-
    gories, 16, 117, 173
combo-pack man, 117, 173;
    description of, 16
commitment, avoidance of, 14
compartmentalizing, by a hider,
    114, 116–117
compulsive actions, 233–234
conditioned learning, 33
conduct disorder, 232–233
counseling, 111; couples, 141–142;
    and violent men, 167, 175;
    when leaving relationship, 27,
    167, 178, 207
criminal records, 176
cultural gender roles, and ignoring
    red flags, 38–40
cyber-dating, 102

D

danger-alert system. *See* red flags
dangerous man: defined, 8; inability to recognize, 9; versus pathological, 22; presentation of, 8; types of described, 14–16; types of women who respond, 9–10; universal awareness of, 9–10
dangerous man risk scale, 209
dangerous men, categories of: abusive or violent, 161–178; addict, 145–160; emotional predator, 179–199; emotionally unavailable man, 89–111; hider, 112–125; mentally ill, 126–144; parental seeker, 73–88; permanent clinger, 59–72
dating choices, signs of bad, 200–210; danger signs, 205–206
dating history, importance of evaluating, 50–51
dating, time out from, 228
decision-making skills, lack of, 75
defense mechanisms, 33
defense strategies: against the abusive or violent man, 174–177; against the addict, 156–159; against the emotional predator, 196–197; against the emotionally unavailable man, 107–109; against the hider, 123–124; against the mentally ill man, 140–143; against the parental seeker, 85–87; against the permanent clinger, 70–71
delusional disorders, 237
denial, 51–52, 225
dependent personality disorder: described, 236–237; parental seeker, 74–75, 86; similarity to other dangerous men, 130
depression: and addiction, 148; as chronic disorder, 25; described, 233; in the mentally ill man, 130; in the parental seeker, 86;

in the permanent clinger, 71; and psychotic behavior, 132
detection of dangerous men, 8–9
discipline, lack of, 86
domestic-violence shelter, 129, 167, 178
drug addiction, 148, 153. *See also* addiction
dry-drunk behavior, 148

E

ego, 52, 74–75. *See also* narcissism; narcissistic personality disorder
emergency safe houses, 167, 178
Eminem, 11
emotional abuse, 164
emotional avoidance, 92. *See also* emotionally unavailable man
emotional development, factors influencing, 20–21
emotional disorders, 232–237
emotional distress, in response to dangerous man, 35–36
emotional predator, 94, 179–199; defense strategy, 196–197; description of, 16, 179–183; and encouraging overdisclosure, 188, 196; motives of, 181–182; and naïve women, 184, 199; professions of, 193; red-alert behavioral checklist, 195–196; and rushing into relationships, 185–186; success of, 185–186; and weak boundaries, 201; who they seek, 183–185; women's stories about, 186–195, 197–199
emotional psychic, 179
emotionally unavailable man, 89–111; background of, 93; defense strategy, 107–109; description of, 14, 89–94; devotion to other interests, 90–91; and naïve women, 95; red-alert behavioral checklist, 106; success of, 97–100; versus

for the emotional predator,
195–196; for the emotionally
unavailable man, 106; for the
hider, 122–123; for the
mentally ill man, 139–140; for
the parental seeker, 84; for the
permanent clinger, 69–70
red flags: and blaming men,
212–213; and cultural gender
roles, 38–40; defined, 32–33;
emotional, 35–36; and family
training, 39–43, 213–214;
ignoring, 33, 36–44, 47–50, 53,
223; mental, 35–36; and mythical assumptions about dangerous men, 217–218; not noticing, 211–212; physical, 33–34,
42, 45; and respect for certain
careers, 43; signs of bad dating
choices, 200–210; and societal
rules, 37–38; spiritual, 34–35;
universal, 214–217; and a
woman's mental health, 43–44.
See also red-alert behavioral
checklists
rejection, fear of, 61
relationship exiting skills, 133,
174–175, 189, 207
relationships: healthy versus
unhealthy, 204; pathological,
18; rushing into, 51, 64, 70,
185–186
responsibility: accepting, 31–32,
56, 212–213, 225; avoidance of
by permanent clingers, 61
restraining orders, 165, 178, 222
romanticizing dangerous men,
11–12

S

schizophrenia: as chronic disorder,
25; described, 237; unmedicated, 132; and violent men,
129, 163
self-esteem, low: and involvement
with the emotional predator,

197, 199; and involvement
with emotionally unavailable
men, 99–100, 109; and involvement with violent men, 166;
and women's mental health, 44
self-help, 17
self-sabotaging behavior,
women's, 52–53
sensory response system, 33
separation anxiety disorder, 86
sexual abuse, 165. *See also* childhood abuse
sexual addiction, 93, 119, 123, 148,
160. *See also* addiction
sexual availability of emotionally
unavailable man, 91–92
sexual predator, 182
sleep problems, 233
sobriety, addict's periods of, 147
social learning, 21
social phobias, 71
social services, 167, 178, 207
societal rules: and ignoring red
flags, 11–12, 37–38; men's
disregard of, 114
society, and teachings about
dangerous men, 11–12, 37–38
Spears, Britney, 11
spiritual abuse, 164
spiritual intuition, 34–35
Springer, Jerry, 12, 97
stalking, 222
stress reactions, 34
subservient women, 39
substance abuse, 237
substance-related disorders, 237
suicide, 132, 233
support groups, 178
system abuse, 165

T

television, portraying dangerous
men as normal, 11–12
therapy, 111; couples, 141–142;
support and encouragement-
based, *xiii*; and violent men,